"REVELATIONS AND ALLEGATIONS THAT HAVE MADE WAVES."

—*Sports Illustrated*

"That Pallone is gay is the secret he poker-faced behind his major-league umpire's mask for more than a decade. . . . As outspoken as baseball memorists come . . . he now spills the spicy beans in an autobiography full of frank talk about baseball and the gay life . . . a life fraught with exhilaration, fear, glamour (affairs with a film star and a ballplayer) . . . Pallone's baseball talk fascinates . . . brimming with bristly baseball lore . . . but the real kicker here is his parallel, and explicit, account of his coming to grips with his homosexuality."

—*Kirkus Reviews*

"THE MOST OUTRAGEOUSLY CANDID TAKE ON THE NATIONAL GAME SINCE *BALL FOUR*. . . . PALLONE IS NOT A SHOWOFF LIKE BOB UECKER, A BREAST-BEATER LIKE DAVE KOPAY. . . . HIS STORY IS FUNNY, TOUCHING, OUTSPOKEN AND SEXY AS HELL."

—*Lambda Book Report*

"A SENSITIVELY WRITTEN, IMPORTANT WORK."

—Larry King, *USA Today*

"SIMPLY REMARKABLE. . . . Fans will appreciate Pallone's anecdotes involving players and great moments . . . his controversial shoving match with Pete Rose . . . his honesty."

—*Rocky Mountain News*

BEHIND THE MASK

My Double Life in Baseball

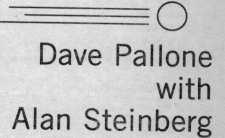

Dave Pallone
with
Alan Steinberg

A SIGNET BOOK

SIGNET
Published by the Penguin Group
Penguin Books USA Inc., 375 Hudson Street,
New York, New York 10014, U.S.A.
Penguin Books Ltd, 27 Wrights Lane,
London W8 5TZ, England
Penguin Books Australia Ltd, Ringwood,
Victoria, Australia
Penguin Books Canada Ltd, 2801 John Street,
Markham, Ontario, Canada L3R 1B4
Penguin Books (N.Z.) Ltd, 182-190 Wairau Road,
Auckland 10, New Zealand

Penguin Books Ltd, Registered Offices:
Harmondsworth, Middlesex, England

Published by Signet, an imprint of New American Library, a division of Penguin
Books USA Inc. Originally published in a hardcover edition by Viking Penguin,
a division of Penguin Books USA Inc.

First Signet Printing, April, 1991

10 9 8 7 6 5 4 3 2 1

Grateful acknowledgment is made for permission to reprint the following
copyrighted material:
Excerpts from ''Controversial Umpire Pallone Resigns,'' by Ben Walker,
Associated Press, September 19, 1988. By permission of the Associated Press.
''Report Links Ump Pallone to Sex Scandal,'' by Leo Standora, *New York Post*,
September 21, 1988. By permission of the New York Post.

 REGISTERED TRADEMARK—MARCA REGISTRADA

PRINTED IN THE UNITED STATES OF AMERICA

BOOKS ARE AVAILABLE AT QUANTITY DISCOUNTS WHEN USED TO PROMOTE
PRODUCTS OR SERVICES. FOR INFORMATION PLEASE WRITE TO PREMIUM MARKETING
DIVISION, PENGUIN BOOKS USA INC., 375 HUDSON STREET, NEW YORK, NEW YORK
10014

CONTENTS

ACKNOWLEDGMENTS

The authors wish to acknowledge gratefully: Maura So-
den for her special friendship and encouragement; Jay
Acton for making the book a reality and for finding the
right forum for our ideas; Marvin Brown for sharing our
sense of urgency and providing that forum; Ed Iwanicki
for his extraordinary patience, attention to detail, and
tough-mindedness in helping us shape our vision; Ed-
ward Novak III for his cooperative spirit and ability to
take a joke; Debra Constantini for her editorial input,
Italian take-outs, and encouragement; and Betty Lund
and Sharon Lenihan for their discreet and dedicated work
on our tapes.

Thank you, one and all.

AUTHORS' NOTE

The following names are fictitious: Francis, Carla, Kenny, Steven, Leona, Ted, Doris, Linda, Roger and Elaine Rossler, Doug, Scott, Randy, Jeffrey, Greg, Wes, Rick, Ned Stoner, Joe, Lane, Mac, Sam Gennaro, Paul. We do not wish to use fictitious names and personal descriptions, but several people specifically requested it. We changed the rest at our own discretion to protect personal privacy. Our hope is that this book will inspire sensitive discussion about the ignorant prejudice that makes it necessary to use these ''masks'' in life as well as in a book.

The person who wants to make it has to sweat.
You've got to have the guts to be hated.
That's the hardest part.

Bette Davis

A BULLET
TO THE NECK

Early Tuesday morning, November 1, 1988, I thrashed in bed, trying to sleep after another nightmare. Something still wouldn't let me rest. But since I hadn't had a peaceful day or night in months, I was almost used to it. I just rolled over and tried again.

When the phone rang, I thought, "I can't take any more bad news." I picked up the receiver and heard a familiar voice. "Dave?" my lawyer said. "It's over."

"What?" I said, stunned.

"I got a call from the DA's office in Saratoga Springs. They dropped the investigation."

"Jesus," I said, "it's about time. What took them so long?"

That question still haunts me today. But at the time I felt tremendous relief; I thought, "Something finally went *right*. Now, maybe I can get on with my life. Maybe I can get back to baseball." In my mind the air had been cleared, along with my name. I felt upbeat again, aggressive, more like *me*.

So I got up, showered, drank two cups of coffee—and phoned Bart Giamatti, president of the National League. It was Giamatti who, in mid-September, had directed me to take a leave of absence the last two weeks of the season to concentrate on the Saratoga Springs investigation.

I got through to his secretary, Mary Lou, at the league office. She checked Giamatti's schedule, called me back, and said, "How's eleven-thirty on eleven/thirty? You should be able to remember that." We both laughed at the dig. But I thought it was strange that Giamatti would wait nearly a month. And I was anxious for his reassurance that I could resume my career. I said, "Mary Lou, is that the earliest date?" "Yes, Dave," she said. "Eleven-thirty on eleven/thirty." I was disappointed; I wanted to tell Giamatti myself. I respected him like a second father, and I still felt the need to prove myself to him. I had thought, "When I tell him the news, he'll feel good for me." But that was out; now he would hear about it from either head of security Kevin Hallinan or league attorney Lou Hoynes.

Over the next couple of weeks, I just tried to relax. I was ecstatic to be free of the allegations. I felt I had a future again, a life. But I was still so goddamn mad. In July, my life had been turned upside down by my meeting with Giamatti and Kevin Hallinan when they told me my name was being investigated in upstate New York. Then, in September, the barrage of loaded headlines and slanted news stories destroyed my name: UMP TIED TO SEX RING; PALLONE BATTLES SEX CHARGES. I thought about something former Secretary of Labor Raymond Donovan once said: "Where do I go to get my reputation back?" I had no idea what Donovan did; I just knew that I'd done nothing wrong, and yet I'd lost *my* reputation, too. That was my greatest fear throughout the investigation. I knew that if my name hit the papers, I was dead. Once people read that kind of crap, they tend to assume that where there's smoke there must be fire. Being cleared doesn't erase suspicion. In fact, most people never knew I was cleared. The media treated it as incidental news. Being investigated was a five-column, bold-face headline; being cleared was a three-line blurb. I was never gonna see the truth in one of those headlines: PALLONE EXONERATED. HE DID NOTHING WRONG. IT WAS ALL A MISTAKE.

I knew I was facing a tougher road than before, if that was possible, but I didn't know how I would handle it. I needed time to prepare. So, through November, the only thing I planned was a February vacation to St. Maarten. I didn't want to think about getting a job yet; I still saw baseball as my future. I discussed this with my close friend Francis, a valued confidant. He felt there was no way they would keep me on. "Baseball's like Hollywood," he said. "They promote their own image. Whatever threatens that image has to go." Kiddingly, I said, "You're talking about the national pastime, you know—God, apple pie, fair play." He chuckled. "The good old national pastime," he said, "is about money these days, not fair play."

Subconsciously, I probably knew he was right. Consciously, I wanted to believe I could make my case to Giamatti: "Hey, the Saratoga Springs thing was a total fabrication. I would never do anything to hurt major league baseball." And I hoped he would say, "I know. Let's get you back on the field." In my heart I desperately wanted to believe that baseball *did* care about fair play.

About a week before our scheduled meeting, I phoned the league office to find out if I needed to bring my lawyer. Mary Lou told me that Mr. Giamatti said it would be a very informal meeting, so attorneys weren't necessary. Then, the day before the meeting, she informed me that Lou Hoynes would also attend. I said fine to that, too, and called my lawyer. He said, "I should go with you." I said, "No, I'll go alone. I don't wanna go in fighting."

Wednesday morning, November 30, was sunny and winter-crisp. I met Francis for breakfast and we talked about the meeting. I said, "Bart Giamatti's a highly intelligent, decent human being. He's always been very fair with me. He becomes commissioner of baseball on April first; maybe he can turn things around for me." Francis said, "He sounds like he might be the right person for the job. Let's hope he can educate the game."

It was gorgeous outside, so I walked over to 350 Park Avenue, where the National League has its executive offices. Riding the elevator to the eighteenth floor, I wondered what Giamatti would say. Would he be sympathetic: "Dave, this was a terrible ordeal for you—I want you to know that we're on your side and we'll do everything we can to help you handle any problems with the press"? Or was I in for a reprimand: "Look, Dave, these things can't keep happening to you—you've got to start watching your step"? I was nervous but hopeful. I hoped that when I left there after the meeting, I'd be going home to prepare for my eleventh spring training in the major leagues.

Waiting in the reception area, I pulled a letter out of my suit coat. It was my written request to the National League supervisor of umpires, Eddie Vargo, asking, as usual, to work just the first two weeks of spring training, and for all my games to be in the Clearwater area, near my winter home. Just then Mary Lou came out to get me, so I said to the receptionist, "Anita, remind me to give you this letter for Eddie Vargo before I leave." For some reason, I decided to hold on to the letter until after the meeting. But as Mary Lou and I marched back to Giamatti's office, I had a big smile on my face. I hadn't felt this relaxed in months.

When I entered Giamatti's office, he and Lou Hoynes were discussing a *New York Times* article about a college dean who'd been accused of plagiarism. Giamatti, a former president of Yale, was very interested in academic issues. When they saw me, they stopped talking—and I sensed the tension in the room. Giamatti looked grim. The instant he looked at me, I knew I was in trouble. His eyes were piercing, not smiling with his usual warmth. I sat down in front of his desk; Hoynes slid back onto the couch.

"Dave," Giamatti began, "I know you're not going to like what I have to say."

I stopped him cold. "What I don't like is the way this meeting is going. This is not a very informal meeting like you said it would be."

Giamatti looked surprised. "I feel bad about that," he said sincerely. "I know you felt the same way about the July meeting when I brought Kevin Hallinan. Why do you think this isn't informal?" Suddenly, an old Georgie Jessel line popped into my head: "Do you ever feel like the whole world is a tuxedo and you're just a pair of brown shoes?" So I said, "Because right now I have the feeling that this meeting is a tuxedo and I'm a pair of brown shoes."

Giamatti managed a smirk. He said, "Well, I'm sorry you feel that way." There was a long silence while he lit a cigarette. Finally he said, "David, we've decided not to renew your contract."

That jolted me. "I don't understand," I said. "How can you do that? I've done nothing wrong."

"Well, we have a sworn affidavit from a juvenile in Saratoga Springs stating that you engaged in sex with a minor. And it doesn't matter *who* it was with."

"Wait a minute," I said. "You know I was cleared of that. I was not charged with anything. I was not indicted for anything. They were just investigating my name—and they dropped the investigation. I'm guilty only of being in the wrong place at the wrong time. That is the only thing I'm guilty of."

Giamatti didn't flinch. "Your ratings have slipped. They're very low."

I said, "You know what you can do with those ratings."

He flashed a small grin, which—based on our past talks about how inept the league's rating system was—I interpreted to mean: "Dave, I know that you're a good umpire and I know the rating system stinks." Then he said, "There's also the Cincinnati bar incident in 1986."

"Jesus," I said, "that's ancient history! We've been through all that. It was just a *rumor.*"

He said, "We just don't feel that you can handle the pressure from all the negative publicity."

"That's absolutely ridiculous," I said. "I've handled the pressure for the past ten years, coming up during the strike and being a scab. How can any other pressure be tougher than that?"

Giamatti leaned back in his chair. He looked troubled. "Look, Dave, we don't want to fire you. We'd like to see you retire voluntarily. We don't want you to be left out in the cold on this. We'd like to see you get your next year's salary plus your severance pay."

Suddenly I understood why he'd waited a month before meeting with me. Baseball needed time to figure out a game plan. "I can't make that decision now," I said.

Lou Hoynes finally added his two cents: "We wouldn't *want* you to make that decision now."

I stood up, looked at Bart, and said, "You'll be hearing from me." Without shaking hands, I turned around and walked out. I was goddamn pissed. I remember thinking: "Why do they believe a kid's affidavit over me? Where's the allegiance after the ten years of sweat and tears I put into major league baseball? Where's the compassion for all the ostracism I suffered when I helped baseball out of their jam in '79? They're not saying, 'This is what we believe. What do you have to say?' They're saying, 'We've decided you're guilty and we don't *care* what you say.'"

As I stormed past the reception desk, Anita said, "Dave, hold on. What about Vargo's letter?" I said, "Never mind. It means *nothing* now." I got on the elevator and ripped the letter to shreds. When I hit Park Avenue, I found a pay phone and called my attorney. "They're letting me go," I said. "I'm going home. Make sure you're in the office. We gotta talk."

That afternoon, my attorney phoned Lou Hoynes and asked him to put in writing the league's reasons for dismissing me. A few days later, we received a letter from Hoynes dated December 1 listing these reasons: (1) concern over information received from the prosecutor in the 1987 Saratoga Springs incident; (2) allegations in the 1986 Cincinnati incident; (3) my recent "low performance evaluation," placing me "third from the bottom in the League"; and (4) concern about my "ability to function as an umpire under the pressure and with the criticism" the league believed I would receive if I returned to the field after the publicity about the Saratoga Springs incident. This letter was crucial, my attorney told me, because now baseball could not invent any other reasons if I decided to take them to court. He said that I was being forced out, basically, over the Saratoga Springs scandal. As far as he was concerned, my constitutional rights had been abrogated, and we had a strong chance of winning a discrimination suit.

In the coming months I was to be faced with the toughest decision of my life up to that time: Should I fight to get my job back, or should I put this whole traumatic

ordeal behind me and go on with my future? The issue
was so clear, yet the decision was so complicated. Yes,
I'd had enough of the ostracism. Yes, I'd had it with the
bullshit rumors and the accusations and the devastating
press. On the other hand, if I left on this note, I'd probably be the only umpire in the history of baseball who
left under a cloud. And what about my last career goal:
working a World Series? That was still tremendously important to me.

I had a hard time accepting that the game I'd been so
devoted to had put me in this position. The way baseball
chose to handle this was eating me alive. They were rewarding my ten years of loyalty with a bullet to the neck.
They bought a phony case against me, added garbage of
their own, acted as judge and jury, and found me guilty—
though they never really said of *what*. Well, they didn't
have to. I *knew*. And it was none of the things they hinted
at.

Baseball had really found me guilty . . . of *being gay*.

THE OTHER ME

My dad, Carmine Pallone, was born in Pescara, Italy, and he came over to Watertown, Massachusetts, with his parents and went to Boston Braves games and dreamed of pitching in the major leagues. In his late teens, he was a baseball fanatic—and apparently a damn good pitcher, because he was offered a contract with the St. Louis Browns. But that was during the Depression, and his father said, "No. You gotta work in the fields." So instead of pitching baseballs in the major leagues, my dad pitched vegetables onto a truck for a dollar a day.

In a way I inherited his dream. As a teenager, I was already thinking, "If I can pitch in the major leagues, that would really make my dad proud." Since he worked at the rubber fabric factory when I was growing up, and did landscaping and other odd jobs on the weekends, we didn't spent much time together. Maybe that's why I wanted to do so well in baseball. I guess I figured that if I could make him proud of me in the game he loved, he might give me more attention. But working two, sometimes three jobs, he had almost no attention left to give.

Despite his limited free time, my dad did everything he could for me, my brother, and my sister. He taught us how to ride our bikes; he played catch with us; he took us fishing; he even taught us a little cooking. Although he always had money problems, I never lacked for anything as a kid. If I wanted a hockey stick, he'd buy me a hockey stick. If I wanted a new baseball, he'd get me a baseball.

He was very handsome, youthful-looking, big-chested, and muscular. But he kept his emotions locked inside—just like me. He could be aloof and cool sometimes when he lost his temper and wanted to be alone. He had a typically hot Italian temper. One time I was sitting with him in the living room and he saw me looking at his cigarettes. He was a heavy smoker—four or five packs of unfiltered Pall Malls a day. He said, ''Are you interested in those?'' I said, ''No, I was just looking at them.'' He said, ''I don't ever want to see you smoke.'' Well, I didn't take it seriously. As a kid, that kind of threat doesn't stop you from doing what you want. But that night, he and my mom had an argument, and he slammed his fist into the wall so hard that he cracked the wall. After that, whenever I was tempted to smoke I thought of that wall. I figured, ''If he can do that to a wall, what can he do to me?''

But he was not violent; he was just strong-willed and tough. That impressed me, but it also kept me from bringing my problems to him. I always thought of my dad as a man's man. When he moved us into our own colonial home in Watertown, he did most of the improvement work himself. He dug up and recemented the sidewalks. He built a storage shed with a cement floor in the backyard. He helped knock out the interior walls of the house when we remodeled. He also did the hard, handyman jobs that most people can't do for themselves. I admired his self-sufficiency. Later, in my major league baseball career, the thought of that would help me handle situations when I had no help from anyone.

The one thing about my relationship with my father I remember with regret is that we never did get close. I was never ''abused'' as a kid in any physical way, and even though I know my dad loved me and had no choice except to work long hours, I still felt neglected by him. I remember one time when we were living in the projects, he was getting ready to walk to the store in Watertown Square and he asked me if I wanted to go. I don't know why, but I said no. Well, this was a rare chance to spend some private time with him, so I changed my mind. But then my mother said no because she wanted me to help with chores around the house. I said, "I wanna go, I wanna go!" but she wouldn't let me. So I sat on the stairs and cried. That little incident happened thirty years ago, but it still haunts me today that I let that opportunity pass.

Since my dad wasn't around, I ended up getting closer to my mom, Michelina. (I'm aware that many straight people think it's a gay stereotype to be distant from your father and close to your mother. But I know plenty of gay men who were very close to their fathers. I don't believe any one experience makes you gay; I believe you're born that way, period.) "Mickey" was a kind, warm, unselfish lady. She would do little things for me, like go out of her way to make special treats for my birthday. Also, I'm probably the only person in the world who likes lemon meringue pie without the meringue, so on holidays Mickey made a regular lemon meringue pie for everyone else in the family and a special "lemon pie" for me. And whenever she took me shopping with her, if there was something special I really wanted, she'd get it for me—even if it meant she couldn't get something she wanted for herself.

I saw a wonderful human being in my mom. I consider myself a very compassionate person today, and I attribute that to having her as a model. In 1973, when Mickey went into the hospital for a cancer operation, she shared a room with a young girl. They knew each other for only four days. Yet when my mother died five months later, this young girl came to her funeral. She also wrote my dad a card saying how wonderful it was that she and Mickey were able to share their feelings, and how much she admired Mickey's philosophy that you should do whatever you want in life because you never know how short it will be. She wrote: "I learned a lot from her in just a few days. I will never forget the compassion she showed me. I feel very fortunate to have met her." That has always stuck with me, because it confirmed that other people—even strangers—saw the same compassion in my mom that I always saw.

My dad didn't normally show much outward emotion or sensitivity, but when Mickey died, it was the only time I ever saw him cry. In fact, although he loved me, he never *told* me so. To be honest, I didn't tell him, either—until it was too late. Yet I *always* said it to my mother.

Although my father didn't spend much time talking to me about life, he did get me interested in baseball. He taught me how to throw a curve, and he often got us bleacher seats for Red Sox games at Fenway Park. Those games were the most exciting part of my youth. I used to sit there and watch the players taking batting practice, catching fungoes, and running around that gorgeous field, and I'd think, "I'll never work in a hot factory. *This* is where I wanna be someday—out on the grass at Fenway Park."

I played all the sports as a kid—basketball, football, street hockey. But I was just average in everything except baseball, so naturally I devoted most of my time and imagination to that. I was such a big Red Sox fan that I got tickets for Fenway games two months in advance. I'd go to sleep at night listening to their games on my transistor radio. I would've rather had a Red Sox player's baseball card than money for a movie. I was so passionate about that team, I played more imaginary Red Sox games than my own real ones. I'd go out to my backyard and imitate my heroes: Carl Yastrzemski at bat, Rico Petrocelli fielding a grounder at third, Jim Lonborg pitching, George Scott bashing home runs over "The Green Monster." I used to imagine, "Gee, maybe someday I'll be out there with them."

I vividly remember one time I got carried away, pretending to be everyone on the field. First I was Yastrzemski hitting a grounder to short and running it out; then I was the opposing team's shortstop fielding the ball and making the throw; then I was the first baseman catching the throw; then I was the umpire, yelling, "You're *out!*" After that, I actually argued with myself. I yelled, "You're blind! Why don't you get a *real* job?" Then I really went wild; I threw myself out of the game. (I don't know much about psychiatry, but was that the *real* start of my umpiring career? If so, who was I throwing out of that game—the pretend Yastrzemski or the future Dave Pallone?)

That was when baseball started taking over my life—and I got obsessed with "the glove." For years my dad had this beautiful, brand-new baseball glove in his bedroom closet. I didn't know where he got it or what it was for, because it never left his closet. I just always wanted to use it. But he said, "You can't use that glove until I think you're ready." One day when I was in seventh grade, he said, "Go up to my room and get that glove. I want to show you something." I went up and got it and brought it back downstairs. He said, "Now, if you oil this down and stick a baseball in it, we'll make a good pocket and you can start using it." I was ecstatic. It never occurred to me then, but that meant he thought I was ready to get serious about baseball.

At that time in my life, baseball wasn't just a hobby or a sport; it was something powerful inside me. I felt I belonged in the game. It was as if somebody had injected baseball into my veins, and from then on it was always in my blood.

But something else was in there, too. Something I didn't understand. Something I would later come to think of as "the other me."

For the most part, my childhood in Watertown was typical for a young boy. I grew up in the projects with a small group of friends, and we spent all our time thinking, talking, and playing sports. From the ages of about eight to ten, our interest in girls amounted to "Oh, yeah—*them.*" They were just part of the environment, but not especially important or even interesting. I mean, how could they be? They didn't play sports with us, they didn't cut up around the neighborhood with us, they didn't go to the movies with us, or to Fenway Park or Boston Garden or anywhere else we went. As far as we were concerned, they basically didn't exist. And I'm sure they felt the same about us.

When I lived in the projects, I did have a crush on a cute twelve-year-old girl named Carla. One day we went upstairs to my parents' bedroom, and, as we watched for my mother out the window, Carla became the first girl I ever kissed. And the first to let me fondle her so-called breasts (there wasn't much to fondle). Of course, *I* didn't have much either, so there was no erection and no ejaculation. We really had no idea what we were doing.

Except for that one little kiss and feel, the only time I related to girls back then was in school or maybe at a party, which wasn't much more exciting. I was raised Italian Catholic: even if I had *thought* about doing anything with girls—which I didn't yet—I was too scared to actually *do* too much. It's different today, but when we grew up we didn't know too much. Yes, once in a while we'd gawk at naked girls in *Playboy* and I might say to my friends, "Nice tits." But, Jesus, that meant about as much to me as "Nice bike" or "Nice peanut butter sandwich." Tits were strange, but they were still something to joke about. I was much more interested in who won the Red Sox game or the Bruins game or the Patriots game. The only real scoring I thought about was runs, baskets, touchdowns, and goals. At that age, that's as typical as a boy's life gets.

At age twelve, though, something else happened. Occasionally I had "encounters" with other boys. When I was living in the projects, I played sports and games a lot with an Italian friend named Kenny. I remember that when we played tackle football, or if we wrestled, we'd sometimes "goose" each other—grab each other's crotch. It felt good, but it didn't mean anything. It was kids' stuff; it was what every kid did—and I was every kid.

Kenny had always been after me to come over to his house and go down his cellar to play Ping-Pong. For a long time something told me not to go. So I'd say, "No, I don't wanna play Ping-Pong. I'm no good at it." I don't know how, but I knew that if I went down there he would try to touch me. For a while, I guess, although I wondered what it would be like, I wasn't ready to experience it. Then one day I went over to Kenny's to play basketball. Somewhere in the back of my mind, I also went over with the idea: "I wanna find out what'll happen if we go downstairs." I wanted to experience it, learn what it was.

We went down into his cellar to get the basketball, and we ended up playing Ping-Pong. After a while we started kidding around, pushing each other and laughing. Then, for a moment, we found ourselves staring at each other. I remember thinking, "I wonder what *his* looks like. I'd like to see him naked." I don't know who or what started it, but we touched each other's penis. Then we went over to this mattress on the floor in the corner and we sat down. We started groping awkwardly until we finally took our pants down to our ankles. I was nervous because Kenny's dad was upstairs and I didn't want to get in trouble. Yet I didn't stop; I *wanted* to do this.

Kenny turned over on his stomach and I laid on top of him and rubbed against him. What struck me was that I felt more pleasure with him than I'd felt with Carla (with Kenny, at least, I had an erection). But right in the middle, Kenny's dad yelled down to us, "What are you kids doing down there? I thought you were going to play outside?" We stopped immediately and pulled our pants up. Kenny answered, "We're getting the ball," and we grabbed the ball and hurried upstairs to go outside.

I'd never done anything like that with anyone—but it *felt* good! I didn't think it was strange or "perverse"—I wouldn't have even known what that meant yet. The idea that "he's a boy and I'm a boy" didn't occur to me yet. But I knew I couldn't tell anybody. I thought of the Catholic prohibitions "Don't play with yourself or you'll go blind" and "No sex or you'll go to hell." I figured they probably applied to what I did with Carla and Kenny, although I didn't know what sex was yet. I just knew it was wrong, or "naughty," to touch someone that way— either a boy *or* a girl. And I didn't want to get caught and punished. But I had no control over my feelings. Instinctively, I wanted to explore boys. All my social training told me I should be more interested in girls than in boys, but since I had never asked anybody else about it, I thought every kid was doing this.

(I still believe today that most young boys "explore" other boys at one time or another in their youth. Maybe it's with a friend or a brother or a cousin. It's innocent play, mostly out of curiosity. We don't hear much about it because most heterosexual men won't speak about it. One reason is that once they learn about homosexual behavior as adults, they block out these childhood memories. They think, "Well, maybe I'm a homosexual because that's what I did when I was ten." But I don't think they have anything to worry about. I think it's just part of the natural process of growing up.)

After Kenny, I thought about boys more than about girls. I wanted to find out more. My next encounter happened when I was living in our two-family home on Edenfield Avenue. I had a younger friend named Steven who lived across the street, and we played ball together all the time after school. One day we were throwing the baseball around in the street when we started talking about our penises. That isn't shocking for thirteen-year-old boys. Most boys that age fixate on their own penises—and they have a natural curiosity about what other boys have, too.

While we were kidding around, Steven said, "How big is yours?" I said, "How big is *yours?*" And we decided to find out. We didn't have any place to go, so we went behind his garage. I was attracted to him, and he was just as curious as I was, so we took our pants down and felt each other's genitals. I remember he had an ejaculation—the first time I'd ever seen another boy do that before. But I didn't have one, and that was all we did. As it turned out, it was the only time we ever did anything like that together.

I had no clue what it meant. Number one: we were still kids. Number two: it wasn't planned. Number three: I figured it was part of having fun, like playing ball or climbing roofs. There was never any kissing or embracing or mutual masturbation—only looking, touching, groping. I wasn't physically mature yet; I was still in puberty. I wouldn't have known that this was "sexual." Besides, I was doing some of the same things with girls—and I didn't think *that* was sexual, either.

That's why my encounters with boys never struck me as odd. When you're twelve or thirteen, you don't think anything is odd, especially if you feel comfortable. Which I did—with boys and with girls. When I was with a girl, it was "Why don't I have the same things you have?"

When I was with a boy, it was "Here's mine. Let's see yours." At that age, I didn't know enough to say, "Are we supposed to feel this way?" I was just as scared of getting caught with a girl as with a boy, because in my Catholic upbringing sex of any kind was frowned upon.

I didn't know what intercourse was yet. I just knew that whatever I was doing, I shouldn't do it in the open. That's why these encounters were so few and far between. Even though it was always with a friend, we'd meet once or twice and avoid it from then on by telling ourselves, "We can't let it happen again. We'll get caught." I had no other guidelines. There was no talk at home about the birds and the bees; we didn't learn about sex in school, and we didn't get any help in church. So we found out by exploring and groping.

In my early teens I knew nothing about "homosexual" or "gay." The only words I knew along those lines were "queer" and "faggot." I never said them, but other kids did, just because they were rotten names. In my neighborhood they called you a "faggot" or a "queer" if you were a sissy—which meant you were "soft" and could be pushed around, or you acted like a girl, or you didn't play sports. I wasn't any of those things. And neither were the boys I had encounters with.

When I was fourteen and fifteen, I had a few more encounters with friends. I remember worrying for the first time about being caught for doing something *wrong* with another boy. I didn't know why it was wrong; I just wanted to know more about why I was attracted to boys. In one of these encounters, the other boy and I went into the storage shed behind my house and masturbated each other. That's as far as we went, although I wanted to do other things. The problem was, I didn't know what or how.

Another time, a boy and I started fooling around in a tent pitched in my backyard, trying to see how far we could go. I remember we were talking about sex in general when he said, "My father says if you're gonna screw, you should be the one on the bottom, because it doesn't hurt as much." I didn't know what that meant, but I believed him. So I said, "Then I wanna be the one on the bottom.'' (When I was mature enough to reflect back on this, I realized that this poor kid's father probably sexually abused him, and that this was what he told his son at the time.) Well, we tried our best to do it, but we just couldn't get it to work.

In high school, I started noticing major changes in myself. As a freshman, I'd been interested in both girls and boys, although I felt more comfortable, physically, with boys, and I thought more about them. But I just figured it was natural because I played sports all the time and my best friends were guys. My sophomore year, I was much more physically attracted to boys. My encounters with them increased, and the exploration was more advanced. It gave me a warmer, safer feeling. I always thought a man was supposed to be a protector. But as a teenager, I felt I needed protection as well. And that's how I felt when I was with boys; they gave me a sense of security and comfort that I never felt with women.

At sixteen, I didn't think I was ''different.'' I knew that boys weren't supposed to ''like'' or be sexual with other boys, and that if it was ever known publicly, they'd be called ''faggots,'' ''queers,'' or ''homos.'' During the 1960s, when I was in my teens, those words were used as weapons. Getting labeled a ''faggot,'' a ''queer,'' or a ''homo'' was considered worse than being called a communist. It was ostracism—something I would learn more about firsthand further down the road.

At that time, whenever I was with another boy, I never wondered, ''What's wrong with me?'' If I went by my religion, what I was doing with boys was a sin. I believed in sin, but I thought of it more in terms of talking back to your parents or using God's name in vain. I never mentioned my encounters with boys in confession—but I never mentioned any sex in confession, with either boys or girls, because I was still afraid of the punishment. I did tell God—privately. I basically said, ''If this is wrong, why does it always feel so good?''

Since no adults knew about my experiences, I never had mature advice. I was very shy about those feelings then. Never once did I discuss with my friends how I felt. So I had no way of knowing that thousands of other boys felt the same as me. I couldn't find one of them to talk to about it. Even if I could have found one, I would have been too scared, too confused, and too inarticulate to explain how I felt anyway.

All through high school "the big encounter" never happened. I was curious about it, but still too shy. In fact, nobody wanted to be the first to mention it. It was a very frustrating time. I was also confused because I was still dating girls, mainly because I liked their company and conversation. And I fooled around with them, too; I made out with every girl I dated. It was never spectacular, but not repulsive, either. I had never had intercourse with a girl, though I did wonder what it would be like. There was still that hurdle.

Finally, in my junior year, it happened one night with a girl I was seeing casually. We had gone bowling and we were driving home in my father's car when I pulled off to a secluded spot so we could make out. I liked this girl as a friend. She was attractive, yet her personality turned me on more than her body. But I really needed to find out how this felt. I knew how I was *expected* to feel from being on the baseball team and hearing guys brag about how great it was to screw a girl. So I told myself, "If what I feel with boys is so good, then sex with a girl should feel really great, because that's who you're *supposed* to do it with."

Well, it felt . . . okay. But not like it was supposed to feel. Even though it was the magical "first time," it wasn't rockets going off or the earth moving or even the car rolling. I tried to enjoy it, but I just didn't feel involved. I felt more like I was going though the motions. It was strange; I found her attractive enough to be aroused, yet something was missing. I never told her that. Afterward, since we hadn't used any protection, we worried about pregnancy. When that fear passed, we were too afraid to have sex again. So we continued to date as friends for a few more months. Then she got interested in another boy, who was more popular—and that was actually a relief. As our friendship had deepened, I had wanted to tell her about my feelings, but I was still too afraid. Now I didn't have to try anymore.

I had one other "relationship" with a girl in high school—a pretty, gentle, intelligent girl whom I took to the prom. She was everything you could ask for, a really great girl. We had become friends and dated a little, but whenever we made out I still felt the same "distance" as before. It just didn't feel as natural or as comfortable as being with a boy—even though I hadn't yet had intercourse with a boy. Eventually, we drifted apart, though we remained friends. I was never able to tell her what I felt, so I was still struggling to find an acceptable outlet for my frustrations. It was the worst time of my life. I felt so helpless; I just kept stumbling blindly, hiding my feelings, trying to figure out which way to go.

Through all this emotional turmoil, my dream of pitching in the major leagues had simmered on the back burner. Now I needed it again. So my junior year I turned my attention back to baseball and I made my high school team. At the time, I still idolized Red Sox players: Yastrzemski, Petrocelli, Lonborg, Scott—and I was old enough to appreciate Dick Radatz, too. I liked how *tough* he always looked on the mound. In that way he reminded me of my dad. I used to say, "My dad takes no shit from anyone, and neither does Radatz." I admired that; on the ballfield I tried to be that way myself. Ironically, years later, this toughness would help me more as an umpire than it ever did as an athlete. In fact, it would pull me through some hellish ordeals.

During my junior and senior years—my "Radatz era"—I could throw pretty hard, but I wasn't a great pitcher. I used to psych myself up by saying, "If I can be as tough as Radatz, maybe I'll be a great pitcher like him someday." I was a big kid then; I had a good fastball. That had made me tough to hit in Pony League and Babe Ruth ball. But high school was a different ballgame. Even at little Watertown High, I faced kids who could actually *hit* a fastball. On the other hand, my senior year, no one ever touched me in a league game.

Here's why: In my first appearance that year, I came in to relieve late in the game. As I marched to the mound, I told myself, "Look tough. Be like Radatz." I did look tough, but it wasn't enough. I was also gonna have to *throw* the ball to get someone out. I wound up and came in with a blistering fastball, letter-high. The batter hit a rope at my head. I stabbed at it with my glove, lost my balance, and fell. When I hit the ground on my shoulder, I reinjured a ligament I'd hurt in hockey and I tore my rotator cuff. End of my baseball dream. And I didn't know then that this was just the first in a series of bizarre falls I would take in baseball.

There is one other event related to my career on the high school team which, in a way, speaks to the issue of why gay baseball players today still don't come out of the closet. My senior year, I was strongly attracted to a teammate. He was extremely good-looking, friendly, tremendously popular with the school's "in crowd." This attraction was different from any I'd experienced before, because I was a little older now, and I was looking for more than just sexual exploration. I was also looking for someone to get close to emotionally—a confidant, a best buddy—someone I could finally share my secret with.

But I knew by then that these inclinations were taboo, especially on a baseball team. I thought it wasn't "manly" to be attracted to another athlete. And I had always considered myself very masculine, so this was a conscious concern. I knew I had to mask and control those feelings, keep them out of baseball, away from the locker room. Which is exactly what I did. I never showed my interest in any serious way. Yes, when I saw this guy naked in the locker room, I fantasized about what it would be like to be with him. But except for a playful slap on the back or the ass, or a wiseguy remark like "My dick is bigger than yours," I suppressed it completely. (Later in my life, I would learn that one of the chief myths—and fears—of baseball team owners is that a gay ballplayer in the team's midst will run sexually amuck, putting the make on everybody in the room. That's preposterous. I knew, even in high school, that a team locker room was off limits. And what gay man in his right mind—especially one who knows he has to hide that side of himself—would be reckless enough to try to pick up a teammate in a locker room just because he was undressing near him? It doesn't happen. I ought to know.)

At the time when I was attracted to my teammate, I'd been repressing ''the other me'' most of my life, because I still felt like I was the only person going through this. There was no way to find anyone else. There were no ''signals'' between boys. And even if there were, I didn't know about ''gay'' life-styles or ''gay'' communities yet, so I had no idea what signals I should be looking for. I was still fighting my own nature. But when I first felt these emotional needs along with the physical attraction, I realized for the first time, ''Hey, maybe this *is* my nature. Maybe this *is* me.'' It wasn't acceptable to society, but it felt good to *me*.

I started thinking more about who I really was. But I was still terribly frustrated and confused. And still alone.

UMPIRE DEVELOPMENT

After graduation, I knew I wouldn't be pitching in the major leagues. I wasn't even gonna get a scholarship to play in college. But my parents suggested I go to college anyway, get a degree, and make a future for myself. So I applied to Lowell Tech to study, of all things, engineering. Why, I don't know. I guess it sounded like it had a future. But the only engineering I'd ever done was restringing my baseball glove. I'd always thought an engineer was the guy who ran a train.

Lowell Tech accepted me for the fall of 1969. But I changed my mind, because I knew I wasn't ready for the regimentation of a four-year school. So my parents gave me the money and I enrolled instead in a six-month computer school. I figured if I wasn't going into baseball, why waste four years trying to figure out what I *was* going into? Six months seemed a lot less time to waste. Of course, it *was* wasted. I was bored stiff. I finished the course and got my degree, but the last thing I wanted to be was a computer programmer. What would that have been like—working indoors with machines, doing the same thing every day? No thanks; not for Dave Pallone. But what the hell *was* for Dave Pallone? At age eighteen I didn't have a clue.

When the summer of 1970 rolled around, I had no baseball, no direction, no ambition, no life. I was living at home and working as a stock boy in a grocery and as a caddie at the Oakley Country Club. Then, one Saturday, my life changed. I was home watching a baseball game on TV as my favorite announcer, Curt Gowdy, did the play-by-play. All of a sudden Gowdy started reading an advertisement for the Umpire Development Program, a training school for prospective major league umpires. I'd never heard of it before, yet for some reason it caught my attention. Gowdy said it was located in Florida and anyone could apply. I remember thinking, "Hey, I wonder if I could get into that *now.*"

I missed the address, so I went into the kitchen, picked up the phone, and called the Boston Red Sox office. They told me that the Umpire Development Program didn't start until the following February, but another umpire course was run out of the Ted Williams Baseball Camp in Lakeville, Massachusetts, and maybe I could go there. So I got that number and found out that their session had already started, but if I came Monday, they'd let me in. I was excited; *something* urged me to go. The only thing was, I needed enrollment money—and permission—from my parents.

My father hit the roof. "You wanna be a *what?*" he said—as if "umpire" meant "bum." He'd said he'd heard of schools for fish, but not schools for umpires. My mother said, "No, wait. Let's hear him out," so we sat down at the kitchen table to debate it. My dad argued vehemently against it. He said, "You're telling me you're gonna waste all that money we spent on computer school? You're saying that instead of getting a *real* job and doing something with your life, you wanna piss away your future on a pipe dream?" I said, "Dad, it's a way I can be in baseball and maybe have a future, too." My mother saw my passion; she said she and Dad would talk it over.

Well, somehow she convinced my dad that if I really wanted to go, they should give me the money and let me go. The next day my dad had to work, so a neighbor drove me and my mother to Lakeville. During that drive, we were discussing umpire school when my mother said something to me that would stay with me forever. She said, "David, I know this is what you really want. I think this is what you will be for the rest of your life." I have no idea what made her say that, especially since I'd been such a troubled kid and drifting at the time. But that small encouragement became my spiritual touchstone throughout my baseball career. In my most devastating crises, in my deepest despair when I was ready to quit, my mother's words kept pulling me through. I don't know how or why. Maybe subconsciously I was fulfilling her prophecy because I wanted so badly to make her proud of me. Or maybe I just needed someone close to me to point the way and say, "Go that way, David. Your life is over there."

When we arrived at the Ted Williams Camp, I met Bill Kinnamon, a retired American League umpire who was the chief instructor. It turned out that he was also the chief instructor in the Umpire Development Program. In our first conversation he told me that I was smart to take this course now because it would put me a step up from everybody else next year, when I'd be ready to apply to the Umpire Development Program. I thought, "This is great. I just got here and somebody important is giving me advice!" But I still felt a little strange. Most of the other guys enrolled in the session were high school and college umpires who came to improve their skills so they could earn extra money working in summer leagues. I was by far the most inexperienced. The only thing I knew about umpires was that I hated them. They were the guys I yelled at during Red Sox games at Fenway Park and the games I played in myself. They wore those drab blue suits and beanie caps with the chopped-off brims that made them look like the wimps we left out of our school-yard games.

Even though I didn't know my ass from my elbow, I liked the Ted Williams course right away. It was very informal—we wore shorts most of the time—and since there were only twenty of us, it was like getting private instruction. The course was for brushing up on basics: proper positioning; the right way to call "safe," "out," "ball," and "strike"; and getting the angles on different plays. Every night we studied the official rule book, and every day we got up early, went onto the field, and prac-ticed. I remember the first time I yelled "You're out!"

on the field. Each guy had to take three steps, stop, and make the call with his fist hammering the air. When my turn came, I took three steps, stopped, and raised my hand in a fist with thumb extended—just like I thought I'd seen in a thousand games. All of a sudden, Bill Kinnamon's voice boomed behind me: "Pallone! Stick that thumb up your ass! It's a *fist*, not a thumb!" That was my first lesson: always a fist, never a thumb. And little did I know then that eighteen years down the road, I would hear myself paraphrasing it to Pete Rose in one of the weirdest confrontations of my career.

In those first umpiring lessons, I was awkward and self-conscious. I'd always been a player; I never imagined what it felt like to be an umpire. You stood differently than a player; you ran differently; you talked differently; you thought differently. You had to be assertive and firm and look like you were right—which isn't that simple to do. I could see that umpiring was a world of its own, and that not everyone was cut out for it. That's what appealed to me. I guess I'd always wanted something different. During that one short week I was really enthusiastic. I thought, "I can do this. This is for me."

Midway through, I sought out some of the college baseball coaches who were involved in the baseball camp, which ran throughout the summer. I sat with them for hours, talking baseball, trying to pick up insights on umpires and umpiring. The next-to-last day, I told Fred Brown, the coach at Bridgewater State College, "I felt like shit out there at first. Now I feel like I've been doing it all my life. I love this. I really hope I can turn myself into an umpire." He said, "If you love baseball that much, and you can't play anymore and don't want to coach, the next best thing is umpiring. *Anything* to be part of the game."

That expressed exactly how I felt. So at night I threw myself into the rules, absorbing as much as I could, even though the session was practically over. I was totally hooked. When the session ended, I went to Bill Kinnamon and said, "I know I want to be a professional umpire. How do I go about doing that?" He said, "Why don't you stay here the rest of the summer and umpire in the baseball camp? You can earn a little extra money and get some real experience.'' I thought it was a great idea, so he talked to the owner of the camp, Bernie Cassidy, and I got the job. They paid my room and board and fifty dollars a week for umping games, and they made me a counselor to boot.

During the umpire course, they had pointed out how important it was to *look* like an umpire. So I decided that now was the time to invest in a uniform, try to look and act like an umpire, and see how I did. The uniform consisted of black pants, a blue shirt, black, rubber-soled shoes for working the plate, and rubber-cleated baseball shoes for the bases. The camp provided mask, chest protector, and shin guards; I had to buy a ball bag, whisk broom, and hand indicator for tracking the count.

The first time I stepped onto a baseball field dressed like this, I had home plate in a high school game. I knew I'd have to be on my toes, because there were only two umpires to a crew, these kids knew the game, and they were vocal about mistakes. It was one of the strangest experiences of my life. At first, I felt grotesque and awkward in the chest protector and mask. They don't look like much, but if you've never worn them, you don't know how clumsy they can make you feel. We were told that our equipment should feel like part of our body—but how do you get used to about forty square inches of extra ''chest'' and a small jail cell over your face that feels like a brick? Never mind the mask itself—I had trouble with the goddamn *straps*. I'd make a call and straighten up and the mask would drop over my eyes. So then I'd tighten the straps and they'd cut off the blood to my head. And every time I'd yank my mask off, I'd lose my hat—which is like a cop dropping his gun belt and badge. If you don't *look* foolish, you definitely *feel* foolish.

Meantime, whether I was comfortable in the uniform or not, this was trial by fire. The only umpiring I'd ever done was when I was a kid in the projects, pitching whiffle-ball games and calling my own counts. I'd really liked that. What appealed to me was the power, the authority of being the guy in charge. But that was just one-on-one, throwing a ball against a wall. Here, in an organized game on a regulation baseball field, the power increased twentyfold. I remember calling a player out on strikes in that game, and he pissed and moaned about it as he walked away. When he stopped and looked back for my reaction, I took off my mask and said, ''You'd better keep going.'' He did—without another word. I couldn't believe how tough I'd sounded. I was Radatz tough. No; I was *umpire* tough.

To me, that was power. That was control. I'd never felt like that anywhere else in my life. It probably had a lot to do with ego and frustration. When I grew up, I always had friends, but I was never part of the ''in'' group. I was still too shy, too much of a follower, not as bold as the popular kids. So I always longed to be accepted, to be the center of attention. Maybe my secret life caused that longing—with all the hiding and the powerlessness and the fear of discovery. Or maybe it was just being shy and not knowing how to change. I don't know. But it wasn't until I started learning how to umpire that I found my true inner strength.

Somewhere in the early innings of that first Ted Williams game, all of a sudden I *became* an umpire. I started thinking and acting like an umpire and doing everything I'd just learned in the course. Late in the game, I called a batter out for stepping on home plate while putting down a perfect bunt. That infraction is always difficult to see, even in the pros. But I caught it my very first time—and I remembered the rule. After the game Roy Engle, coach of the team the call went against, came up to me and said, ''I'm amazed that you made that call, Dave. You can be proud of it. It was a great call.'' I was shocked. I felt terrific. For the first time I was in complete control of something.

Off the field, though, was a different story. My feelings about women were the same, while my feelings about men had grown stronger. I'd had no interest in anyone involved with the umpire school, though a couple of the younger baseball camp counselors caught my eye. Nothing happened, though. I was too busy trying to become umpire material, and still too cautious to approach anyone. I just put my sex life on hold. No women, no men. Just umpiring.

At night, sometimes, a bunch of us counselors would go to the bars. (As of 1970, I had not been to a gay bar. I never thought about it, didn't know if they existed, wouldn't have gone anyway. It would be thirteen long years before I would have the courage to do that—and even then, I'd be scared shitless of being discovered there by someone associated with baseball.) We'd sit around drinking beer and talking about baseball, women, and getting laid. As far as I was concerned then, it was great to just be one of the guys. Yes, I was lonely. Yes, I was frustrated. But I knew I had to control my feelings about any man I was sexually attracted to, or even thought if being sexually attracted to, because I was totally dedicated to establishing a career. So, unlike in high school, everything else was secondary.

In these bars, though, I had to resort to pretense. I always let somebody else be the "macho" guy who tried to pick up a girl. I would never try to be that person. Instead, I'd do the dance routine—I'd ask a woman to dance and I'd make it look as though I were hustling her by keeping the conversation going and laughing and kidding around with her on the dance floor. This way no one would say, "Why's Pallone sitting over there by himself? Why isn't he trying to get girls like the rest of us?" I figured that if I at least danced, I could always come back to the guys and say, "She turned me down. She wouldn't go back with me. She was too afraid"—or any other believable excuse I could invent. I always shifted the blame to the girl, and no one seemed to doubt me. At the table I would always carry on lively conversations with women just to make it look like I was interested in them. And although I might be enjoying them, I was not looking to take them home for sex. I was more interested in finding out what it would be like to go all the way with a man. But nobody knew that—not even the girls I was talking to.

At summer's end I was exhilarated. I'd done pretty well as a novice umpire, and I'd made some new friends. Apparently Bill Kinnamon saw something in me; he told me flat out that he thought I would be accepted to the Umpire Development Program for the coming February session, and that I should mention his name as a reference on the application. When I got home, I told my parents everything that had happened to me at the baseball camp, and that I'd decided to go further. I knew in my heart that this was what I should do, and my parents seemed to agree. I was surprised that my father didn't try to argue me out of it. I remembered when he'd said, "You wanna be a *what?*" and I thought it would really be something if I could succeed at this and show him that I had made the right choice after all. I still wanted to make him proud.

I applied and got accepted (no doubt with Bill Kinnamon's help; I found out later that I was one of only sixty accepted out of twelve hundred who applied), sent in my deposit, and waited for February. I felt positive that whole winter, even though I worked dreary jobs to raise the six hundred dollars I needed for the program, like bus boy, bank teller, and clothing-store clerk. I even shoveled snow for five bucks a walk. I had a purpose now—direction, ambition, a focused goal. I felt that if I could make it as an umpire, that incredible sense of power and control I'd felt on the field might somehow carry over to my personal life. I thought, "Hey, I'm really finding myself now. I know where I wanna go. Maybe my whole life will change for the good. Maybe it's all gonna work itself out."

Many years ago, Don Adams did a comedy routine where he played an instructor at an umpire school giving the opening speech to the new trainees. He said: "Men, all of you are here to become umpires. Some of you will make it and some of you will crack. Those of you who make it will go on to bigger and better things. Those of you who crack . . . will become *umpires!*"

I always think of that when people ask me what it takes to be a major league umpire. A lot of fans believe that you must be "cracked" to want to be "the man everybody loves to hate" on a baseball field. I mean, why would anyone want to go to work every day knowing he's gonna get booed and second-guessed and be generally unappreciated? Who needs that? Well, obviously, *umpires* do. That's because umpires—the good ones, at least—need to test themselves under pressure. They like to be in situations where the heat is on.

Of course, at age nineteen, what did I know about that? My first day in the Umpire Development Program in Florida, when a veteran umpire told me, "Kid, the reason I do this work is because I love the heat," I swear to God I thought he meant the *sun*. I had no idea what umpiring was all about yet. At the time, if you asked me to name a current major league umpire, I could name only one: Emmett Ashford—and I thought he was the most ridiculous figure I ever saw on a baseball field. He was always jumping up and down and waving his arms and looking ridiculous. I remember a call he made at Fenway on a line drive over first. As the ball sailed past him, he jumped up and down and waved his arms and called it fair, even though it landed four feet foul. I couldn't believe that call. I thought, "Boy, umpires are jerks." A classic Dave Pallone irony: how could I have known then that I would eventually try to *become* one of those "jerks"?

Chub Feeney, a former president of the National League, used to say that you could take anybody out of a bar and make an umpire out of him. Bullshit. You might as well say that you can take anyone out of a bar and make him an astronaut or a cardiologist. Number one: you're talking about a specialized profession of trained experts. Number two: only sixty people get to the top of that profession—so *something* weeds them out. Granted, some of the ignorant, bigoted jackoffs I worked with in the major leagues probably *belonged* in a bar, but that's not where umpires are made. A major league umpire learns the tools of his trade in two places: first at a sanctioned umpire school, and then under fire on a baseball field.

The first week of February 1971 I flew to St. Petersburg, Florida, to begin my five-week "basic training" course. It was my first plane ride, my first extended stay far from home, my first attempt to make a career. I was nervous as hell. I knew that no one got into the minor leagues—never mind the majors—without first graduating from one of these affiliated schools. So there was no room for screwing up. And even if I did well, only half of us would get jobs when it was over. But I knew I wanted it, and I knew I'd do well. My attitude was: "Nothing can stop me now."

The training was intensive from day one. We did class-room work on rules and regulations every morning, and then went out to the baseball fields. First, they had us do vigorous calisthenics to get us going. Then we ran laps. And if you got out of line, they made you run more laps. Next, we split into groups and worked with our instructors, who were minor league umpires—Nick Bremigan, John McSherry, Frank Pulli—on the verge of making it to the majors.

Every morning, we'd start with our safe/out routine. We'd line up along the outfield foul lines and, one at a time, run three steps, stop, crouch with hands on knees, raise a fist, and call, "Out!" Then we'd run three more steps, stop, crouch again, signal with our hands straight out at our sides, and call, "Safe!" It was interesting that they always stressed waiting before making the call. "Never rush a call," they said. "Pause a second to register the play. Then make the call." I worked very hard on that, because when I first started out I was overanxious to make my calls. Well, that turned out to be another Dave Pallone irony: who could have predicted that my mastery of the waiting technique would eventually result in the wildest controversy of my pro career?

The reason we ran so much in the safe/out drill was because, in the minor leagues, you worked on two-man crews and you'd always be on the run to cover the bases. That's why the instructors always had us practicing positioning drills. They would divide us into a "home plate" group and a "bases" group, and they'd show us where we had to be on different plays. For instance, on a base hit with a runner on first, the home plate umpire would go halfway up the third base line, in case the runner tried for third. Or on a bunt, the home plate umpire would follow the batter up the first base line to make sure he stayed within the forty-five-foot lane. Along with correct positioning, they emphasized hustle, alertness, willingness to make a tough call, and proper technique. They covered everything.

After that the instructors took us to the batting cages, where we called balls and strikes thrown by pitching machines. They taught us the strike zone and critiqued our positioning and style. Next we worked on mechanics—technical things you wouldn't learn anywhere else, like how to remove the mask without knocking your hat off (or pulling your face off with it). Losing your hat made you appear clumsy, they said. Everything should be done with ease and grace. They showed us how to remove the mask and chest protector at the same time. (That was when the outside protector was used in the American League; today, it's no longer used.) You always removed the mask with the left hand, dipped the right shoulder, stuck the mask under the protector, grabbed the protector's handle, and swung it away from your body like a shield—all in one quick move. They wanted you to look as graceful as a matador sweeping his cape across the bull. On the other hand, they didn't want you losing sight of the baseball while you fiddled with your gear. So we were instructed to work on that every night in front of a mirror until we had it down.

The Umpire Development Program was so thorough, they even worked us on the correct technique for brushing off home plate. They said, "Keep your asses *down*. An ass in the air is a stupid ass." And they took it a step further. They pointed out: "Always face the crowd when you brush off the plate. Never aim your ass at the fans." I thought that made sense, too. "Yeah," one of us joked, "it's better to aim your ass at *pitchers*. They think umpires are assholes anyway."

Another thing the instructors stressed was style. They explained that appearance always made the first impression, and since we would be in the public eye, we needed to make a strong, positive impression. "If you look sloppy out there, people will think you're a sloppy umpire," they said. "If you look good, people will think you're a good umpire." Bill Deegan, a former American

League umpire instructing in the program, taught me more. He told me, "If you have a clean, crisp style, you always look like you're right. If you have a clumsy style, you look like you're wrong." Off the field, I had always been conscious of my personal appearance, especially the way I dressed. I liked to look crisp, stylish, sharp. So this was easy for me to apply to my umpiring style. I always made sure my uniform pants were tapered exactly right—not too long, not too short. Too long makes you look like a slob; too short, like a wimp. I liked my jackets dry-cleaned and pressed, my shirts starched, my shoes shined.

Frank Pulli also helped me understand how important it was to call your strikes with style. That hadn't occurred to me; I was too busy just trying to feel comfortable. But I realized that part of conveying your umpire's personality was in the way you used your body and voice. Pulli said that when you had a close call, you had to "sell it" by looking like you *knew* you were right. That way, he claimed, most people would think, "Well, it was close, but he must be right. He's so *sure* of himself." The idea was: communicate conviction, firmness, self-confidence. This was probably the most significant lesson I learned in the Umpire Development Program. It formed the heart of my style, and it got me out of jams a lot of other guys could not have handled.

I liked the program for many reasons, but the chief one was that they taught you not only the physical techniques of umpiring but also the mental aspects that could give you an edge. I think that's why guys like Frank Pulli have succeeded for so many years in the major leagues; they know so much more than how to just call balls and strikes and "Safe" and "Out." They know the psychological aspects, too—things you can't read in a book. I told myself that when I made it to The Bigs, I would use the psychological edge whenever I could.

One other thing I liked: the instructors were all business. They stressed the need to discipline yourself to really learn these things. That's why, after the first week, every time we screwed up on the field they made us run laps. "Punishment," we used to kid, "is swift and severe in the Umpire Development Program. Only the tough survive.'' That was true. It was obvious that if you didn't have mental toughness, you couldn't get through this program—never mind the pressures of big-league baseball. (Years later, I was talking during spring training to a major league player with whom I'd had a few encounters, and we were discussing why certain minor league ''phenoms'' made it to the big leagues while others didn't. ''What do you think the key ingredient is?'' I asked. He looked at me and pointed to his head. He was right. At that level, almost everybody has big-league ability. But ability means nothing if you don't have the inner strength to handle the pressure and stress. I learned firsthand that the same is true for umpires. It's far from a simple job. And you don't just sail from umpire school to the major leagues. You gotta have what it takes, mentally, right from the start, or the game eats you up and spits you out. Hey, it eventually did that to me—and I *had* what it took.)

Finally, we started working some actual ballgames. We worked local college games, and occasionally we went over to Lakeland to work Detroit Tigers intrasquad games or to Winter Haven to call Red Sox games. That was thrilling. I mean, there I was at age nineteen working home plate with my childhood idol, Carl Yastrzemski, at bat. I could not believe I was actually doing that. Yes, umpires are fans; how can we be involved in the game we love so much and *not* be fans? But we learn to separate our personal emotions from our job. I remember thinking, ''This is what it feels like to be in the spotlight, to be right there with the big names.'' As I said, I had always longed to be the center of attention. And though I really wasn't the center in this case, I was sure as hell inside the circle.

That feeling of importance gripped me. I became surer and surer throughout the five weeks that this was how I was going to make my mark in life, and that I would pass the course and get a job. Toward the end, naturally, I sweated it out. But guys like Bremigan, Pulli, and McSherry had taken me under their wing and given me extra tips and encouragement. They kept reassuring me, ''You're gonna make it. You'll get hired.'' And they were right. Thirty of us were hired to be minor league umpires—and I was one of them. Some of us were also hired to work spring training and then "extended spring training" in St. Petersburg. Extended spring training was something that four major league teams—the Mets, the Phillies, the Cardinals, and the White Sox—had just started that year for the purpose of giving their rookies some post-spring training work. It allowed umpires to get more experience, too—and to earn some needed extra cash. I was extremely excited. I thought, "I've found a profession."

But off the field, I still hadn't found *myself*. The only thing I was interested in while I was in St. Petersburg was becoming an umpire. I still wasn't sure about my sexuality, so I kept thinking about girls and—whenever I went with the guys to the bars—dancing with and talking to girls like everyone else. Part of me kept saying, "This thing for men is probably just a phase. It won't last." But another part said, "This has to change. I gotta be able to tell my feelings to *somebody*."

Meantime, I told no one and dated no one. I had no sexual life at all; I kept it on hold. My frustrations kept building, but I knew my inner feelings had to remain hidden. A couple of the younger guys in the program (who never made it into pro baseball) attracted me, but I just told myself, "You cannot pursue this here." Deep down, I knew that I wanted to go further with men, because I needed to compare it with what I'd felt that one time I had sex with a girl in high school. So I was thinking about it and wanting to do something about it; but I suppressed it because I was in this all-male, "macho" world of baseball. What was I going to do—jeopardize my career before it began?

"No way," I told myself. "I *want* this career."

(4)

BEHIND THE MASK

I had a stormy eighteen-year career as a professional umpire. Crazy incidents followed me everywhere. Things happened to me that didn't happen to other umpires who'd been around twice as long. I could never figure it out. After a while I *expected* the bizarre. I understood how Ralph Branca felt after he served up Bobby Thompson's "shot heard 'round the world" in the '51 playoffs. After the game, Branca sat on the clubhouse steps saying, "Why me?" Well, at the end of my career I was thinking the same thing.

Most of my memories of the eight long years (1971–78) I spent in the minor leagues are of trials and tribulations related to my troubles later in the majors. By that I mean the minors was where I formed my umpire's persona and style, which attracted so much conflict in my major league career. Yes, some of it was my fault; but plenty of it wasn't. Either way, every conflict in the minors added to my reputation later. And I *always* had a conflict. Even my facial expression caused me problems. That's how crazy it was for me.

Reflecting back now, I know that my immaturity in my twenties, and my inner turmoil over "the other me," and definitely my explosive temper made me a hardass umpire, and probably helped polarize people's opinions about me throughout my career. Add to that the fact that I didn't get to the majors the usual way, and you have a volatile mix. And that's what my career was—volatile. But let me add this: I think I was a damn good umpire. I knew my stuff; I never ran from controversy; I stood up to everything they threw at me to try to drive me out. I am totally convinced that had I not been forced out of baseball for being gay, I would still be umpiring in the major leagues, still earning respect—and probably still getting into conflicts.

Like everybody else in the business, my initiation was the minor leagues. It was a weird world, not the "glamorous" life people might imagine. The closest we ever came to glamour was reading about Hollywood in the newspapers. We did ball-busting travel in junker cars to out-of-the-way towns you couldn't even find in bed-and-breakfast books. We lived in rundown rooming houses straight out of Hitchcock for three dollars a night with boarders straight out of Rod Serling: angry vets, spacey addicts, drunks who sat on the porch all day smoking and flipping the finger at strangers. We used common hallway bathrooms with rotting tubs, rusty water, and pull-chain toilets that dimmed the light bulb every time they flushed. Picture it this way: the major "metropolises" on the circuit were places like Pawtucket, Toledo, and Charleston, West Virginia.

Not every town was depressing; some in upstate New York were beautiful. But as rookie umps we didn't get to sightsee the beauty, because we never got days off—unless it rained. We were so fatigued sometimes, the places were a blur. We didn't often see the nice parts of town, because a lot of times the ballparks were across the tracks. Although it was exciting to be part of professional baseball, it was sometimes hard to get fired up to work games for teams called the Tides, the Mudhens, and the Charlies. In rookie ball we didn't earn enough money to whistle while we worked. Those first couple of years I made six hundred dollars a month, which on paper figured out to about twenty dollars a day. But after taxes and expenses took about half of that, it was more like ten dollars a day—and only if I skipped lunch. It ain't called the *minor* leagues for nothing.

I remember when I was working with Lanny Harris (he

made it to the majors with me in the '79 strike) in the Double A Eastern League one time when we had three weekend games in Thedford Mines. If any one place characterizes my memories of the minors, Thedford Mines is it—a dreary, asbestos-mining town tucked into the hills of Quebec. Sometimes the asbestos dust in the air was thick enough to block the sun. For restaurants, they had fast-food outlets and classic greasy spoons. There were two hotels; the players stayed in one, and we stayed in the other—a dingy, smelly, knotty-pine dump. But we had to save our money, because Lanny was supporting his wife and three kids, and I had to fuel my '73 Buick Regal—the horse we rode to all our games.

Between the two of us, we had maybe forty dollars for our room, food, and a tank of gas to get us to our next scheduled stop, in Pittsfield, Massachusetts. How can you live on that? We could only afford a room with one bed, so we switched off each night: one of us on the bed and one on the floor. We went to a market and bought a loaf of bread, a pound of bologna, some mustard and tomatoes, and that's what we ate every day.

This particular weekend, all the miners were on strike, which meant the whole town was on strike. There was no place to go for entertainment, nothing to do but umpire our games. Money was tight in town. Only twenty people came to the games—and they all sneaked in. The ballpark was pitiful: makeshift, portable stands; wooden home plate; flattened pitcher's mound; rickety outhouse near the dugout where local "Sallies" gave certain players one-minute blow jobs between innings. Night games were like playing under pen lights. Outfielders risked not only getting beaned by flyballs but also disappearing forever into the Twilight Zone on long base hits.

I hated Thedford Mines; I kept telling myself, "No, this can't be real. It's just a nightmare—or a Boris Karloff film." This particular trip, all I wanted to do was get the hell away from there and down to Pittsfield, where my close friends Al and Connie Bianchi were always ready to put me up overnight and feed me home-cooked meals and share friendly conversation.

We finished the Friday and Saturday games, so that left

only Sunday—which suddenly seemed ten years off. Lanny and I decided to kill the night by driving to the Kentucky Fried Chicken joint and treating ourselves to one order for the two of us—four pieces of chicken and a couple of soft rolls. We got the food and drove around, trying to eat away our depression. I said, "Wouldn't it be nice if we got rain tomorrow, and we could leave early and make Pittsfield by one o'clock and have the whole afternoon to enjoy? Then we wouldn't have to hang around this place anymore." Lanny said, "It's not going to rain tomorrow. We'll be right here umpiring our game." He was about ten years my senior, wiser, more experienced, and more resigned to serving out our term in Thedford Mines. I, on the other hand, had an idea for early release.

I said, "C'mon, let's go to the ballpark," and I drove us over there. In the lighted parking lot I told Lanny, "I'll be right back. Don't ask questions. That way, when the FBI grills you, you can plead ignorance." He laughed, and I got out to engineer our escape. The place was silent and deserted—pretty much like game time. I jumped the fence and jogged around the first-base dugout to the water hose, which I uncoiled and dragged onto the field. The rain tarp was already covering the infield as a precaution. It was a joke, though; the tarp was so worn out, it had a dozen rips and holes. But I guess in Thedford Mines it was better than nothing—although nothing ran a damn close second.

I peeled the tarp back, placed the nozzle of the hose on the infield between first and second, and laid the tarp back over it. Then I returned to the dugout, looked around, and turned the water on. All of a sudden, water started spritzing through the holes like seltzer after you shake the bottle. I knew if it pumped all night, there was no way they could play tomorrow's game.

When I returned to the car, Lanny was laughing his ass off. He had seen the whole thing. I said, "I sense 'washout' in the baseball forecast." He said, "I can't believe you did that. If anyone finds out . . ." I said, "Hey, if *you* don't tell, *I* won't tell. However, if you do tell—then you must die." Back at the hotel we started worrying that somebody might find out anyway, so I suggested that we leave immediately. Lanny said that would point the finger right at us. The Voice of Reason—or Too Much TV.

The next morning the phone rang at ten. It was the GM of the Thedford Mines team. "No game today," he told Lanny. "Some vandals put the hose under the tarp last night and soaked the field. It's unplayable."

Our luggage was already packed in the Buick, so we drove immediately to a gas station, where I told the attendant not to spill a drop because we only had five bucks left. That bought us a full tank and some candy bars, and we blew out of there for Pittsfield. A rainout never felt so good.

The next day, though, it felt terrible. I had second thoughts about what I'd done. So I rationalized that given the circumstances in Thedford Mines that weekend, probably no one regretted missing the game—including the teams. That was the best I could do. Of course, these things did not go on routinely. Sometimes you just felt you had to do something crazy to survive the craziness. Maybe it was a lame excuse; but like in almost any other profession, life at the bottom can wear down your sanity.

In fact, when I first started out in the Class A New York-Penn League (which a reporter once called "the Big Mac-Motel 6 League"), the existence was so meager that even washing clothes was a hardship. Since we worked every day, we didn't have time for a Laundromat, so we mostly wore dirty, smelly clothes. We thought, "Well, if we can hold off till Friday, we can have two more snacks." Food was the top priority; my spare change went for potato chips, candy, and coffee before detergent and bleach. I had three pairs of underwear my first season. I wore each pair twice a week, and on the seventh day I laundered.

I had no preparation for the minors. I didn't make many friends there, and I was often paired with somebody I didn't like. For instance, my first partner in the New York-Penn League in 1971 was Jim Griffin, a decent enough guy in his late twenties whose personal habits irritated the crap out of me. This will sound stupid, but it bothered me that he used baby powder after he showered. The reason was that the dust settled on everything I owned—which was basically my clothes. Appearance was very important to me, and I was meticulous about my clothes and how I looked. Another thing I disliked was the overcautious way he drove. Meekness always aggravated me—especially in umpires. Plus he smoked, and I hated being trapped with a smoker.

One other barrier was that he enjoyed drinking beer and looking for women. I didn't mind going out for a beer, but I wasn't interested in hunting women. Over the winter I'd fought the undertow pulling me toward men by telling myself that maybe those feelings weren't real. I thought that maybe I just needed to transfer those attractions back to women, and that would do the trick. So I dated a few girls I knew at home, thinking I could get a relationship going with somebody I already liked. It didn't work. Something was always missing: ease, romance, even lust. But I liked being around women, and I kept hoping they might change me.

The problem was, each time I kissed and fondled a girl, I stopped myself from going all the way. I did feel some pleasure, but it was always like my first sexual experience in high school—it never felt the way I thought it was supposed to feel. I'd grown up on that stuff about bells ringing and rockets going off when you found the Right One, so I guess I was looking for those kinds of signs. I kept figuring, "Maybe she isn't the Right One. Maybe the next girl will be." I mean, no one ever said, "By the way, Dave, the Right One for you might be a *man.*"

So, from the start, Jim Griffin and I didn't have much in common. We'd go to a bar and he'd say, "Maybe we'll get lucky tonight." I'd say, halfheartedly, "Maybe we will," but I had something else in mind. While he was sizing up the waitress with the nice legs, I was sneaking glances at the handsome bartender with the great smile. Of course, I could never tell Jim that. In most male bonding situations, the standard subjects are probably sports and screwing girls. In professional baseball, those subjects aren't just standard, they're almost automatic. Can you imagine what the response would've been if, back in 1971, I had announced to my fellow umpires, ''I hope I can find a handsome man to take me home tonight''?

In the sporting world at that time, there was almost no talk about ''gays''—why would it come up? But whenever it was mentioned it was almost always in a tone of ridicule. So I knew the guys would suspect anyone who didn't talk the talk, never mind play the role. That's why those first awkward weeks on the circuit with Jim Griffin were significant for me. Here was my first chance to room with somebody at close quarters and maybe get to share my innermost secrets—but unfortunately we didn't get along. That meant we had to spend the next three months traveling, eating, working, and living together without sharing friendship or trust. We never became good friends, just fellow travelers for a while on a road that forked.

He made me realize even more how careful I had to be around baseball people. I consciously reminded myself, ''No way can you reveal your feelings here. They might shun you; they might report you; they might get violent. You gotta hide it and keep it hidden.'' I was like a one-way mirror; I could be a foot away from you and look you in the eyes, yet you couldn't see me.

All that early pretense in public places was the real start of my double life in baseball. I always hated pretense, but there was no alternative. It protected my secrets, my family, my friends, my career. But it also made me feel guilty. So my toughest chore every day during the baseball season wasn't my umpiring; it was living a lie. I thought if I could throw myself into baseball, I could hide my confusion and frustration, even from myself. I figured I could handle it—as long as I could hide behind my mask. When I think of the deception in my baseball life, something Satchel Paige said comes to mind: ''Don't look back. Somethin' might be gainin' on you.'' Well, starting with my first year in the minors, I developed a permanent crick in my neck from looking over my shoulder to see if the truth was catching up to me.

Meantime, Griffin and I muddled through the '71 season together. We weren't poor umpires, but we weren't particularly good, either. That season was one long lesson in screwing up and trying to learn from it. Typical for me was a game with the Oneonta Yankees in which a Yankee player tried to score from second on a hit, and the catcher tagged him in plenty of time, yet I called the runner safe. Well, here came the opposing manager, neck veins bulging. "How the fuck can you call him safe?" he said. "The ball beat him by twenty miles!"

I said, "Yes, the ball beat him. But your catcher didn't tag him with the ball. He put in his throwing hand and tagged him with his *glove*. That's no tag—he's safe."

"Yeah?" he said. "Well, what the hell are you smilin' at? It's not fuckin' funny."

I said, "I'm not smiling."

He said, "Then what's that fuckin' *smirk* for?"

"That's the way I *look*," I said. "I'm not laughing." I knew I had this facial expression. I felt that if I looked angry or mean during an argument, it would just add fuel to the fire, whereas if I looked calmer and more subdued, the argument would settle down faster. So I always had this relaxed look, and people took it the wrong way a lot. But I couldn't consciously change it.

I had several ridiculous arguments that first year, and I remember exploding a lot and throwing too many people out. Hindsight tells me now that it was probably a combination of my temper and my personal problems seeping through. The best thing about rookie ball was that the season lasted only three months—which is why it's called "Short A" ball. Even so, for me, that first "short" season was a helluva long three months.

The following year I was asked by Barney Deary, head of the Umpire Development Program, to serve as a junior instructor at the their Umpire Development School in St. Petersburg. I was mainly a "gofer," but I did help some of the students with their basics, including a fellow Bostonian named Steve Palermo. That was such a great feeling; just a year ago I was like him. After the school session ended, I looked forward to my second spring training in Clearwater, hoping to improve my work. But I dreaded another lonely season on the road with a stranger. The big surprise was that at extended spring training I was paired with Palermo—who became my partner for the upcoming regular season. He was a good guy back then, and we got along great. We had similar dispositions and goals: we were both lonely on the road, both fiery Italians, both serious about the work, both aiming for the majors. I thought we could become an excellent team, because we also shared that tough demeanor on the field and the ability to take control.

But I was worried that I wouldn't be able to concentrate strictly on umpiring. I was twenty but still in the dark about my sexuality. There was a war inside me: should I be with women or men? In the off-season, I'd dated two women casually because I wanted company, and because I was feeling social pressure from family and friends: ''Who are you going out with?'' ''Do you have a girlfriend?'' So I took the women to lunch or to parties, more like I would with friends. Sex was not an issue; I just said, ''With my career, I don't have time for a serious relationship.'' Yet, at spring training, I couldn't stop wondering what it would be like to have intercourse with a man. I asked myself constantly, ''Why can't I just have that one experience and find out about it once and for all, and then I'll know?'' After two years of sexual frustration, I needed to do something about my personal life. I thought I might be gay, but I didn't know for sure. I just knew I had to find out.

One night after an exhibition game, I went out with a group of umpires to a bar in the Holiday Inn. Some of the major league umpires were there; they liked to buy drinks for the minor league guys because they remembered what the grind was like. So everybody was having a good time, while I sat there sipping an amaretto, depressed about my nonexistent sex life and my loneliness. I phased in and out of conversations, thinking, ''I gotta find out about myself, one way or the other.'' That's when I noticed this older woman drinking alone at the bar—dark hair, buxom figure, attractive, around forty. She was wearing a black paisley dress and electric earrings that blinked on and off. I thought, ''Boy, God just read my mind. Here she is—Miss Easy.'' I knew I could pick her up without much work. (It's funny; I could always attract women, because—according to them—I had that tall, dark look of Mr. Right. Another Pallone irony: I used to hear that and think, "That's nice. But when do I meet *my* Mr. Right?")

Normally, I wouldn't have gone after an older woman. But that night it occurred to me that a more mature woman might be just the person to help me feel something that younger girls had failed to make me feel. I thought, "Maybe I've been missing something important because I've never been with a woman of experience." I mean, at twenty, how do you know about these things? The only things I ever heard from the guys on the baseball circuit were the typical war stories about sex with groupies or "chippies." But those stories didn't speak to *my* dilemma. And they didn't tell me anything useful about women. They told me more about men—though not what I *needed* to know.

So I approached the woman at the bar, sat next to her, and started polite conversation. The more I talked, the surer I was that I could leave with her. When she started getting drunk, I knew it was time to make my move. I asked her if she'd like to go for a drive and she said sure. We went out to my car and drove awhile, and she did everything she could to arouse me. But nothing happened. In my mind, I attributed that to nervousness. I was anxious as hell because I knew that this was my big test. I was determined to find out the truth about myself, no matter what.

When we got to her house and she asked me in, something clicked inside me and I said, "Thanks, but I don't think so. Not tonight." She said, "Oh, come on. Loosen up a little," and she started seducing me again. I tried to get into it and let myself go, but I didn't feel excited. She blamed herself: "I'm not turning you on, am I?" I was embarrassed—mostly for her. I said, "No. But, listen, it isn't you. It's me."

"What's wrong?" she said. "You don't want me? I thought you wanted me." She was confused, not angry.

I said, "I thought so, too. Maybe it's just not my night." And I remember thinking, "Jesus, that's the understatement of the year." She looked at me with her big, cloudy eyes and those blinking earrings, and she said, "Then why'd you drive me home?"

"I don't know," I said. "I found you attractive and I wanted to be with you. It just didn't work out. It's my fault. I'm really sorry. I feel bad I wasted your night. That's not what I wanted to do."

"So, what *did* you want to do?" she asked sincerely.

"I wish I knew. I'm really sorry. I hope you understand." She shrugged and said, "That's okay," and she got out of the car. I thought, "Damn it, Pallone. You can't do these things to people. Get your act together."

When she got inside her house, I left. And then it hit me: "Maybe I just *found* myself. Maybe this means I'll never feel what I'm supposed to feel with a woman. Maybe it means it *has* to be with a man. If that's true, then it isn't just a phase—it's something I was born with. And this isn't 'the other me' anymore; it's the *real* me." There was a sense of relief in believing that. But I was still unsettled, still unsure. I knew I still faced the ultimate test: going all the way with a man. Only then could I know for certain that everything I was feeling now was really true. I thought, "Okay, I know this much: I won't feel anything with a woman. But what the hell do I do *now?*"

By the end of the first month of the '72 season, Steve Palermo and I had established ourselves as the best crew in our league. Apparently, though, that didn't matter, because all of a sudden one day, Wallace McKenna, the league president, decided to break us up. He called me and explained that a lot of the teams in the league had complained about our short fuses, so it would be better to split us up. I got pissed. I said, "Are you saying the *managers* run this league? If you split us up, you're makin' a big mistake." He said, "Are you looking to get fired?" I said, "Go ahead and fire me—I don't give a shit. The life's not that great. We shouldn't be split up. We're the best fuckin' crew you have." I was making it known, even as a novice, that I would speak my mind regardless of the consequences. I decided early on—and it would become my trademark in the major leagues—

that I would allow no one to push me around. Finally, Bill Kinnamon was called in to confer with Steve, myself, and McKenna, and as a result we were not split up. I think Kinnamon respected my backbone—and I intended to stiffen it even more.

Palermo and I continued to have a great year and a terrific camaraderie. We did everything good partners normally do together: we went out to eat, we went shopping, we hit the bars, we went to movies. It felt great compared to my first year. But as friendly as we were, I couldn't tell Steve my secret. Two reasons: The first was that it felt so good to be liked and to have a real friend, I didn't want to risk losing that friendship and ending up lonelier than I was in '71. The second reason was that I was attracted to him sexually, though I never let him know it. My brief fantasy was that he would be my bed buddy as well as my close confidant. It was easy to imagine, because we were like roommates in college, sharing everyday experiences and everyday talk. But it was just my fantasy; Steve was obviously straight, and he was deeply in love with his girlfriend. That was okay; I would've settled for a friendship close enough for me to trust him with my secret. But I was too scared to take that chance. I also knew that once a friend doesn't necessarily mean always a friend. So I let the issue ride.

It was a damn good thing I did. About a month into the season, Steve wanted to quit. He said he missed his girlfriend back home and that it was a tough, demeaning, horseshit life and he couldn't stay with it. I felt the same way about the life, but I couldn't imagine quitting. We went to the bus station together and I argued, "Steve, it's crazy to quit. You're throwing away a major league career. You'll be there within five years, without question, because you're a great umpire." And finally I talked him out of it. I guess Palermo owes me one, because he made it to the majors in 1977, two years before me. But we don't talk anymore—mainly because he resents me for how I eventually got to the majors. And since we're no longer friends and I find him arrogant and self-centered now, I'm glad he didn't know my secret back in '72. But in fairness I want to say this: today, Steve Palermo is deservedly considered the best umpire in the American League.

That same year, a Double A umpire named Randy Marsh (now in the National League) had to leave for two weeks of service in the Army Reserve, so Barney Deary selected me to take his place. This was a big move for a guy working the bottom of the barrel in rookie ball. The fact that Deary considered me more qualified than anyone else gave me a big ego boost, and just in time. I thought, "This is unbelievable. I'm going to Double A my second year, even if it is only for two weeks." That's when it hit me that they had really noticed my work, and I actually did have a chance to move up someday to the majors.

That was the one sustaining thought I had as a minor league umpire: "Someday I'll be in the bigs." But I knew that in order to get there, I was gonna have to *be* somebody. Down there, it wasn't enough to be a good umpire, or even a great one. The competition to move up was stiff. You were always competing against the same guys you lived and worked with, which created a cutthroat atmosphere. You never knew who was ahead of you in line, or even if there *was* a line. You came into the minors knowing that your first stop could also be your last. So finally I figured, "I'd rather be noticed than invisible. If I don't make it to The Bigs, it won't be because they don't know my name."

The first place I made an impression was Geneva, New York, in 1971. I was still pretty raw, still learning the ropes. I don't remember the score of that particular game, just that it was close and the Geneva team lost, and I made several close calls against them. In the minor league parks, you always had a number of "lifer" fans—people who came to every game, year after year, not so much to enjoy baseball as to let off steam from a tough day at work or a bad night at home. Unfortunately, a lot of these people came loaded for umpire.

Two weird events happened in that game. The first involved my underwear. We always wore our shin guards under our pants, so in order to get the pants to fit, we had to wear flares—and they had to be black. Well,

I liked the more tailored look, so I tapered the flare, which also tightened the pants. Big mistake. Early in the game the fans started in on me, even though I hadn't done anything yet to provoke them. I couldn't figure it out. Then I heard someone yell, "Nice underwear, Pallone. Is that a truce flag you're wearing?" Then I understood: my pants had ripped right up the ass seam. Worse: I'd committed the dumb rookie mistake of wearing white underwear. Every time I called a pitch, I flashed my patch of white and got a barrage of insults from the fans. I guess the lesson was: if you don't want to make an ass of yourself, always wear black underwear with your black pants—which, after that, I always remembered to do.

But, Jesus, the ridicule got under my skin, which was tissue thin then. And my aggravation contributed to the second event: a case of severe rabbit-ear-itis. Apart from the underwear fiasco, I was catching nonstop flak from a lady in the front row. She was in her sixties, and she busted my balls the whole game. In the New York–Penn League back then, crowds were measured more in terms of empty seats than by ticket stubs, so everyone in the place could hear this lady giving me lip: "Go back to Little League! You stink, you bum!" I was close to detonating, but I told myself, "Forget it. She's nuts. She's not worth it."

As the game wore on, so did her abuse: "Punch a hole in your mask, ump! You got one in your pants, and we all know you got one in your head!" Normally, I wouldn't tolerate that kind of personal attack from a *player,* never mind a sixty-year-old female "lifer." I could have tossed her out of the ballpark at any time, but my Italian pride wouldn't let her get the best of me. Finally, the game ended and I hurried for the dugout. I couldn't wait to get away from her. But when I reached the steps, there she was at the rail, waving her camera and screaming at me, "Hey, ump—you're the worst! You need glasses! Get a hard hat, you dummy!"

When I heard "dummy," something in me snapped. I reached up, snatched her camera, and smashed it against the dugout roof. Plastic flew everywhere; people were shocked. I looked right at the woman and said, "The name's *Pallone,* lady. That's spelled P-A-L-L-O-N-E, in case you wanna call the league and complain to *them.*" Then I disappeared into the dugout. I'll never forget the astonished look on that lady's face. I only saw it for a second, but she had to be thinking, "Oh, my God. He's coming up here now to break my neck." I never saw her or heard her voice again, so I credited myself with literally running a terrible fan out of the game. But even today I love fantasizing that she's still standing by that dugout—nineteen years later—shocked out of her life, trying to remember how to spell my name: "Did he say *one* 'L,' or two?"

At the end of September '72, I was selected to work "winter ball"—the Instructional League—in Sarasota with Steve Palermo and Mike Reilly (now an American League umpire). It was a two-month schedule for players from all leagues, including the majors, who needed to rehabilitate injuries, learn how to switch-hit or change their batting styles, try new positions, or just brush up after long layoffs. To me, it meant I was moving up in the ranks, because only the better umpires got that assignment. I started feeling proud of my umpiring. It felt like my career was working out.

The November day I returned home from winter ball, my mother was busy hanging the curtains in my room. As usual, they were freshly cleaned and pressed—her way of welcoming me home. We talked about my work and our Thanksgiving plans, and then I found out she'd been feeling ill and had a lot of pain, although the doctors didn't know why. But she told me not to worry about it, everything would be fine. I believed her.

During December, Mickey's pain increased. In January, she had to go in for surgery. When I went to visit her in the hospital, a nurse took me aside and told me she'd worked with Mickey's surgeon for years and it was the first time she'd ever seen him stop an operation to cry. She said he had found a tumor the size of a grapefruit in Mickey's intestine, and that the cancer had spread to her liver. He cried because he knew that if they had caught the cancer while it was confined to the intestine, they might have been able to save her life. This devastated me. I could not accept it.

I went back to my winter job in the Grover Cronin department store and tried to hope for a miracle. In the meantime, Mickey prepared for chemotherapy treatments. One day in February, she called me at the store and asked me to meet her at the hospital. "Your father has had a heart attack," she said. Two days later, Mickey went in for her chemotherapy. So there I was, starting off what promised to be the best year of my career by going to the hospital on my lunch hour to visit my mother and father in the same room, both gravely ill. I remember how frightening it was to see both of them in the hospital like that, not because of accidents but because of nature. It was a stiff dose of perspective; suddenly I didn't give a damn about baseball anymore. Yet, ironically, there was no question that it was the challenge in my umpiring that had been teaching me the kind of inner strength I needed to pull me through this ordeal.

My dad's heart attack scared the hell out of him. He stopped smoking, recovered, and went back to work, while my mother kept up her treatments and held her own. They both seemed to rally through the winter, so when March came I decided to go to spring training in Florida. I had just learned that my assignment for '73 was in the Class A Carolina League—another step up the ladder to The Bigs.

I struggled through spring training, worrying about my parents. I could not get my mind on my work. One night early in June, I called Mickey from a pay phone in Kinston, North Carolina, to see how she was doing. She said things were fine and she was doing really well. She mentioned her latest project: redecorating our house. She was finally getting everything she'd wanted for years: woodwork refinished, kitchen repainted, new carpeting, new drapes, new furniture. She sounded really happy. But she told me she had to go into the hospital again for more chemotherapy. There was a pause, and then, out of the blue, she said, "David, I just want you to know that I think you're going to do so well in your career. I know things will work out really well for you. Remember that."

I didn't realize it then, but Mickey knew she wouldn't be coming home again. She was saying her last goodbye to me. Three days later, June 6, I was in Winston-Salem when my brother phoned. His words were: "David. Mommy died." I couldn't comprehend it. "No, no, no," I said, and I broke down. I'd never felt so shattered, so alone. The next day I flew home. I spent the entire flight staring out the window, crying. I could not imagine Mickey not being at the house to greet me.

When I got home, my father was away making the funeral arrangements. When he finally came back, I hurried out and embraced him in front of the house. But he didn't put his arms around me. I never knew why; probably because he was still in shock. As strong as he was, it was obvious that he felt a little lost without my mom. It's strange; the memory of that missed embrace has lingered in my mind all these years—like my missed chance to walk with him to Watertown Square as a kid. That's how important my father's love was to me, especially at that awful moment in my life.

After the funeral, I stuck around home awhile to look after Dad. Finally, Barney Deary called to ask me how things were going at home. I said they were much better and he said, "I was wondering if I could ask you to come back. We need an umpire in the Eastern League, and I think you're the right person for it." I got excited; that was Double A, another step up, and after only two months in Class A. So I said yes.

When I returned to work in the Eastern League, I wore a black arm band in my mother's memory. But every time I walked onto a baseball field, I thought of her and lost my concentration. Her words to me the day we had driven to the Ted Williams Camp kept haunting me: "David, I know this is what you really want. I think this is what you will be for the rest of your life." I couldn't adjust to the loss. Finally, I called Barney Deary and told him, "I can't do it. I have to leave." He said, "You're making a big mistake. You shouldn't leave. There's too much at stake." "I cannot do my job right," I said. "I have to quit."

I went home and worked my old job at the department

store. One day, a saleslady introduced me to a woman named Leona, who had learned that I'd lost my mother. She asked me to come visit her family at their home sometime. A week later, I took her up on the offer, because I sensed that she was someone I could talk to. We had coffee and apple pie, and I met her husband, Ted, who was an architect. We talked about our families, and I knew that we would all be close. Over the summer they treated me like one of their sons, and I considered them my "adopted" family. I visited frequently to talk, mostly to Leona. She became the guiding hand I needed after losing my mother. She had that spirited Italian frankness I liked, and an open ear for me, and the same comforting compassion I used to get from Mickey. Their home was also a refuge from the feeling I had at my home—"I can't stand it here because I miss my mother so much." The warmth of that whole family gave me strength to come through my sorrow, and hope that I would find others out there who would also care.

That winter, I thought more about returning to baseball. I spoke to Barney Deary's brother, Fran, and asked him what his brother would say if I called him up and asked him to let me come back. Fran said, "He knows you're a good umpire. Why don't you call him and ask?" So I did. I told Barney, "I know I quit. But I really didn't want to quit. I was going through a terrible time. I'm over it now and I hope you'll let me come back." He said, "See you in spring training."

So in '74 I got spring training in Clearwater again and I resumed my career. I knew one thing: if I could come through the loss of my mother, I could come through anything. And I was more determined than ever to justify her faith in me. I dedicated my career to her, because she was the one who gave me the confidence and support I needed to succeed at it. In my heart I wanted Mickey to know, somehow: "Yes, Mom, this *is* what I really want. And yes, I *will* do it for the rest of my life."

HEAD ABOVE
THE CROWD

For some reason, much of what I remember about my last five years in the minor leagues involves blowups, arguments, and fights. I was always in a fire storm. What continually shocked me was how a single spark could light the whole place up. For example, when I worked the Double A Eastern League I had a game in '75 at fabulous Wahconah Park in Pittsfield between the Pittsfield Rangers and the Quebec Expos. We had a "crowd" of exactly 119, but those 119 were excited because a "bonus baby" on the Rangers named David Clyde—just sent down by the Texas Rangers—was making his Wahconah Park debut.

It was a miserable, rainy night, and nobody was thrilled to be there. I was working the bases, and every time I looked at a fielder's face I thought I saw the same message: "Let's get this over with and go home." Which was fine with me; I hoped we had a quick, easy game, too. But in an early inning, that hope went out the window. Quebec had runners at first and second with nobody out, and the batter—a guy by the name of Felix Peguero—bunted. The catcher scooped it up and threw to the shortstop, Bump Wills, who was covering third for the force out. I'd anticipated the bunt, so I was right on the play. I called the runner safe.

Bump Wills went nuts. The Rangers' manager, Jackie Moore, bolted out to argue with me and take the heat off

Wills. But Moore cursed me—and I didn't tolerate that. So I threw him out on the spot. My personal rule was: You can curse, as long as you don't direct it at me by starting off with "You" or "You are." If you say "That fuckin' call was terrible," that's fine. If you say "Where the fuck was that pitch?" that's okay. If you say "Bullshit call," that's okay, too. But if you say "You're fucking terrible" or "You're an asshole," you're gone.

Moore knew that, so he started to leave. All of a sudden, here came Bump Wills to argue with me again. He said, "Hey, man, what's your problem? That guy was out. Get in the game." I turned around to him and said, "Get your ass back to shortstop or *you* won't be in the game." That brought David Clyde off the mound toward me. He said, "Don't talk to my shortstop like that. You blew the fuckin' call." I said, "And you get your ass back up on the mound and pitch the ball."

Wills could barely control himself. He said, "You're an asshole, man." That was it: instant ejection. "You're gone," I told him—and he lost it completely. As I turned to walk away, he spun me around and threatened to hit me. It was rare when a player touched an umpire, so it caught me off guard. Now I lost *my* temper; I shoved Wills back and knocked him on his ass. I shouldn't have done that. It was reflex, but very unprofessional.

Meantime, David Clyde came up behind me and clamped me in a bear hug—and suddenly the whole Rangers bench emptied onto the field, including Jackie Moore, who wasn't allowed out there anymore. I looked at my partner, but he was standing at home plate like a cigar store Indian, and I realized, "Great. He's too scared to help."

I was scared, too—but I was a typical young, hot-headed Italian. I thought, "I'm not gonna let these guys get me. I'll be killed, but I'm takin' 'em *all* on." I finally broke free of Clyde's bear hug, ready to take on anybody else who wanted to try me—which was about twenty-five pissed-off Rangers. That's when one of the most extraordinary things I've ever seen on a baseball field took place. The entire Quebec Expos team poured onto the field and rushed to my aid. One second it was twenty-five against one; the next twenty-six against twenty-five. These guys weren't gonna fight over an umpire, but they obviously came out to even up the odds.

After everyone calmed down and we got the game under way again, I returned to my position. We finished out the half-inning, but I was getting vicious verbal abuse from fans in the first-base stands. They were really aggravated. As we started the next inning, some of those fans threw rocks at me. They yelled, "We're gonna get you, Pallone! You better check your tires! We're waiting for you! We're gonna kick your ass!" They sounded serious. So I stopped the game and directed the public-address announcer to get a policeman over to the first-base gate—which he did. Things calmed down, and there were no more incidents.

In my career, I took a lot of ridiculous criticism, but one of the dumbest things I ever read was in Roger O'Gara's newspaper column in Pittsfield a day or two later. O'Gara, who was also the official scorer at that game, wrote this about my request for a cop at the first-base gate: "He alleged that some excitable fans were making threats there. It's difficult to conceive how an assembly of only 119 can get out of hand, but here was Pallone asking for help."

What was really "difficult to conceive" was how anyone could have made such a reckless statement. How many people throwing rocks constitutes getting "out of hand"? It sure as hell doesn't take 119. I don't know what world O'Gara imagined he was living in, but in the world I knew it took only one crazy person throwing one rock or one punch to cause needless injury. Yes, it was only a handful of people threatening me. And no, it wasn't a riot. But how could I have known who really meant me harm and who didn't? Was I supposed to take a poll on my way out of the ballpark: "Okay, how many of you are *really* gonna do it, and how many are only kidding?"

O'Gara knew when he wrote his column—in fact, he even mentioned in his column—that the league president, Pat McKernan, reviewed the incident, suspended and fined both Jackie Moore and Bump Wills, and exonerated me. I mention this because media criticism of public figures is a key element in my story. Throughout my career, I ran into a lot of emotionally biased press—some of it motivated by ignorance, some by personal dislike for me. I have no idea what O'Gara's motivations were; and though his mindless statement did me no harm, it was irresponsible garbage that told me to watch out for worse later.

Part of the reason I had these kinds of conflicts was that I brought them on myself. I know that. I brought them on by continually sticking my head above the crowd. That's where people can take potshots at you. I'm not complaining. I knew it came with the territory, and I was willing to be controversial and disliked. But that's because I was also willing to try to do the best job I could—whether or not I looked good or got high ratings for doing it.

I did things as an umpire that others wouldn't do, out of either timidity, or weakness, or incompetence. I was willing to do whatever had to be done, under the rules, even if it cost me a better reputation. In fact, one of the first guidelines I gave myself in professional baseball was: "Call your own game. Let everybody know you're running the show." I demonstrated that repeatedly in the minors by establishing that when you had Dave Pallone umping your game, there were no unwritten rules. So watch your mouth, mind your business, and play baseball.

Even though I'd put in five years in the minors, my temper kept putting me on the spot. I thought it was the worst in the Eastern League, until I had a little disagreement with Joaquin Andujar in a 1975 game in Bristol, Connecticut. He was pitching for the Three Rivers team, affiliated with the Cincinnati Reds. Previously, I'd enjoyed working his games, because he was so talented and such a great control pitcher. I knew he would eventually be a star in the majors. Like all the top pitchers, Andujar knew how to control a nine-inning game pitch by pitch. Unfortunately, the only thing he couldn't control was his hot Latin temper.

Andujar was pitching a superb game in the late innings, totally in command of a 1–0 gem, mowing 'em down left and right, when a breeze blew some debris onto the field. It obviously distracted him. All of a sudden he loaded the bases and found himself in his first jam. He went to three and two on the batter, so the next pitch might mean the ballgame. He looked in for the sign and was getting set to start his delivery when a piece of paper landed at his feet—and stayed there. He stared at it so long, his infielders got restless. Finally, it unnerved him so much, he broke his hands and bent down to pick it up. As soon as he did that, I called a balk and the run scored.

Andujar went absolutely nuts. I thought he was gonna kill me. They had to tackle him to *keep* him from killing me. He threw the wildest fit of rage I'd ever seen on a baseball field—over a piece of paper. I thought, "And they say *I* got a temper?"

Andujar argued loudly that it wasn't a balk, that it should have been an automatic time out because all he was trying to do was clean up the field, and what the shit was wrong with that, why couldn't he do it if he wanted to? I tried to explain that in breaking his pitching motion to pick up the paper, he'd committed an obvious balk. But the only obvious thing to him at the moment was the need to strangle me to death for costing him a run. He called me every colorful word in the Spanish language— and a few in English I almost didn't recognize.

So now I had to toss him out of the game. Naturally, he went crazy all over again, and they had to gang up on him and literally drag him to the dugout to get him off the field. I was looking around for cops, just in case.

We eventually resumed play, and Three Rivers lost by that one run. The next day, their manager, Russ Synder (who'd missed the game), came over to me and said, "I heard you had a little problem with Joaquin yesterday. What happened?" "I wasn't trying to have a problem," I said. "But he decided he wanted to become a janitor and pick up papers." Snyder chuckled. "What's wrong with that?" "Nothing," I said. "He just changed professions at the wrong time."

On the lighter side, Dick McAuliffe changed professions at the *right* time. In 1974 he had played for the Red

Sox, but in '75 he left the Sox to manage their Bristol Double A team—and I had one of his first games. When he brought his lineup card to home plate for the pregame exchange, he couldn't have known that I had an old grudge to settle with him. This meeting was pure irony.

When I was a kid, I collected hundreds of baseball players' autographs. In Boston, all the kids who wanted autographs would gather at the hotel where the players stayed and wait by the lobby door for them to come out. The Detroit Tigers were the hardest to get, because they used to go through the kitchen and out the back door. I knew this, so one time I went up the alley to the back door and camped there. When they came out, I got Gates Brown, Al Kaline, Norm Cash, and a few others. But when I asked McAuliffe, he said, "I can't sign now." I never forgot that. And little did he know that this snub from the sixties would come back to haunt him in 1975.

So there we were, standing at home plate together for the first time as "equals," and he didn't know who the hell I was. I took McAuliffe's lineup card and I said, "Dick, do you know that we met once before?" He looked at me, trying to remember. I said, "I don't want to make you feel old, but I remember when you were on the Tigers and your team used to come out the back door of the hotel in Boston, never the front door." He said, "Yeah, we did. How'd you know that?" I said, "I was one of those kids waiting at the back door for autographs." He nodded blankly. "One time I asked you, 'Mr. McAuliffe, could I please have your autograph?' and you said no. You were the only one who would *never* give me your autograph. And now, after all these years, I have it on a lineup card."

This irony caught him off guard. He said, "What made you think of that?" I smiled and said: "I just wanted to warn you that if by some chance I should make a close call against you tonight, you'll know why." He looked at me a second, thought it over, and handed me his pen. "Mr. Pallone," he said politely, "could I please have your autograph?"

* * *

Light moments like that were hard to come by for me. After my experience with Miss Easy from the bar in '72, I knew that women were not for me and that I was probably gay. But I couldn't sleep with a man, because I didn't know where to find the right one. I knew there were other gay men, but where the hell were they? Even if I had wanted to be promiscuous (there was no AIDS scare then), I didn't know where to go or how to draw another man to me. I didn't know about gay bars or gay communities or gay literature. I had zero information.

I kept up a front every year. The typical baseball dialogue was, "Hey, Dave, you got a girlfriend yet?"—"No, not yet." "You dating anyone back home?"—"No one special." Which isn't suspicious for a guy in his twenties. And since I spent most of my minor league seasons with just one other ump, I didn't see the other guys. Once in a while when we did meet on the circuit, we'd get together for beers and there'd be talk about picking up women. But mostly we'd talk about what happened to us on the field that week; what arguments we had; who we threw out and who stuck it to us; who was an asshole and who wasn't. And with my ability to attract women in bars, and having my "dancing act" down pat, I got by pretty well.

Each year I was attracted to some ballplayers, and once in a while to another umpire. But these were casual attractions, not driving impulses. It was no different from a straight guy watching a woman walk by and thinking, "Gee, she's attractive." I was attracted, but I didn't lose sleep over it. On the other hand, the constant longing to be with a man frustrated me every day. Even if I had found someone—which I never did in the minors—I couldn't take the risk. I was so committed to my career, I wouldn't put anything else ahead of it. So I neglected my sex life totally. Who knows, maybe that's why I was so explosive on the field.

Once the '75 season ended, I returned to Boston—and more loneliness. I lived at home with my father, and I still missed the love and caring of my mother. I hardly ever went into the city, so I had too much time to dwell on my problems: "How do I find someone to get close to? . . . Will I ever have sex again? . . . Where can I go just for some friendly company?" When I went into professional baseball, I lost touch with the guys I grew up with in the projects and went to high school with. Since I didn't go to college, I never really had a buddy I could call to say, "Hey, what're you doing? Let's go to the hockey game" or "Let's got to a movie" or "Let's get a beer." That was something I was always searching for: the camaraderie of hanging around with someone I really liked, the kidding around, the talks about things that really mattered to me. Maybe it seems like a given in the average person's life, but my life was never "average." Simple companionship seemed like a luxury to me, not a given.

I missed that outlet even more so because I had that kind of easy camaraderie during the baseball season with partners like Steve Palermo and Lanny Harris. But they always lived somewhere else. That's why being home for winter got rough; I spent a lot of time alone. Which meant that my sex life was with me, myself, and I.

Yet I felt the weight of society's pressure to keep up appearances. People were always asking me, "When are you gonna get married?" or "Who are you seeing these days?" I knew that if they saw me occasionally with women, they wouldn't keep asking those questions. And if I didn't have to answer questions, I wouldn't have to lie. That's why I started seeing a girl I knew from the computer school I went to years before. We would see each other maybe twice a week for coffee or maybe a visit with other friends. She was friendly company and someone I could "front" to the public. But after about a month, she wanted to get more serious physically, and I wasn't interested in that. So I had to stop seeing her, though I couldn't tell her the real reason why.

I was frustrated in Boston; so when Barney Deary called me in September, I welcomed the opportunity to work winter league ball through January in the Dominican Republic. I knew it would distract me from my problems for five more months, as well as enhance my chances of making the majors, because if you were picked to work the winter league, the brass considered you one of the better umpires. Also, I thought of the Dominican as an exotic locale: sun, water, a chance to unwind and still work baseball games. What I didn't know was that the Dominican was even more nerve-racking than the minors, and a weirder world.

I got off the plane in Santo Domingo with two dollars to my name, so I had to report to the league office to get more cash. On the way over, I saw this young boy sitting in the street crying. I went over and asked him, *"¿Qué pasa, señor?"* and he answered in Spanish that he was hungry. So I gave him one of the two dollars, which was worth a lot at the time to a poor Dominican kid. Then I left for the office to pick up my pay. On my way back to the hotel, I passed the same boy, only now he was eating bread from a bag. When he recognized me, he gave me a big smile. I felt like a king. I realized that, in so many ways, I'd been thinking of myself as a victim of circumstances I couldn't control—the torture of my double life. Yet here was this young kid in a different dilemma, and he was thrilled to get a dollar for bread. I looked at the kid's smile and I thought, "Now, there's a *real* victim. I should appreciate more of the life I have."

It was clear that the Dominican—at least in 1975—was no exotic resort. Another umpire told me: "It's a great place to eat bad food and get a good tan." It was also a great place for baseball—if you liked chaos. They took their baseball seriously, like Europeans take soccer. Their fans were the true meaning of the word "fanatic." They were absolutely nuts. For example, Dominicans typically carried guns to ballgames. It was like a gun bazaar in the stands. The league had to station armed police everywhere, even on the field. Pretty strange to be calling balls and strikes and glance at the stands and see the police leading somebody away with their machine guns aimed at his back. Meantime, it was also Las Vegas South in the stands. The fans gambled openly on everything imaginable. They bet on how many times the manager would go to the mound in an inning; what the next pitch would be; how many hits a team would get; which player would make the first error; how many times the umpire would whisk off home plate. Jesus, I used to wonder how many times I almost got shot because I only whisked the plate three times and somebody bet *four*.

Everything in the Dominican was different. I remember in '75 (before he became manager of the Dodgers), Tommy Lasorda managed the Licey team—Los Tigres del Licey. He was very big in the Dominican; everybody loved him. He was sort of the Frank Sinatra of winter ball down there. He charmed the crap out of the president of the team and the Latin players by speaking fluent Spanish all the time; he had a hotter temper than theirs; he stood up for his players; and he took no shit from anyone. The Dominican umpires, on the other hand, took shit from *everyone*—especially from Lasorda.

Since we had only four American umpires to handle the two games every day, we worked in pairs with two Dominican umps. One time, one of my umps made a slow call on the bases. Lasorda charged out in all his glory, cheeks puffed, eyes bulged, cursing in Spanish every step of the way. He didn't care if he was right or wrong; he loved putting on a show. The fans loved it, too. Well, Tommy ate my guy alive. Before I could get out there to help, he was picking his teeth with my guy's bones, spitting out his feathers. It was vintage Lasorda: Soon to Be Seen in a Major League Stadium Near You. I waited for my guy to throw Lasorda out, but he wouldn't do it—too scared. This was Tommy's home ballpark; he was so popular here, he could get away with anything. The Dominican umps lived there; they had to go home after the games. So they figured: "Why piss anybody off and risk losing my job—or maybe even my life?"

Finally, Tommy started to leave. But he stopped at the mound for a grandstand play. He yelled at the top of his lungs, "Jesus Christ almighty!" and he picked up the rosin bag and threw it thirty feet in the air. That did it. I said, "Tommy, you're fuckin' gone," and I threw his ass out. He went crazy; he argued with me in English and Spanish and, I think, even some Italian. I thought the stadium was gonna collapse from the screaming and booing. I half-expected machine-gun sprays from the stands. But I didn't care. I would not tolerate anyone showing me up like that on the baseball field.

Since '75 was my first time in the Dominican, it took a lot of getting used to. Our faithful chauffeur, Baca, helped us adapt. He was a big, jolly old man—six feet, about two hundred and fifty pounds, bald head, childish sense of humor. Every time he tooted the car horn to pick us up, he'd make a sound in his throat just like the horn, so that after a while you thought he *was* the horn. He drove us to all our games in either Santo Domingo, San Pedro, or Santiago. The first time we went to Santiago, he stopped at this roadside shack for lunch. It was right out of a grade-B movie: flies and ants on the bread, chickens clucking and pigs snorting in the backyard—future suppers. I never saw filthy, ramshackle farm stops serving food like that in America, so when I first went into one, I thought, "Oh, my God—I'd *never* eat crap like that." But I kept seeing these places and I got hungry and the food was cheap, so I started ordering it—and I actually got used to it.

One thing I never got used to, though, was the atmosphere of violence—which eventually ruined my first year. We'd only been there one month (the season went four) when I got a call from Eric Gregg, an umpire I'd met at the Umpire Development Program, who was one of our group of four. He said, "Oh, man, we had a *big* problem last night." He explained that when he'd called local favorite Bobby Valentine (then a major league player, now manager of the Texas Rangers) out on a half-swing, Valentine threw his bat at him, igniting a brick-and-rock-throwing riot that got so out of control, they had to cancel the game—and now the *season*. He said Barney Deary was "evacuating" us because some fans threatened to shoot the *"estúpidos americanos"* umpires.

We agreed it was a pretty good reason to *ándale*. Hey, this wasn't Pittsfield. You couldn't just tell the PA man to station a cop by the gate to watch the fans. This was the Dominican, where they could put a bullet in your ass *now* and not even *ask* questions later. And who knows, maybe the cops were part of the threat. It wasn't hard to imagine them stopping us at the airport and forcing us at gunpoint to turn over the gringo who committed the crime. Then what? Take him behind home plate and shoot him? Made sense: Ejecting Bobby Valentine from Home Game. Punishment—Trial by Execution. Well, *muchas gracias, señores*, but *mañana* for that.

So they evacuated us out of there, and I was back home for Thanksgiving. What the hell—I could use the winter to brush up on "normal" baseball.

Just before spring training, I got great news: another promotion. I would be working the 1976 season in the Triple A International League—one step away from The Bigs. I quickly figured out that Triple A was sane. I would come to the ballpark and there would be a clubhouse guy I could pay to shine my shoes, or get my uniform cleaned and pressed, or even do my laundry. That meant I didn't have to look for a Laundromat or wear filthy, smelly underwear two days in a row. To me, that was a major perk of my new assignment.

But as I started to think about Next Stop Major Leagues, I must have made myself a little more tense than usual. That's the only way I can explain, even today, what happened to me a couple of months into the '76 season. Mysteriously, out of nowhere one day, I fell into a slump. Of course, players suffered through slumps all the time, but I'd never really had one as an umpire. I didn't know what the hell was happening.

I was working at the time with an old-time minor league veteran, Joe Searles, so I asked him for advice. He couldn't help me; he didn't really care. He knew he was never going to the majors; he was just doing the job, day after day, like a good soldier. So I called Frank Pulli, who was then in the majors. I told him, "I need some help. All of a sudden I can't do anything right. I don't know a strike from an automobile anymore. I know you can't physically see what I'm doing, but I can't figure out what's wrong. What do you think I should do?" He said, "Maybe you need to change your mechanics a little. Try raising up higher behind the catcher. Or maybe getting in the slot a little more—away from the catcher, so you can get a different angle." He gave me a million good tips. Unfortunately, none of them worked.

No matter what I tried, I couldn't get a good plate job. Out of a hundred pitches, I'd miss thirty or forty. Obvious strikes, right down the middle, I'd call balls. I'd talk to myself the entire game: "Jesus, bear down. This is not you." And pitch after pitch, inning after inning, I would try something different. As soon as I had a decent game—meaning I only missed twenty pitches instead of forty—I'd try to memorize everything I did and then do it all again. Ridiculous; it didn't work. I was like a guy trying on a hundred pairs of shoes, and all of 'em fit, only I didn't know it. Eventually, I had my eyes checked, I took a physical, I even had my teeth examined. I was in great physical shape; I probably could've played defensive back for the Detroit Lions. The only thing I couldn't do was call accurate balls and strikes.

Now batters started to complain: "Where was *that* one?" "Wasn't that *outside?*" "Wasn't that *in the dirt?*" And pitchers and catchers couldn't hold off anymore: "What was wrong with *that* one?" "Was that too *high?*" "Too *low?*" "Too *wide?*" "Too *tight?*" Finally, they got pissed. I'd miss a perfect strike and a catcher would grumble "That's *fifteen* so far," and he'd be gone, because I couldn't let a catcher keep count on me and show me up like that. You let them get away with that and they crucify you.

But I couldn't keep that up. I started losing confidence. A catcher would say, "Damn. What was wrong with *that* pitch?" And I'd be so frustrated with myself, I'd admit, "I don't know what was wrong with that pitch." He'd say, "What do you mean you don't know?" I'd say, "I didn't see it." He'd look at me: "Am I not giving you a good shot? Should I get lower?" I'd say, "You're doing everything right. It's me. I'm in a slump and I'm trying to work my way out of it, but I don't know what's wrong." Sometimes, if a team was losing, their catcher would tell his manager that I admitted I was missing calls. The manager would then jump all over my case, hoping I'd give calls back.

Jim Beauchamp, who managed the Charleston Charlies

in '76, was a master at this. Every game I had the plate, he'd start yelling from the dugout, "That's fucking terrible!" Well, you can't let anyone challenge you like that. So I'd take my mask off and look over at him and say, "I don't wanna hear any more out of you." But he'd do it again on the next pitch, baiting me into throwing him out. Which I always did—even though that's exactly what he wanted. He knew that once he got thrown out, he could come out of the dugout to argue balls and strikes, which you can't do when you're in the game. We did this little dance game after game, me making my point to him, and him putting pressure on me in the hope that I'd wear down and start giving his team some breaks. Neither of us ever won.

My slump lasted about a month, which was a long time for an umpire. By then, I'd earned the rap as a lousy umpire—the last thing I needed in Triple A. This was my first year within shouting distance of the major leagues; I wanted to establish the exact opposite reputation. I guess I wasn't happy just sticking my head above the crowd. I always had to stick it *way* up there, just to see how close I could come to the bullets whizzing by.

6

GETTING THE MESSAGE ACROSS

Just as suddenly as I went into my mysterious slump, I came out of it, and I was myself again. But I knew that I'd lost some respect and I'd have to rebuild my reputation. While I was busy doing that, I developed a crucial umpiring concept that I picked up by observing veteran umps. A story Ken Kaiser—one of the tougher veterans and now an American League ump—told me crystallized this concept, which I call Getting the Message Across. Kaiser, who was a former pro wrestler, had spent a lot of years in Triple A, and he felt he belonged in the big leagues. Maybe that's what toughened him; I don't know. But he developed a reputation in the International League as an umpire who would screw you over fast if you tried to screw him. In other words, he could make you wish you never saw him.

He told me about a game when he was working the plate and the batter was this miserable kid who'd already made Kaiser's shit list several times. He was one of those pain-in-the-ass batters who gave the umpire a hard time on every called strike. Well, these guys are no mystery; Kaiser knew exactly which button to push. After the first pitch came in, he took an extra few seconds before calling it strike one. "Jesus Christ," the kid groused. "Why don't you take a little more time to call the pitch?" That was the absolute worst choice of words. Kaiser looked at him calmly and said, "Was that a little too slow for you?

Well, I'll try to make it up to you. I'll try to be a little quicker.'' Kaiser was that way; he could plant a grenade in your ear and pull the pin without you knowing it. The kid stepped back in, ready for the next pitch. The pitcher went into his windup and was about to throw when Kaiser suddenly yelled, ''Strike two!'' Two seconds later, the pitch came in high for an obvious ball. But Kaiser didn't change his call. The kid couldn't believe it; his jaw dropped three feet. Kaiser removed his mask, looked the kid in the eye, and said, ''Is *that* quick enough for you, kid?''

I loved that story because it reinforced my feeling that to be an effective umpire, you sometimes had to get the message across: *Don't fuck with me*. I liked the concept because it was a personal way of saying, ''Justice is served. How many helpings do you want?'' Right after Kaiser told me his story, I had a game with Jim Beauchamp's Charleston Charlies that provided an unexpected opportunity for me to serve a *double* portion.

The Charlies had an outfielder who, like the hothead kid in Kaiser's story, complained about every called strike. ''You know,'' I used to tell him, ''you're an umpire's nightmare,'' but it wouldn't faze him. He continued giving me shit. He was fearless—and also brainless. Every umpire knows that you have to handle these characters in your own way. I'd waited all year for an opening to drive my message across to this guy, but until now it had never presented itself. By chance, I arrived early at the ballpark, and he had just finished batting practice. As I passed his dugout, I happened to see him shellacking his bat, which is illegal. He didn't know I saw it, and I thought, ''I've got him.''

I had home plate that day, so I couldn't ask for a better situation. I bided my time, waiting for him to come up in the right spot. I figured ''Why get him on a harmless fly out or ground out? Get him when it *counts*.'' His third time up, he tripled. Since nobody was on base, I didn't have to cover the play at third, so I beat the Charlies' batboy to the bat and I picked it up. When the guy dusted himself off at third, all excited about his big hit, I pretended to examine his bat. I was playing a game with him now, because I already knew about the shellac. He had this nervous look on his face: "What the hell are you doing?"

I called Jim Beauchamp out of the dugout. "Jim," I said, showing him four inches of the shiny wood, "look at this bat. There's a shine all the way up to here. The guy's cheating. This is illegal." He said, "No, Dave, that's the way the bat came." I said, "No, that's *not* the way the bat came." He got damn mad: "How the hell do *you* know?" I said, "I know because they're not manufacturing bats with *shellac* these days. And that's what this stuff is. You can shave in the reflection. Your boy is gone. Get him off the field." Beauchamp was stunned; maybe he knew all along about the shellac. I didn't care; I'd nailed *both* of them with one shot. Meantime, as the kid departed from third base, I looked at him and said, "Maybe you'll get the message now."

I got him great—and it had immediate positive results. It was like fixing a leak in the sink; just like that, the faucet was sealed. I had that kid the whole next year and he took my called strikes silently, like a pro. I never had another problem with him. I'd obviously gained his respect, and he gained mine. I'd say *that* was a message worth getting across.

The most important message I got across in 1976, I got across to *me*. Even though the last thing I thought I needed during the '76 off-season was involvement with *women,* that's exactly what I got. And it was more than I could handle. But the irony of these two strange events was that they ended up spinning me around and pointing me in the direction of my ultimate destination: a love affair with a man.

In September, I had my usual off-season blues at home—no close friends, nobody to unwind with. Home was so lonely, I was always searching for new people to talk to. Plus, my hormones were up. It may be hard to believe, but I hadn't had sex with anyone since *high school.* I yearned for contact with a man, but that was still just yearning. The next best thing, I figured, was to be with people having fun somewhere. So one night instead of spending another lonely night at home, I drove to Oliver's, a popular Boston watering hole. I could lose myself there in the live music and the college crowd. And who knows, maybe I'd get a bonus.

The place was jumping when I arrived. I ordered a beer and went to the game room to play pinball. After one game, I noticed a beautiful, black-haired girl watching me play. She flashed me a warm "Hi, how are you?" smile, like a friendly acknowledgment. It impressed me; I've always liked assertive people who don't need go-ahead signs from anybody else. Before my next game, she came over to me and said, "How're you doing here?" "Well," I said, "I'm not doing too good. I'm not the greatest pinball player." She laughed and watched me play poorly again. "Maybe I can change your luck," she said. "Wanna play some doubles?" "Sure," I said. "Set 'em up."

I had no ulterior motive; I felt friendly and relaxed, and I was really in the mood for company. As I put the money in, I introduced myself and found out that she was Doris, a junior drama student at Boston University out for a few beers with some of her friends. She asked what I did for a living, and when I told her I was a professional baseball umpire, she beamed and asked me something a lot of people ask: "What team do you umpire for?" I laughed: "Not for a team. I work for a league—this year, the International League in the minors." She said baseball was one of her favorite sports, so we played pinball and traded predictions for the upcoming playoffs and World Series.

For a while I felt like I was in college, too, and that being in a bar talking to a pretty coed and playing pinball was the most important event of my week. And I was thinking how nice it was to drift away from my own life awhile and be with someone as friendly as Doris. "Are you a Red Sox fan?" I finally asked. "God, I love the Red Sox!" she said. "But they always break my heart." She smiled sweetly and I said, "I know what that feels like."

After pinball, we sat at a table with six of her BU friends—three guys, three girls—and we drank beer, listened to the music, and talked. The guys were very interested in my profession. "Do you know Carl Yastrzemski?" "Yeah, I've worked a couple of spring training games with him." "Really? Well, what do you think of the Sox this year?" It was wonderful; here I'd come to a bar alone and now I was welcome in this group of strangers who found everything I said interesting. The conversation flowed directly at me, and it made me feel wanted. I guess I still needed to be the center of attention; it made me feel that I was important to people, and accepted.

At about one A.M., Doris said she was tired and had classes tomorrow morning. I offered her a ride home and she said, "Fine." As we drove to her place, I was thinking about what a great night I'd had. I felt three-dimensional for a change. I was using my *whole* personality: joking, teasing, laughing, telling stories. Tonight, I wasn't just the confused soul in search of a life. Doris asked me up for a drink and I said, "Sure, why not." I had no thought of sex with her; I never thought of that with women anymore. I went upstairs for more of the friendly conversation that had already made my night.

Inside, we had a couple of beers and talked some more on the couch until she gently leaned against me. Suddenly, we were kissing and I could feel circuits shorting inside me; I was *aroused*. It wasn't *that* surprising, because I was comfortable with her, I was still high on beer and camaraderie, and I was just plain damn horny. In fact, I was so sexually starved that although I was thinking, "This is ridiculous. What am I doing?" I let it happen anyway.

We went into her bedroom and undressed in darkness. I watched her silhouette move to the bed, and I followed her there—still aroused, and still wondering what the hell was happening. I remember touching her and enjoying it, but wishing she were a man. Then, all of a sudden, in my mind she *was* a man. We had intercourse, and I helped her reach orgasm. I thought it was funny and crazy that I cared—but I did.

The next morning I woke up feeling physically gratified but also guilty, as though I'd used her. It never occurred to me that *she* might have used *me*. I couldn't

believe I'd gotten so aroused, until I remembered the
fantasy I had of being with a man. I thought, ''My God,
it was so great to fantasize about having a complete sexual experience with a man. It's probably gonna be so
fantastic when I finally do have sex with a man I really
care about.''

Some people might ask, ''Well, Jesus, Dave—if you
thought you were gay, and if you fantasized about a man
while you had sex with a beautiful girl, and if you constantly yearned for sexual intercourse with a man, why
didn't you approach *men* in those bars and go home with
a *man,* instead of wasting time with women?'' For one
thing, this happened in 1976. While the gay scene, especially in New York and San Francisco, was much more
out front than ever before, I wasn't part of that scene, so
I didn't know it. Also, I didn't see gay men looking
openly for sexual partners in straight bars. As far as I
knew, gays like me stayed inconspicuous in straight bars,
for fear of hitting on the wrong person.

So that night, if one of the college guys talking to me
at Doris's table had been thinking, ''Gee, I wonder what
it would be like to go home with a professional baseball
umpire,'' I probably wouldn't have known it. One other
factor: As frustrated and confused as I was then, I thought
the only way of having a sexual encounter with a man
was if we already knew each other, got drunk together,
ended up falling onto a bed just before passing out, then
got up the next day and denied it ever happened. I was
totally naive about this; my hidden life had been too in-
sular.

I never saw Doris again. I realized, though, that I
hadn't really seen her in the first place. What I saw was
my own desperation. The whole thing was absurd. I suppose if I had really understood my problem, I might have
sought professional help. But I always thought things
would straighten themselves out. And I didn't think I
could talk about it to a stranger. I wanted the chance to
reveal myself to someone who mattered to me first, and
then see what happened. I wished it could be someone
in my family, but I thought that was still out of the question. Which was probably a big mistake.

Meantime, I was headed for a bigger one. Less than two weeks after my night with Doris, I was visiting a close friend who said, "David, you should really meet this girl next door. I think she'd really be nice for you." I said fine. Why? For one thing, I didn't want to be impolite to a friend trying to do me a favor. Anyway, what could I say: "No thanks—but can you introduce me to a *guy*"? Also, I hated hearing all those questions from family and acquaintances that I had no answers for: "Who are you dating now, David?" "Don't you have a girlfriend yet?" "Aren't you thinking about marriage?" And I was sick of telling people that I went on dates even though I almost never did. And I was always looking for a friendly girl to keep me company, especially in public. For all those reasons, I said yes. "Besides," I thought, "what harm can meeting her do? I'll meet her, I'll leave, and things will go back to normal."

A few days later I showed up for dinner at my friend's house. The girl next door came over for coffee and dessert. Her name was Linda; she was petite, pretty, shy. Yet when we were introduced she had this warm, gentle smile that radiated interest right away. It was the same open smile that Doris had, only more subdued. Linda and I talked about her job as a receptionist in her father's insurance company and a little about my work. The more she talked, the more I sensed that she would be really nice to be around. I was still so lonely, and here was a girl who exuded loneliness, too. I knew that she was looking for someone.

Over the next few weeks, we dated casually and deepened our friendship through conversation. She showed a feisty side when she gave her opinions, which I liked. She talked passionately about how she didn't really get along with her father and didn't like the woman he was dating; how she disliked living with her brother and sister-in-law and their kids, not because she didn't love them but because she had absolutely no privacy; and how she sometimes felt so trapped that she daydreamed about running away. I understood the feelings of being trapped in a life that wasn't your own. I could see that she needed to be needed, that she was searching for the same things

I was: a companion to confide in, a shoulder to cry on, a sense of emotional security, someone to guide her toward a new existence.

We started out as innocent friends, but I grew to enjoy talking to her so much that I told myself, "Screw it. I haven't had this kind of closeness in years. My interlude with a man is probably never gonna happen. I can't take it; I don't wanna wait anymore. It's time for me to put a stop to my confusion. If I go after Linda wholeheartedly, maybe it'll all come together for me." So I started seeing her more often: movies; suppers cooked by her brother, followed by fun romps with his kids (who were so friendly and accepting, I started hoping that I would someday be a father); walks in the park; private dinners in local restaurants that we could both afford. Once in a while she would pick up the dinner check or send me a card during the week: "Hope you have a great day today. Thinking of you." These little things made me feel special. They helped confirm that yes, we were a couple. That may seem silly, but I had nothing to compare this with, no previous relationship to teach me the ropes. And when you needed affection as much as I did, the smallest gesture came across in marquee lights: I LIKE DAVE PALLONE AND I DON'T MIND SHOWING IT. That stuff reached me.

I was feeling happy that fall, because I was finally with someone who needed me. She was only twenty-three; she looked to me to be the strong one, the leader, the guiding light in the relationship—probably because I was older and I traveled a lot and was more experienced. I looked to her mainly for close companionship. I hoped that she would end up being that special friend I'd always wanted to tell my secret to. The whole idea of keeping up my double life made me desperate for emotional stability. The sad thing was that Linda had begun to see me as *her* stabilizer.

I didn't know it consciously then, but I was more infatuated with the *situation* ("I have a girlfriend—society's pressure is off") than with the relationship. I was enamored of the idea that she was the companion I needed and that I would now be free of having to find another woman to keep up appearances. I disliked myself for that, but I fooled myself into believing it was okay, because I really did care for her as a person and I enjoyed her company.

But anything more than that was a mirage, a mind game I played with myself. I *did* care for her; I called her often, I sent her flowers, I visited her at the office to take her to lunch, I even introduced her to my father. But some of those things I did not so much to show my affection as to keep up my charade. I always felt like part of me was trying too hard, *acting* at falling in love, playing a role that I could only imagine. Even though I was twenty-five, the only love I had ever known was the love of my parents. I did not know what love for a companion or girlfriend felt like. I thought of loving someone in terms of wanting to be with them all the time, wanting to share my innermost feelings with them, always wanting to see them, touch them, talk to them—all the things I was missing my whole life. But I didn't feel that way about Linda. I was not in love with her; I just *wanted* to be in love with her.

As our involvement carried through October, I remained a gentleman with her. She liked that, so there wasn't any pressure sexually for a while. In November, the kissing got more sensual—but it didn't turn me on, which disappointed me. I guess I'd hoped that my encounter with Doris might have changed something. I was wrong; I still felt no passion, although I was willing to overlook my real sexual needs because I wanted to please Linda. I knew deep down that I should have stopped right then and said, "No, wait. I just want us to be close friends. I don't want to spoil the friendship." Had I done that, I would have spared her the pain that came later. However, I let it go too far, because I thought if I didn't show her some physical affection, I would lose her and never have the chance to find out whether or not I could have loved her. It was selfish and immature; but that's how desperate I was.

I fell back on the same old self-delusions: "Maybe I really *have* been missing something all this time. Maybe Linda really *is* the right one. Maybe I'll learn to enjoy sex with her over time. Women keep coming into my life; maybe Linda is God's message to me—'This is who you're supposed to be with. This is what you're supposed to do.' " I ignored reality and hoped against hope that I would eventually be physically attracted to her. It was the most terrible thing I could have done to anybody, including myself. But I fooled myself. I tried to abandon the idea that I was gay. I told myself that if I worked hard at developing what I had with Linda, my longing for men would disappear. "If I try hard enough," I thought, "I can change our friendship into love."

Here was another quandary I ignored: early on, I started looking forward to someday being able to tell Linda that I might be gay. Yet wasn't this the very thing I was now expecting her to help me *exorcise?* It was insane. I was trying to escape something I couldn't escape, something I didn't really *want* to escape, something I didn't even know I was trying to escape from: *the real me.* (So many homosexuals go through the same ordeal, trying to change what they are—but they can't. It's a farce; I don't believe that you can change what you're born to be. Unfortunately, many people belive that homosexuals *aren't* born that way and can *always* change. In my opinion, that is a dangerously naive myth. I think homosexuals know in their hearts that they *were* born that way, that they didn't just choose it one day or fall into it by circumstance. If I had understood and accepted that in 1976, my life would have been dramatically better. But I didn't—and I paid the price.)

As we dated into December, Linda never pressed me for anything more serious, probably because we'd known each other only three months. But in my mind we were at a point of no return, physically and emotionally. I thought I needed to make a firm commitment or else risk losing her. So I considered getting engaged. I said to myself, "If I get engaged to this girl, I will get to keep her around longer. People do grow to love each other over time. Maybe that's what'll happen to me, and I'll finally find out what true love really is."

Shortly before Christmas I asked Leona to accompany me to Boston and help me select an engagement ring.

Linda knew nothing about it. On Christmas Eve, she and I had a quiet candlelight dinner. We talked about everyday things, including the 1977 baseball season. She wasn't looking forward to me going away for the season. After dinner we drove back to her house. I could see Linda's brother in the window, waiting up. So I looked Linda in the eyes, took a deep breath, and said, "Well, I had hoped to do this inside where it would be a little more romantic, but your brother is waiting up for you." She didn't understand until I pulled out the ring. "Linda," I said, "will you marry me?" That didn't feel right. Here was probably the most important question in our culture, and I was asking it without really feeling it, without being carried away, without being part of it. This was supposedly the biggest emotional moment in anybody's life, something that was supposed to feel *sublime*—yet I felt like I was outside myself, watching myself go through the motions.

Linda's eyes went wide; she was stunned. "Yes," she said, and we embraced. "I love you," I whispered, and I was surprised at how easily the words rolled out. But I remember thinking, "You don't mean it." Linda didn't know that; tears came to her eyes. "I love you, too," she said—and *she* felt it. We kissed sensually, and bells *did* go off—except they weren't the bells of True Romantic Love. They were alarm bells: "This is wrong. Don't do this." But I ignored the alarm. I didn't want to hear it; I didn't want to face it yet.

The next morning I woke up at home thinking, "Jesus, this is really wrong. I don't love her. Giving her that ring was the most ridiculous thing I've ever done in my life. How am I gonna get out of this?" I felt low—almost like one of those foreigners who come to America and marry an American just to stay here.

I needed time to think, so I continued to see Linda as if nothing had changed. I wanted to believe that my first reaction was typical, that everybody got cold feet at first. I hoped that I would come around. But once February broke and my mind turned to baseball and I realized that I was gonna have to start putting up my "macho" front again, I knew I had to settle things with Linda. I felt,

"I'm leading this poor girl on. I have to break this off before I leave for spring training or I'll ruin my baseball life, too." I dreaded the pain I was about to cause us both. I'd already had so much of it.

One evening we were in the car and she mentioned the wedding and I said, "I'm uncomfortable about it." "Why?" she asked. "What's wrong?" I was tempted to tel her the truth and the hell with it, get it out in the open. It occurred to me that it might actually make it easier for Linda to take, easier for her to understand why I had changed my mind. But I thought, "What if she takes it badly? What if she gets vindictive later and tells people? I haven't even told my own family. I can't do it; I can't tell her."

So I said, "I don't know what's wrong. I'm missing the closeness we had. I'm losing it." I didn't have any experience with this kind of emotional scene. I was juggling strategies, trying to choose between being as honest as I possibly could under the circumstances and not hurting her. I didn't know how to handle either of those, never mind both at once. She said, "Do you think we're going too fast? Is that it?" I said, "Yes, that's part of it. It was probably a mistake to get engaged." She said, "What do you mean, it was a mistake? You love me, don't you?"

I'd already crossed the line, so I said, "Linda, I don't think we should see each other anymore. I cannot be engaged to you. I feel that this isn't going anywhere, and I would be leading you on if I try to keep this going. It's the wrong thing to do." The wrong thing to do was what I'd just done and the way I'd done it. But it was too late. Now I just wanted to cushion her pain. She was extremely upset, very confused. "Why, David?" she said. "What is this all about?" All I could say was, "I know you'll probably never understand this, but I'm doing this for both of us. It would never work."

She started to cry and I noticed the ring. I said, "Lookit, I gave you the ring on Christmas Eve, so that makes it a gift. I want you to keep it." She looked at me desperately. "I don't understand this," she said. "Can't you just tell me why?" I squirmed; I wished to hell I could say, "I lied, Linda. I *do* love you. It's gonna work out. Just give me some time." But I couldn't say that. I told myself, "Pallone, you asshole. This is the worst thing you've ever done to anyone." That didn't help. It didn't relieve her pain or my guilt. Nothing could.

We didn't talk for the next two weeks. But before I left for spring training, I gave Linda my number in Florida. Pretty soon, she began calling me to find out if I had changed my mind, and to ask if we could see each other when I got back to Boston and talk it over some more. I said, "No, we can't. We have got to stop." Yet I called her every few days anyway now, because I felt so terrible about it. I would not discuss the relationship, though. I thought if I just called once in a while, she wouldn't be so devastated. I was wrong.

The International League got under way, and when I had my first games in Pawtucket, not far from Boston, Linda came on her own to all three games. The first two games, I noticed her in the stands, just watching. But she wasn't around afterward, and she didn't call me. At the end of the final game, I was leaving the ballpark with my new partner, Mark Brewi—a very handsome young man—and there was Linda waiting for me. Mark knew that we'd just broken up, so he went his own way. Linda and I walked to her car in the parking lot. I noticed the ring was still on her finger. She said, "Why are you doing this to me? You're not talking to me anymore and I don't understand why. Can't we work this out? Why don't you want to even *try* to get back together?"

I said, "Linda, this is not gonna work. You have to get me out of your mind and I have to get you out of my mind. I didn't do this to hurt you. I know it ended up that way, but I never wanted that to happen. I care for you. You've meant a lot to me. I just don't love you." She looked down; it was killing her to hear this. It was hurting me to say it, but I didn't know what else to say. She started to remove the ring, so I said, "No, I want you to keep the ring. I told you, it was a Christmas gift." She said, "I don't want your goddamn ring. You can *shove* your gift," and she threw it at me.

I felt like the scum of the earth. I couldn't find a hole

deep enough to crawl in. I just went to my car and cried. I was sick about it; I felt angry, guilty, sorry, ashamed. I thought how stupid I'd been: "Here was a woman who was my fiancée, yet she was never really my girlfriend. That was *my* fault." I promised myself that I would never hurt anyone again like I'd just hurt Linda. To this day, I hate thinking about what I did to her. I consider it my ultimate sin against another human being.

It's important to understand why I could not go through with the engagement. At that point I didn't know for *certain* that I wanted to be with a man for the rest of my life, because I hadn't even spent one night with a man yet. My mind was telling me to love Linda and to marry her because that would be good for both of us. But deep down inside, my body was telling me that I was much too attracted to men and that I needed to find out more about that. I finally realized, "How can I marry this girl before I have that one experience with a man?"

As for my sexual life, I told myself I could never again carry on a "romantic" relationship with a woman until I had experienced the ultimate with a man. I knew I would continue to keep up appearances by being seen with women, but that was it.

One final irony—which confirmed the *real* message I got across to myself—concerned my partner, Mark. When he and I traveled to our next series, he asked me about Linda and I told him it was over, though I didn't get into the real reason why. He sympathized; he was married, and he knew how complicated these things could be. I appreciated his empathy and sensitivity. And I remember that as he went out to the field for the game, I thought, "Just my luck. He's straight."

For weeks I felt like shit over what had happened between Linda and me, but luckily baseball kept me too busy to think about it much. A few weeks into the '77 season, Mark developed a circulation problem in his legs, so I was assigned two college umpires while the league tried to find a temporary replacement. Since these college guys were not expected to work home plate, I worked it nearly every game. That was very tiring; I had to be on my toes all the time to keep fatigue from clouding my judgment. But I did some of my best work under that pressure, and some people went out of their way to praise me. That hiked my self-confidence. When Mark returned, I had improved my home-plate technique significantly, so we looked pretty good around the league.

I had also reined in my temper for once, and, with a couple of exceptions, I kept it reined in the entire season. I realized I needed better rapport with everyone if I was gonna be considered major league material. Because of that and the improvement in my work, I gained more respect around the league. Before a game in Pawtucket, as we dressed next to the Red Sox manager's office, I overheard Joe Morgan say, "Who do we have today— Pallone and Brewi? They're the best crew in the league. I'm glad we have them." I felt a shift in attitude all around me that year: fans stayed off my case; red-ass players accepted my calls; managers stopped giving me a hard time on controversial plays, and most of them— particularly old "enemies" like Jim Beauchamp—were much more friendly toward me. All in all, 1977 was a turning-point year for me. I had a relatively incident-free season, and I never had more confidence in my ability to control a game. I was still troubled off the field, but one consolation I had was knowing that I was getting much better as an umpire. I believed I was right on target for the major leagues.

At season's end, a disappointment: I wasn't invited to work winter league ball. I was hoping for Puerto Rico— the "place to be" in winter ball—but I didn't even get the Dominican. Who knows why? Just because *I* thought I had a great year didn't mean the league thought so, too. But halfway through the season, circumstances changed. Barney Deary called me and said that one of our umpires had been arrested in the Dominican and that we needed to replace him. "You've been down there before," Barney pleaded. "Would you go down and try to get things under control?" I said, "Absolutely." I was only too glad to escape from home again.

I got down to the Dominican and met with Randy Marsh, who had been in charge. As far as I was concerned, he hadn't done a real good job controlling the other umpires and letting them know they couldn't just quit because they were nervous or homesick. So I talked to the others myself. I said, "Look, everybody here has a shot at making the majors. Let's get it together and finish out the season tough." Which is what we did.

I replaced our arrested umpire (who was subsequently fired), and I enjoyed myself because a lot of players remembered me from '75. They particularly remembered the game I booted Tommy Lasorda for throwing the rosin bag in the air. That impressed them so much, they came up with a nickname for me: "Jefe"—the Chief (for "chief umpire"). I liked it because it made me unique. It gave me power and control—things I was missing in my personal life. It was also my Dick Radatz dream come true, only as an *umpire,* not as a player. I was no longer Dave Pallone, one of the *"estúpidos americanos"* umpires from '75. Now I was Jefe, the Chief, the toughest umpire in the Dominican Republic. Warning: Do Not Mess with Jefe.

That reputation came in handy at the end of the season during the playoffs—*off* the field. About two days before the playoffs started, I got a surprise call from Leona and Ted to tell me they were in the Dominican with friends. I was excited; it would be great to have my adopted family see me work. Strange as it was, neither my mother nor my father ever saw me umpire in professional baseball, so this would be an exciting new experience for me. But first I decided to show Ted, Leona, and their friends a good time. So I got Baca to recommend a chauffeur with a station wagon to drive the seven of us to Casa de Campo, a huge resort area a couple of hours out of Santo Domingo. It had a sprawling golf course, a swimming pool where you could swim up to a bar for tropical drinks, gourmet food—you name it. So we spent the day in the sun, swimming, golfing, drinking, eating—deluxe relaxation à la "Jefe" Pallone.

The drive back to my game that night was another story. I was in the back of the station wagon with my legs dangling out the window like a college kid on spring break in Fort Lauderdale when, all of a sudden, here was the *policía* blasting their horn. Our chauffeur cursed them in gutter Spanish. I thought it was hilarious until they pulled us over and two angry-looking cops got out with machine guns strapped to their shoulders. Our chauffeur got out and the three of them talked Spanish too fast for me to understand. But I could see they were giving him a hard time. Leona urged me to find out what was going on, so I got out and asked one of the cops, "*¿Qué pasa?*" He looked at me like he was thinking, "Who is this American asshole talking 'Qué pasa' bullshit and trying to pull a fast one on us?"

The chauffeur took me aside and explained in broken English that they were telling him he had an expired license and wasn't supposed to be driving the car. "So what do they want you to do?" I asked. "Not drive the car," he said flatly. "*What?*" I said. "Are you saying they won't let you drive us *back?*" The chauffeur nodded yes. I said, "Shit. They can't do that. I have to be at my *game*. What can you tell them?" He spit, "I can tell them '*Vate al carajo!* [Go to hell!]'" He turned to do it, but I held him back. "No," I said. "Let *me* try something first."

So I went over to the second policeman and I pointed to myself and announced, "*Árbitro de la Liga Dominicana del Beisbol Profesional* [I am an umpire in the Dominican Professional Baseball League]." It was a mouthful; somebody in the station wagon applauded. The policeman was impressed. "*¿Árbitro?*" he said. "I said, "*Sí, sí. Jefe. Árbitro Jefe.*" Both policemen looked at each other, eyes bulging. Their demeanor changed instantly. Now they had Jefe—which was like having El Presidente. I thought, "The power of *beisbol* finally comes to my aid!"

So instead of detaining us, they commanded our chauffeur, "Get in and *drive* him!"—and they gave us an official police escort all the way back to Santo Domingo. We were cracking up in the car; my visitors couldn't believe that baseball was so big there.

We reached the ballpark in plenty of time. It was sweltering outside; people were drinking and milling around and raising hell. The stadium held only about ten thousand, so playoff tickets were harder to come by than tickets for the Super Bowl. People were running around, wheeling and dealing for seats. I accompanied my friends inside, where they noticed the policemen with machine guns, and the crowd—about fifteen thousand in the ten thousand seats—squashed together in the stands, drinking, betting, yelling. Leona and Ted were concerned about where they and their friends would be sitting. I told them I'd arranged for their friends to sit in one of the two private, air-conditioned owners' boxes upstairs, and for Leona and Ted to sit in the other box. I saw to it that they had an escort to the boxes, and then I left to get ready for the game.

It was the first game of the playoffs. Manfredo Moore, the president of the league, was there, along with the owners and presidents of both clubs, politicians, big business people—everybody and his mother. It was *the* big event, because the winner of the playoffs would go to the Caribbean World Series—Dominican Nirvana. I had first base that day, and when I went to my position to get ready, I looked up to see if everybody was in the boxes. Everyone was, except for Leona and Ted. I scanned the stadium frantically. Suddenly I spotted a white handkerchief waving at me from the very top row. It was Leona and Ted packed behind the standing crowd, waving for help.

I was furious. I knew that Leona was probably going absolutely nuts, because she didn't like baseball and was claustrophobic and nervous in crowds. At this same moment the pitcher threw the first pitch. It sailed right over the backstop screen near Manfredo Moore. I made an instant decision. I called time and stopped the game and ran over to his seat. Nobody had any idea what was going on; they were booing and screaming—and only one pitch had been thrown.

Normally, umpires didn't have access to Moore and wouldn't approach him during a game anyway. But I didn't care that he was the league president; *I* was in charge of that game, and he was about to find that out. I pointed to the waving handkerchief in the top row and said in English, ''Do you see those people up there? That's my mother and father. They came all the way from the United States to see me work this game and they were supposed to sit in an owner's box. I'm taking everybody off this fucking field unless you send armed guards up there right now and get them down here to sit right next to you." Moore looked at the top row, then back at me. Immediately, he dispatched four armed policemen to retrieve Leona and Ted.

The crowd went crazy, hooting and howling and straining to see who the big criminal was. The guards went all the way to the top row and accompanied Leona and Ted back to the president's box, where they were welcomed as honored guests. Moore nodded graciously to me, and I thought, "Boy, being Jefe is like being Al Capone. They treat you like a goddamn king." Then I resumed the game. Two innings later, Leona and Ted were gone. Leona was too nervous; she couldn't handle the crowd.

After the playoffs, Barney Deary recommended to the World Series Committee that I be selected to work the Caribbean World Series. Manfredo Moore called me in and told me that I had been selected—undoubtedly with his vote. So Jefe went to Mazatlán, Mexico, to close out a terrific season. The series was a plum; you were considered the best in your league if you went.

In 1978 I had to put in another season in Triple A. I was paired with Bill Emslie, a friendly guy whom I'd worked with in the Dominican in '77. Bill knew some major league umpires, particularly Richie Garcia, so whenever they worked in Boston, we used to go and watch their games. It just whetted my appetite even more; pretty soon, even though I'd come into my own in Triple A, I kept wondering how long it would take to make that one last step up to the big leagues.

I remember 1978, though, for two things that happened to me *after* the International League season ended. One was a bad break in my career, the other an unexpected breakthrough in my life. First, the breakthrough. Since I had another good season in '78, I finally got my first shot at winter ball in Puerto Rico. It was a totally different environment from the Dominican; most of the major league umpire scouts and supervisors went there, not only because there were more teams with major league prospects to watch but also because it was a beautiful and convenient vacation spot. It promised to be a great opportunity for me.

Another opportunity presented itself off the field. One Saturday in mid-December, I came out of the beachside condo I shared with another umpire, Derryl Cousins (now an American League ump), and I started jogging along the beach. As I watched dusk descend, I was thinking how much I hated jogging, but that I needed to do it to stay in shape and relieve my emotional stress. I went about two miles and started back to beat the darkness. As I approached the condo, I noticed a strikingly handsome young Puerto Rican man sitting in front of the tennis courts. I thought of approaching him, but then I had second thoughts: "What if he doesn't speak English? What if he isn't receptive to me?" But I figured, "I gotta find a man *sometime*. What can I lose?" And I got up the courage to try.

As I made my approach, he smiled warmly, and that took the edge off. He was obviously open to meeting a stranger. In my rusty Spanish I asked him his name, and he smiled and said in decent English that it was José. He asked me the same thing, and I told him my real name—which surprised me. But I was new at this; I made a mental note and let it go. "Where do you live?" I asked.

"In San Juan, past all the hotels. Where do you live?"

"I'm staying in this condo. I'm here from Massachusetts in the States."

"Are you having a vacation?"

"Yes. But I'm also here to work in baseball. You know about baseball, don't you?"

"Of course. I see them play sometimes. I like it."

"Well, that gives us something in common. Look, I have to get cleaned up from running. Would you care to come up for a beer?" Although I didn't expect Derryl back for hours, this was still a big risk. Yet something urged me to take it.

"Yes, thank you very much," he said, and we headed inside. My adrenaline surged; if anything happened, it would be the first time since I was a teenager. I showered and came out to talk with José, and I was more nervous than I'd ever been. I *felt* like a teenager. We each had one beer, we talked a little, and then we sat on the floor listening to the ocean pounding the shore at high tide. Eventually, we were facing each other, supporting our heads with our hands. He asked, "What do you do for baseball?" I said I was an umpire. He said, "That is a very important job here. You must be very strong." I didn't know if he meant strong-willed or physically strong, but I liked it.

I said, "I don't know how strong I am, but I do know you are very beautiful." He smiled shyly and stretched out on his back. I gently put my hand on his chest. When he didn't resist, I knew it was time. I thought, "It's finally gonna happen."

The next hour was pure sexual passion. I was free to be myself and follow my impulses without faking anything. I touched José because it *felt* good, not because I thought I should. And I knew it was the *real* me touching him: the excited boy who groped with other boys in the shed, not the tortured guy behind the mask with women. The groping was gone; now it was instinct. I felt the nervousness, yes, but not the fear. It didn't feel wrong anymore, and I wasn't looking over my shoulder. I could finally let real physical passion carry me away.

What did it feel like? The same as heterosexual passion: breathlessness, dizziness, heat. I lost my inhibitions and almost my consciousness, and I became what my body felt. And something else: I knew instinctively that while I was doing this, I was the person I had always imagined myself to be.

José wanted to stay the night—I wanted that, too—but I explained about my roommate coming back. He asked if he could have another beer, and although there were plenty in the fridge, I told him we were out. I felt nervous now about Derryl coming back early. He knew that I had no friends here; how would I explain José? So I hurried him on his way. At the door José said, "Dave, I want to come back to see you again." I said, "Yes, I'm on the beach almost every day. We'll meet again." I meant it.

When José left, I went onto the balcony and listened to the ocean and stared at the stars. I thought of the two times I'd had sex with women and how terrible I felt afterward, compared with how fulfilled I felt now. I remembered the questions I asked myself after those encounters: "Will I ever know what real sex feels like? Will I ever have a true love life? When will I ever know who I am?" Now I had no questions. I just had the incredible afterglow that millions of human beings had felt before me—and now I was *part* of that. I thought, "I finally know what it's like to smile after sex." I reflected on the experience: it was so *natural*. I didn't have to fantasize about being with someone else, like I did with women. It was like an injection of new life; I could start over from here. All the waiting and hiding and pretense were worth it. This wasn't about love—I understood that. But this would make love possible in the future. Because now I knew who I was. For the first time in my life, I knew absolutely: *I was gay.*

INTO THE BIGS

Over the next ten days I didn't see José, but I felt sure I would see him very soon. But then came my bad break—and I lost that chance forever. Dallas Parks, another umpire working in Puerto Rico, and myself went home for the Christmas and New Year's holidays. We were allotted only five days apiece, and we had to go one at a time, so we had to select who went when. Since Dallas had a wife and a kid in Maryland, I thought it was only fair that he should be with them for Christmas. I would go for New Year's.

He flew out on the twenty-fourth—Christmas Eve day—with the understanding that he would return on the twenty-ninth, when I would leave. On the twenty-ninth, it turned out that his plane was due in just after mine was scheduled to depart. If I waited to actually eyeball him on arrival, I would miss my plane and lose one day. Knowing Dallas to be a man of his word and a reliable guy, I didn't think twice; I just took my flight.

Instead of going back to Boston, I spent my vacation visiting friends in New York—my first time in the Big Apple. I had a great five days, and I was looking forward to beginning the new year on a good note when I got back to Puerto Rico. I felt that if I finished strong down there, I might get my shot at The Bigs.

One rude awakening coming up. When I got back to the condo, Derryl said there was a problem and that I'd

better call Barney Deary right away. I called Deary, and
he told me the league had notified him that Dallas Parks
never got back on the twenty-ninth, so they were short
an umpire for one game. They were under the impression
that I wasn't supposed to leave before Dallas returned.
As a result, the league had fired me and wanted me to
go home. I couldn't believe what I was hearing. I explained about the agreement Dallas and I had had, and
the timing of our flights. I said, "Dallas is an adult. Was
I supposed to hold his hand to make sure he came back
on time? *I* was back on time. I kept up *my* end of the
agreement. Why am I being punished for somebody else's
screw-up?"

Deary couldn't discuss it further. He said he would
look into it, but in the meantime I should leave. It made
no sense to me then, and it still makes no sense to me
now. How was that a fair decision? Why was I the one
in the spotlight? Yes, I should have exercised better judgment and arranged to leave only after I was certain that
Dallas was back. But what about *his* responsibility in
this? What was *his* punishment for missing a game? None
that I ever heard about. (At that time, Parks was under
option to the American League. That meant they had the
exclusive right to hire him in the major leagues. He was
American League property, so they had a stake in his
career. I don't know if this influenced the Puerto Rican
League's decision to fire *me*, but it's an interesting factor.) And I felt that since both of us were at fault, Dallas
should have come to my rescue and told the league, "I
was wrong, too. I should have been there when I told
Dave I'd be there." But he was a very non-confrontational
guy, and as far as I know, he never backed me up to the
league.

Meantime, the Puerto Rican League cut off my pay,
gave me air fare home, and kissed me off. Needless to
say, on the plane home I was a mess. In one day my
whole career went down the drain—and I couldn't figure
out what the hell crime I had committed to deserve that.

Shortly after I got back to Boston, I got more good
news. The Umpire Development Program—which over-
saw all minor league operations—was concerned about a

rumor alleging that I had actually gone to New York City over Christmas to pay off a fifty-thousand-dollar gambling debt. Where the hell did they get that? No one would tell me. It was unbelievable; I didn't have fifty thousand *cents*, let alone dollars. How could I possibly owe anybody that kind of money? And if I had borrowed that kind of money, that could easily have been proved. I did some gambling, sure; for recreation, a lot of the umpires went to the casinos in San Juan. When I went, I played blackjack or roulette. But losses on an average night would be twenty to twenty-five dollars, because I didn't have a lot of money to bet. For me to lose fifty in one night—shit, that could be a whole week's worth of food. I went for broke one night and lost all of a hundred dollars. On my salary, after blowing a hundred dollars in a night I couldn't have bet Monopoly money, never mind the real thing.

Now I was asked to prove to the Umpire Development Program exactly where I was and whom I had visited in New York City over Christmas. I was embarrassed, not only for me but for the friends I'd visited, because the investigation was ludicrous. In the end, it proved without a shadow of a doubt that there was no gambling debt, the rumor was nonsense, and I had nothing to hide. Nevertheless, the minor leagues didn't offer me a contract for 1979. So I would have no spring training, nothing. I was in limbo. At first I thought I was a victim of circumstances and that it wasn't fair. But then another Pallone irony intervened to spin my fortunes around again.

In 1978 the Major League Umpires' Association hired Richie Phillips—who also represented the National Basketball Association referees—as its legal counsel. Phillips's first order of business was to pull the plug on the accepted way that umpires ''negotiated'' their contracts every year. Actually, there never *was* any individual negotiation. Traditionally, the league presidents just mailed new contracts to their umpires every year with the understanding that they must sign them by the first day of spring training or be released. In a way, it was like the old ''option clause'' arrangement allowing owners to unilaterally renew a player's contract year by year, binding him to his present team for life. The players' union finally put a stop to that—and got free agency in the bargain.

Well, until Richie Phillips decided to negotiate for the fifty-two major league umpires, the league presidents called all the shots on salary and benefits. And until 1979, no one ever held out. Now fifty out of fifty-two umpires were holding out—in other words, going on strike. (AL ump Ted Hendry and NL ump Paul Pryor signed contracts; Hendry didn't know about the strike, but Pryor did.) What the strike meant to me was that while all the minor league umpires except me were down at spring training, the major league umpires were holding meetings with all the Triple A umps to ask them not to cross the picket line. ''We need to stick together,'' they said—which was bullshit, because they never gave enough of a crap about the guys in the minors to let them into the Umpires' Association. Yet they told these guys, ''Stand behind us on this, honor the picket lines, and we'll do everything in our power to help you get to the majors.''

The standoff came because the American League president, Lee MacPhail, and the National League president, Chub Feeney, would not negotiate. They felt they had a binding contract with the umpires' union, which included a no-strike clause. Phillips focused strictly on salaries; he was asking an additional $520,000 for the fifty-two umps. At the time, major league salaries were a disgrace. A first-year umpire was making less than $18,000 a year. Finally, it was obvious that the standoff wouldn't be broken in time for the start of the season, and replacement umpires would be necessary. Baseball made a terrible decision, even though it was my open door to The Bigs. (In my opinion, they could have avoided the inevitable ''scab'' situation if they had hired only amateur umpires until they settled the strike. That way, professional umpires in the minors wouldn't have had to cross a picket line of their fellow professionals in the majors and suffer their ostracism.) Nevertheless, both leagues went after crew chiefs from the high minors and paired each chief with three amateur umpires—mostly guys who'd worked at least college ball.

My guts were grinding because I wasn't at spring training to see all this unfold. But that was the great irony I mentioned earlier. If I *had* been there, the major league umpires might have persuaded me, "Dave, if they ask you to come into the majors during the strike, don't do it." If that had happened, I wouldn't have gotten in at that time, and then maybe I *never* would have made it.

As the season approached, I grew more distressed over my release. I decided to call Richie Phillips and see if there was anything he could do. I said, "I know you're the lawyer handling the umpire strike. I'd like to talk to you about my situation," and I explained it to him. He said, "Let me look into it and I'll get back to you." But he never did. At first that made me angrier. But looking back now, how could he possibly have found time for me? I didn't have any money to pay him, and he had a much bigger fight on his hands. And anyway, why should he worry about Dave Pallone, who wasn't anybody to the major leagues? I wasn't even an umpire anymore.

I felt as low and miserable as I could possibly feel. I had no prospects, no power to change the situation, no one who cared that I had gotten shafted. Or so I thought. Late in March, with the strike impending, I got a call from Barney Deary. He said, "There is definitely going to be a major league umpires' strike, and they're going to need some experienced umpires. I recommended you for one of the jobs." Boy, *that* was a shock. I said, "Barney, what are you saying? I was *fired*, wasn't I?"

He said, "Listen, forget about that, Dave. This is the opportunity of a lifetime."

I asked him for the details. He said, "We have cut a deal with the major leagues that any umpire who signs with them will get a guaranteed two-year contract, so you would definitely be there at least two years. You would be judged strictly on your ability, as far as extending your stay further. I know you can do the job. For what it's worth, I don't think the major league scouts have really evaluated you fairly. I think you belong in the major leagues, Dave, or I wouldn't have recommended you. I think you should take the job."

"Well, thank you. I *am* interested. But I need a chance to think it over. What's the next step?"

"A gentleman by the name of Blake Cullen will be calling you. He's the supervisor of umpires for the National League. You can tell him if you want the job or if you need time to think it over."

Barney Deary had liked me ever since we first met at the Umpire Development School almost nine years before. He always told me what a good umpire I was, and he was a fair man, someone I'd always respected. I believe he was trying to help me get to the majors in his own way because he felt that I had gotten shafted by the Puerto Rican League.

I talked the situation over with my father. For years as a factory laborer, he'd been a union man, and now he'd worked his way up to management; so he knew both sides of the story. I remember him telling me, "You always have to do what's best for you. Of course, I believe in unions. I had a union job almost my whole life. But you don't have a job now, rightly or wrongly. You worked all your life to get where you're going. No one is gonna put bread on your table for you. You have to make the decision that either you want this profession and you're gonna take it while you have the chance, and the hell with the people who call you a scab, or forget baseball altogether and get into something else—which is something I don't think you wanna do."

I had to consider all the options. What if I could get back into the minors—maybe with Barney Deary's help—and still get to the majors without crossing the picket line? On the other hand, what about what Barney had said about the major league scouts not giving me a fair shake? Even if I did get back, I might have died on the vine for ten more years—and I couldn't take that. Yes, I wanted to be principled and honor the picket line. I didn't want to have to think of myself as a scab taking advantage of somebody else's misfortune. But how much principle had baseball shown *me* lately? And wasn't my father right: who else was going to put bread on my table if not me? I couldn't buy bread with principle. Plus, if I said no to the supervisor of umpires for the National League—who was calling me personally to ask if I wanted to work in the major leagues—what were the chances that he'd ever ask me again? Oh, sure: "Dave, this is Blake Cullen. You remember me. I called you five years ago and you turned me down because you wanted to honor the picket line. The job is still yours, because baseball needs more principled men like you. We don't care if you *have* been sweeping floors the last five years."

Forget it. This was real life, not Disneyland. There was no way on God's green earth I would ever get a chance like this again—even if I was still working in the minors. Minor league umpires had no union and none of the benefits or security that major league umpires already had. We were just meat; as far as they were concerned, we didn't count. And as much as the major league umpires said they would help the guys in the minors who didn't cross the line, there was no history of that and no guarantee. Besides, umpires didn't do the hiring; league presidents did.

From where I stood—no job, no career in baseball, no future prospects—this looked like a godsend. It wasn't a one-shot-and-out deal; it was a two-year contract in The Bigs. Wasn't that what I'd worked for all my life? Eight years in the minors and I'd never been invited to a major league spring training. Was I supposed to wait *another* eight years for that? What if this *was* my last chance and I didn't take it? Could I live with that the rest of my life— never knowing how good I might have been in the major leagues?

I analyzed it up and down and inside-out. I supported the umpires' position on better salary and benefits. I knew what the players were making, and that baseball still considered umpires a necessary evil rather than partners in making the game better for everyone. I knew that if I were a major league umpire, I'd have walked out, too. And I probably would have resented a Dave Pallone if he crossed the picket line. All that was fine—but what *about* Dave Pallone? Why did I go into baseball in the first place—to spend my career in the minors? No way. And, Jesus, had I invested all those years in the game only to see them flushed down the toilet over one missed game in Puerto Rico? Was I supposed to accept the end of my career at twenty-seven just because Dallas Parks couldn't keep his word?

I knew what the veteran major league umpires would think of me if I grabbed the gold ring this way: "He came in the back door. He didn't get here on merit—he only got in because of the strike. He should have waited his turn like the rest of us." Bullshit. Everybody understood that a lot of time it took more than "merit" to get you into the major leagues. Dallas Parks used to say, "Umpiring is the most competitive profession in sports, because so many are trying to become so few. It's a long road, a lucky road, and an ass-kissing road." Everybody knew at least one umpire who made it to the majors in a questionable way.

Sure, I could've taken their view and said, "Okay, guys, I don't want to break your unwritten code. You go have your careers and I'll just take a back seat again and become a nothing for the rest of my life. I'll take my eight years and my hard sweat and all the shitty little towns with their three-dollar rooming houses and the greasy chicken and bologna sandwiches, and the terrible pay, and all the loneliness, and I'll throw 'em in the river and go be a factory slave or a grocery-store clerk so you guys can be happy, collect your bigger salaries and better benefits, and live in your nice homes for the rest of your comfortable lives. I will do that for you because you have a noble cause and you're looking out for me, too, and I'll benefit from everything you get when I make it to the majors. And if I *don't* make it to the majors—well, then, at least I'll know I did the right thing."

More bull. None of those guys was worried about me doing the right thing. None of them was concerned about me, period. And why should they be? They didn't *know* me yet; I was nothing to them. They had to be concerned with Number One.

If, in fact, I had been under option to the American League or the National League at the time, and if I was expected to be in the majors within a year, then I could have said, "No, I won't cross the picket line, because I know I'm going to be up there soon myself." But that wasn't my situation. I had no job, no future, only myself.

So I decided to take care of myself. I decided I owed it not only to me but also to my mother and father, who had sacrificed so I could have this chance.

When I had considered all that, just to be sure I asked myself, "What would somebody else do in my situation?" And the answer was: "Take the job, you bet your ass. And thank you very much."

The day after the call from Deary, Blake Cullen called me at home. He said, "Dave, I'm supervisor of National League umpires and I'm hiring new umpires for this season. As you know, there is a strike and we're calling some people we feel would be interested in a job and qualified to do the job. You're one of those candidates, so we would like to offer you a two-year contract to work in the National League."

I said, "Thank you, Mr. Cullen. I heard about the situation from Barney Deary."

"You don't have to give me your answer now. If you like, you can have a day or so to think it over."

"I already thought it over. I'll take the job."

It was a crazy arrangement. Legally, I could not work in the majors without having a minor league contract, so Barney Deary arranged for the International League to send me one for 1979, even though I'd been released. I signed it on March 31, with opening day about a week off. Then the majors bought my option from the International League.

Two days later, I flew to New York to meet with Blake Cullen and Chub Feeney in the National League offices at Rockefeller Center. I wore a suit and tie, and I was nervous but elated. They welcomed me on board, I signed the contract, and they gave me a couple of checks for per diem expenses and salary. Feeney asked me if I had any second thoughts. "Absolutely not," I said. "This is where I belong." Just like when I had started in the minors, I wanted to let them know from day one who I was.

Feeney seemed pleased. "We're going to have you open the season with the Expos-Pirates game in Pittsburgh," he said. "Pittsburgh might be one of our toughest places, because it's a big union town. But with everything we hear from Barney Deary, and what we know of your reputation, we think you're the man for the job." I said, "I appreciate the confidence. I know I can handle it." They told me that Tom Gorman, one of their umpire supervisors, would be meeting me in Pittsburgh and that I would be staying at the Hilton. I thought, "It's amazing. Last time I worked, I was on the Holiday Inn circuit—and I thought *that* was great."

Just as planned, they hired eight minor league umpires, each in charge of a crew of three amateur umpires provided by the home teams. They went this route, I think, because they knew they were going to eventually settle with the Umpires' Association and they would then have to find a way to integrate us, at least for the two years guaranteed in our contracts. They planned to offer two-week vacations as part of a settlement (at the time, major league umpires got no in-season vacations), so they decided to create a permanent pool of "vacation umpires" who would rotate in for vacationing regulars. That way there was room for eight more guys—and nobody who crossed the picket line would cost anyone else a job. I didn't need more justification, but I admit that when I learned about this arrangement, I was even more certain that I'd made the right decision.

I got to Pittsburgh, registered at the hotel, and relaxed in my room. Later, Tom Gorman and I went to the Rusty Scupper restaurant for dinner. As we walked in, I recognized two of the Montreal Expo players: Steve Rogers and Gary Carter. I remember Carter saying hello and welcoming me to the major leagues, and then Tom and I sat down to eat. He was a highly regarded former National League umpire whose job as supervisor was to watch young umpires work, critique them for the league, and troubleshoot problems. It was nice to have him to talk to the night before my first major league game. He said, "It's going to be tough out there tomorrow. It's opening day, the umpires on strike—but you can do it. Things will improve slowly, and the strike probably won't go two weeks, so don't worry about it. Just do your best and enjoy yourself while you're here. Things will work out for you." Very supportive, very sympathetic. I thought, "Gee, these people really *care*. If everybody running this league has Tom Gorman's class, I'm in the perfect place.''

It wasn't until I got back to my room that I started having second thoughts. Although it was still early, I tried to sleep off my stress. But I couldn't have slept if you paid me. I kept thinking, ''Jesus, am I doing the right thing? Maybe if I leave now . . .'' I decided to call Frank Pulli and talk to him about it. I had looked up to him ever since I met him in umpire school. He was also a staunch union supporter and had been instrumental in getting Richie Phillips to represent the umpires' union. I knew I could count on him for solid, practical advice.

Frank's wife answered and surprised me when she said, ''Dave, you didn't sign a contract, did you?'' It struck me like, ''Say it ain't so, Joe.'' Obviously, Frank had heard about my situation.

''Yes,'' I said, and she got very upset. ''But I want to talk to Frank about it.''

When Frank picked up, I said, ''Look, you know my situation. I *feel* that I'm doing the right thing. I signed a contract with Feeney, but that doesn't mean I have to go through with it. What do you think I should do?''

''Call Richie Phillips.''

''I'll be more than happy to call Richie Phillips. I talked to him once, but I never heard back from him.''

Frank gave me Phillips's home number. ''You call him,'' he said, ''and then we'll go from there.''

Well, getting through to Richie Phillips the night before opening day was like getting through to the President the night before his inauguration. His line was busy for three solid hours, so finally I said, ''Fuck it. I signed a contract. Go for it.'' And I went to sleep.

The next morning, I met Tom Gorman for breakfast, grabbed a taxi, and went to Three Rivers Stadium. I remember driving past a line of picketing umpires and not stopping so there wouldn't be a conflict. Inside the stadium, I met my other three umpires, all local guys. I also talked briefly with Blake Cullen about protocol on the field, and then we went to our dressing room to get ready.

I didn't have an official National League uniform—just what I had left over from the minors. Putting on the wrong coat and pants felt more like getting ready to work a pickup game in the sandlots than the first major league game of my career. Uniforms were important to me, because they were part of my power on the field. "If you look sloppy," I remembered from umpire school, "people will think you're a sloppy umpire." I wanted to at least *look* professional.

The clubhouse man was supposed to take care of us before the game, but he was a union member, so he wasn't friendly to us. That was fine; he was entitled to his opinion. But then he went too far. I asked him to get us some coffee and to shine our shoes before the game, and he said, "I don't have to do that stuff. I'm on the umpires' side. I don't work for scabs." That got me madder than hell. I said, "Does that mean you're not gonna do *anything* for us?" He said, "Yeah, that's right."

I immediately got hold of Blake Cullen and told him, "I don't have to take this kind of bullshit. Either this guy does the fucking work that I want done, when I want it done, or I'm walking out of here right now." I never considered being meek; I was going to be the same Dave Pallone as in the minors. Cullen understood; he went right out and got Pete Peterson, the general manager of the Pittsburgh Pirates, and brought him into our dressing room. Peterson looked at this clubhouse guy and laid it on the line. "Either you do what you're supposed to do in this goddamn room," he commanded, "or you can get the fuck out and we'll get somebody in here that wants the job. You understand that?" The guy understood so well, I was drinking hot coffee five minutes later while he polished our shoes.

Something else had irritated me about his attitude. All the stadium workers were union. If he was so adamant about us crossing the picket line, what the hell was *he* doing there? Why did *he* cross the picket line? Why didn't he stay home? In my mind, the more support the umpires got from other unions—even the ticket vendors or the food vendors at the ballpark—the more pressure on the other side to settle. Hey, the *players* had a union; what if *they* decided not to cross? No players: no game. No game: lost revenue. Lost revenue: umpires win. I'm not that versed in unions, but I think all strikes are related. If airline pilots support stewardesses in a strike, the stewardesses win. So I couldn't understand how this union clubhouse guy could stand there and say to us, in effect: "I'm on the umpires' side, but I'm gonna work anyway, because I gotta pay my bills." That struck me as hypocritical—and it helped set me off.

My three partners witnessed all this, so they had a good idea what kind of crew chief I would be. It wasn't an act; I had made up my mind before I walked in there that I would survive, and that no one would push me around. So when this guy refused to work, I thought, "I'm not gonna start off my major league career taking crap like this. If I let a clubhouse man push me around, what the fuck am I gonna let a *player* do?

After I established my attitude, I told my three partners what I expected of them. I talked about how they should go out on flyballs, where they had to be on certain plays, who I would ask for help on half-swings if I needed it. I said that I would help out on controversial plays but I would not intervene in an argument unless absolutely necessary. "You guys have all worked. This is nothing new. Don't let anybody intimidate you. Yes, it's the major leagues, but you have to treat it the same way you treat your other games. We're gonna go out there and do the best damn job we can, and let the chips falls where they may." Here I was giving a pep talk and I had never worked a major league game either. Maybe I knew more than them based on my minor league experience, and maybe not. Yet I know that as crew chief the most important thing I could do was to take charge. So I did.

I think the way I handled the clubhouse man, together with my pep talk, boosted my crewmates' confidence. They marched out with their heads up, looking tougher than when they walked in. I thought it was ironic that they seemed calmer than me on the way to the field. I never got nervous in the dressing room; my butterflies always started when the door closed behind me. Walking through the tunnel to the third-base dugout, I had that queasy rush that said, "Hold on. Here we go."

When I hit the field, my first sensation was the noise.

Here was a crowd of about thirty-five thousand people, whereas the most I'd ever worked in front of was ten or twelve thousand in Columbus, Ohio, or maybe fifteen thousand in the Dominican. The excitement of opening day, despite the cold weather, was really in the air. It not only sounded like a major league stadium, it smelled like one, too. You could almost bite into the aroma of hot dogs—which reminded me of my trips to Fenway Park as a kid. I stopped to look around, and I thought the atmosphere was exactly like it was in Fenway for the final playoff game of 1978 between the Yankees and the Sox, when Bucky Dent won it with his amazing home run. I saw that game, and I felt the same kind of electricity now.

The hardest part was having to wait through the two national anthems, Canadian and American—too much time to think. (I knew I did my best work when there was *no* time to think.) I was anxious as hell to get that first pitch behind me. Meantime, I assured myself: "Do the job you're capable of doing. You can do it." After the anthems, I introduced myself to the managers, Dick Williams and Chuck Tanner. They were all business—no jokes, no jabs, no snide remarks. It got me into the right frame of mind.

I had home plate, and in the bottom of the first inning I could tell the difference between the majors and the minors just in the pitching of Montreal starter Steve Rogers. He had an impressive assortment of stuff, and he worked the strike zone expertly, so I had to be sharp. And Gary Carter was a clever catcher. He knew how to intimidate an umpire—subtly. A pitch came in and I knew it was a ball, but Carter remarked, "What was wrong with that pitch, Dave?"—as if he'd been asking me that all his life. It was such a subtle manipulation, if you didn't have enough experience it could get right past you. It was all in his manner and tone of voice. First, he always greeting you with that big, friendly "How ya doin'?" smile. And when he questioned a call, he had that easygoing, down-home, back-porch tone that always registered as: "Gee, Dave, I've known you a long time and you're such a good umpire, you probably just missed that one pitch. But I'm sure not upset, buddy, because I know you're gonna get everything else right. And don't worry, I'll be right here to help you out if you need it.''

I needed Gary Carter's ''help'' that day like I needed a heart attack. I told him, ''Gary, what was wrong with that pitch was it was out of my strike zone.'' He nodded like he understood—no pissing and moaning to show me up. But then, a few pitches later, in a strategic spot in the count, he came back with, ''Boy, Dave, I thought that one was close enough to call a strike. Miss by much?'' I said, ''Gary, it wasn't a strike. So let's just play the game and get on with it.'' He gave me his understanding nod—but he started the routine again two innings later. It was something I always let him get away with because of his friendly tone. I let him try to get an advantage while I called *my* game anyway.

Steve Rogers had his own way of trying to intimidate umpires. I learned this over time, of course, but he would make faces on the mound if he didn't like a call. When he thought you missed a strike, he would wince and squint his eyes at you, as if to say, ''Jesus Christ, you blew that call *bad.*'' I never responded to that stuff, so I let him do it. But if he turned it into Shakespeare in the Park, I'd stop it immediately, because then it was like telling everyone, ''The stupid umpire *must* have fucked up, because look at how upset I am!'' That was out of the question with me. In fact, before this series was over I would handle a classic case of Shakespeare in the Park when one of my partners fell victim to *The Tempest* According to Rodney Scott.

But this first game went smoothly. It lasted ten innings and the Expos won by a run, and we didn't have a single dispute or controversial call. Nobody made any cracks about scabs or the strike or our ability. Maybe everybody had been told to lay of the umpires, but as far as I was concerned, they really had nothing to beef about anyway. I'll never forget walking through the door of our dressing room and being greeted by my three partners with big smiles, enthusiastic handshakes, and ''You did a super job.'' Then Blake Cullen came by, looked me straight in the eye, and said, ''You can work for me *anytime.*'' He must've thought I did a great job, because he didn't have to say that.

Leaving the dressing room, more praise: "Good job" from Joe Lonnett, the Pirates' third-base coach, and a slap on the chest and "You did a terrific job today" from Chuck Tanner. Here were the manager and the coach of the losing team complimenting me on my work, so I *had* to feel good. Dick Williams's team had won, but I still appreciated his comment to reporters, which was something like, "I don't have any comment about the umpires except that you're not going to get a better job no matter *who's* working."

I was so relieved. I had psyched up before the game by trying to think of myself, in a way, like Jackie Robinson. I imagined that all eyes in baseball would be on me that day—and if I screwed up, it would be like *all* the new umpires screwed up. I'd decided it was my responsibility to set the tone for all of us. So I wanted to be as good as I'd ever been. And when it was over, I did feel that I'd had my best game ever. I felt I had proved myself, and so had my crew.

Game two: Although the normal rotation called for each umpire to work home plate once every four games, I had the most experience, so I would be working home plate every other game. In this game, I had first base and the amateur ump who had home did a very adequate job. But he got into trouble with the Expos' second baseman, Rodney Scott. It didn't seem like much to the untrained eye—just a player getting dramatic after a called strike he didn't like. The pitch was so close that from first base I couldn't tell one way or the other, so it certainly wasn't something to make a deal about. Yet Scott ranted and raved and threw his arms up in the air and really got on this umpire's case. There was no question that the umpire was nervous. He couldn't handle Scott's performance, and he couldn't get him to stop. I made up my mind right there that I would not tolerate this. But I told myself, "Wait for the right time. Pick your spot"—which came up the next day.

Game three: Dave Pallone behind the plate again; Rodney Scott at bat. As fate would have it, I called him out on a pitch that was, let's say, close enough to be a strike. Scott obviously disagreed. He started giving me *The Tempest* when I took my mask off sharply, stared him in the eyes a few seconds (later in my career, I would learn to prolong this stare for an even tougher effect), then turned my back and walked toward first base. In doing this, I sent Scott the message: "You screwed my partner over yesterday. I don't like it, and you will not screw me over the same way." Meaning: "Be ready to swing the bat."

Rodney Scott knew exactly what I was doing, and he couldn't believe it. He started giving me some flak, but I cut him off. "You better knock it off right now and get your ass out to second base or you won't see the rest of this fucking game." He saw the wisdom in that, so he went straight to second. Dick Williams knew what was going on, because he stood at the edge of the dugout and screamed at me, "I bet you feel real good about that." I turned to stare at him, and he said, "Yeah, you feel good." He was right; I felt *very* good, because I knew I had sent them an important message to start my major league career: "Don't fuck with Dave Pallone."

It wasn't just an ego exercise. I knew that I'd still be umpiring here after the umpires settled their strike and that they were certainly going to ostracize me, probably for a long time. So I had to prepare myself to be alone out there. And I decided if I was going to be alone, I wouldn't be unarmed. I would not be pushed around, period. This wasn't just *my* attitude; it's been part of the game since Doubleday invented it. In every era, if umpires couldn't get their message across, they didn't survive. But it's only been over the last twenty years or so that umpires had to assert themselves even more forcefully. If you watch old-time films, you see umpires getting dirt kicked on them, being ridiculed, occasionally getting punched. Today, the abuse is more sophisticated. Players and managers kick dirt, punch, and ridicule *verbally* now. It's just changing values in society; if authority is not respected in society, why should we expect it to be respected on the baseball field? You have to *earn* the respect. That's why when a modern-day umpire argues, he has to get the message across in no uncertain terms. Once people know that you will not take shit, they stop yelling and screaming at you; so you can concentrate on doing your job—and you can do it so much better.

I always had that reputation going for me in my conflicts with players during my career. And year by year, it did help me gain their respect. I only wish it could have been that simple in my relationships with my fellow umpires. With a few exceptions, it would turn out that earning *their* respect wasn't worth my time. They were about to hold a grudge to my head, like a gun, for ten straight years. Maybe they thought they could intimidate me out of the league. Big mistake. They couldn't push me without getting pushed back.

They were about to learn that their intimidation would backfire. In fact, it would only fuel my desperate need to succeed.

A SCAB'S LIFE

Who wouldn't want to be a major league umpire?

Who wouldn't want a job where: you never punch a time clock; you get a five-to-six-figure salary and top-notch benefits for just six months' work; you do almost all your work outdoors in spring, summer, and early fall; you have control over your work space and the power, within rules, to do anything to anyone; you can brighten someone's life with just a two-dollar-and-fifty-cent baseball; you're an indispensable part of one of America's most powerful and lucrative industries; on any day, you can become part of history; you meet interesting celebrities who introduce you to other interesting celebrities who say that what you do is more exciting than what they do; you get to sit at the best tables in exclusive restaurants and barter for free rental cars, airplane tickets, and theater seats; you get to meet four of the five living Presidents; you're offered a speaking role in a movie; people you see only a few times a year invite you to golf at their clubs, swim in their pools, and dine in their homes, and end up your devoted friends for life?

Most people have routine jobs, doing basically the same thing every day, nine to five. Occasionally, they might work on a special project for weeks or months at a time, but the work is the same every day for the term of that project. As a major league umpire, your project changes all the time. Every day you work a different game; every game you work a different position; every play you get a different angle; every few days you work in a different ballpark. There's endless variety in the job, so you rarely get bored. Monday, you might have a day game; Tuesday, a night game; Wednesday might go extra innings; Thursday could bring a rain delay; Friday, you might have a bench-clearing brawl. Who knows, you might even have to cancel a game due to an earthquake.

Just about everything a major league umpire does is different from what he did the moment before. When you work behind the plate, every call is different, every count brand new. In the field, one play might be a routine call; the next, an ''instinct'' call; the next, a call you haven't made in fifteen years. The hard part is knowing what to do on *every* call, especially under such pressure. In the business world, when you're on a project you can stop and say, ''Well, how can I rectify this problem?'' In big league umpiring, you usually can't stop to think. You make most of your decisions *now*—and they must be right. The unwritten law for an umpire is: ''Be perfect on the first pitch—and get better.'' Well, how can you be perfect? And how can you perfect perfection? Yet that's the challenge. And that's why the work is so demanding and rewarding—and unique.

What is major league umpiring all about? It's about having the instinct to be in the right place at the right time, the confidence to trust your judgment, the guts to sell that judgment, and—if you're lucky—a special ego bonus: a show of respect from your peers or the people you're working for. In any given baseball season, there are many satisfying moments like that, especially in the major leagues. Sounds great—*if* you have the talent and the luck and something else they don't teach you at Umpire Development School: hard fuckin' teeth. Because with all its great benefits, the job that *I* bit off was a lot more than I ever hoped to chew.

I hate labels, like the word ''scab.'' They're brands on your soul; once you get them, you carry them for life. Unfortunately, my entire professional life was tainted with labels that prevented a lot of people from seeing who and what I really was. ''Scab'' should have been included in my job description, because it defined me throughout my career. Once I crossed that picket line, it was like taking the raft across the river Styx: One Way, No Return. No matter how justified I thought I was in taking the job, or what I did to prove myself, most of my peers saw me not as Dave Pallone, National League Umpire, but as Dave Pallone, the Scab. When I think back over the ostracism that label brought with it, I think of the Salem witch trials. Those people needed scapegoats for their own insecurities, so they invented witches to burn. In a way, I think, that's what being a scab was like.

Everywhere I went my first year, I had problems because of the scab issue. After opening at Pittsburgh, I went to Philadelphia, and I expected something to happen—a big argument or a crazy controversy. I thought people would start testing me, if not for being a scab, then just because I was a rookie umpire. But it didn't happen right away. For example, I made a call against the Pirates on a close tag play at the plate and Chuck Tanner ran out to argue. I thought, "Get ready. The honeymoon's over." But Tanner was calm and reasonable—which I'd later learn was typical of him. But at this point, expecting the worst to happen and getting nothing, I had a false sense of confidence. I felt like I was on a roll and thought, "Hey, maybe I underestimated everyone. Maybe the shit *won't* hit the fan."

Then somebody turned the fan *on*. One night in May, I was working second base in a game at Houston between the Astros and the Cardinals. Bottom of the ninth, man on first, 4–4 tie, Houston tried a sacrifice. When the Cardinals went for the force at second, shortstop Gary Templeton had to stretch for the wide throw, which I felt took his foot off the bag before he had the ball. I called the runner safe right away. Templeton started arguing with me, and then out came the Cardinals' manager, Ken Boyer. The shit was flying on the breeze.

I was fending off Templeton and Boyer when Keith Hernandez came over from first base. I nailed him instantly: "Get your goddamn ass back to first base. You don't belong over here." He blew his stack and jostled me, and my cap fell off. That never looks good, but at that point I was more concerned with my health. I flicked my hand at Hernandez: "You're gone." Boyer jumped on my case and cursed me, so now *he* was gone. Then Ted Simmons came all the way out to second base from home plate. I got that "ganging up" sensation—like those times they circled my wagon in the minors. So before Simmons could open his mouth, I said, "Get your ass behind home plate and don't give me any shit." He said, "I just wanted to tell you that you made the wrong call. Maybe you should understand what you're doing out here. That guy was out. That's an important call." This really got under my skin. "Get the fuck outta here," I said. "You're gone, too. Now you don't have to worry about if I was right or wrong." That was a quick ejection, but I thought he deserved it. First, he had no business being out by second base. The fact that he felt he could take that liberty with me told me he thought I was just some pushover virgin up here for a cup of coffee. Second, by coming out all that way he was prolonging the argument, which made me look bad. He knew that; they all knew it. Third, when the play happened, he was at home plate. How the hell could *he* see what *I* saw?

So now I had three guys gone: Hernandez, Boyer, and Simmons. All of a sudden Cardinals converged on me from everywhere. When I tried to walk away, they cut off my retreat. Twice more I tried to avoid confrontation by walking away in different directions, but they kept blocking my way. That didn't scare me; it just made me more determined.

Finally, I had everybody cooled off enough to resume play when Joe Niekro started yelling at me from the Astros' dugout, "Hey, you threw *Hernandez* out, too!" Other Astros joined in, yelling and pointed toward first base. I turned and saw Hernandez still standing there, like nothing had happened. I told him, "Didn't I tell you you're gone? Get the hell outta here." He acted outraged; he charged over to me, claiming he had no idea I had thrown him out. He gave me the once-over a second time and I said, "I don't need to listen to your shit. Get off the field—and don't make me tell you again."

Hernandez stormed to the Cardinals' bench, cursing

under his breath, and coach Red Schoendienst started hollering at me. That triggered a frenzy on the bench: they hurled towels and warm-up jackets onto the field; they yelled vicious insults; they openly gave me the finger. It was merciless; they felt I didn't deserve to be there and that I'd cost them the game. They were trying to run me out of the stadium.

So I marched over to the Cardinals' dugout and I said, "That's it. You're *all* gone. Every one of you, get in the clubhouse." They were shocked. It was the "unwritten law" syndrome again: *nobody* clears the bench—especially in the majors. One of the coaches was so amazed, he said, "You can't do that," but it sounded like a question. I said, "That's interesting, because I just did it. Now get the hell outta here or we won't start this game again." They knew I meant business; they started filing out without another word.

Clearing the bench didn't mean that everybody was ejected. It simply meant that everyone except the starting nine, the manager, coaches, and trainer had lost the privilege of sitting on the bench for the rest of the game. It turned out that the Cardinals lost 5–4 in the sixteenth— but the call that triggered the rhubarb had no effect, because Houston didn't score in that inning anyway. Still, when I got to the dressing room I was pumping adrenaline for twenty minutes. I thought, "All *that* over Gary Templeton lifting his foot off the bag? Jesus, what the hell's gonna happen *next?*"

There were so many incidents, on and off the field. I remember flying into San Francisco a day early for a three-game series. I took a ground-floor room at an airport hotel, and since the other guys on my crew were all local, I was alone. That night around ten, I got an angry phone call: "You're a *scab,* Pallone. How's it feel to be a back stabber?" I hung up immediately; I knew it was a union umpire. About fifteen minutes later, another call: "You like being a *scab,* Pallone? Well, we don't like *you.*" It was the sort of pathetic crap you might hear from a twelve-year-old.

The phone kept ringing, so I unplugged it. I didn't want to do that, because I never knew when Chub Feeney or Blake Cullen might call. But since a lot of umpires stayed regularly at this hotel, I wasn't sure that the desk clerk wasn't in cahoots with the ones harassing me, so I couldn't trust him to hold my calls.

Once the phone was disconnected, I had some peace—for a little while. When I shut the light to go to sleep, something heavy crashed against my door. This happened, off and on, for a half hour. When it stopped and I was almost asleep, a group of men outside my window started yelling things like "You won't get any sleep tonight, Pallone" and "Don't worry about that game tomorrow. You got home plate; you should be real rested for that." The silliest shit you can imagine from so-called adults. They probably wanted to say other things, too, but I'm sure they didn't want to get arrested.

It bothered them that I wouldn't give them the satisfaction of coming to the window and looking out. So they increased the noise, trying to keep me awake. I thought, "Jesus, do they really think this will change my mind?" I tried to ignore it, hoping they'd accidentally piss off some karate experts in a room near mine.

I slept fitfully, but I was asleep at six A.M. when someone knocked on my door and startled me awake. It was room service with a big tray of food: pancakes, eggs, sausage, bacon, potatoes, toast, coffee, juice. Except I never ordered it. One of the union umpires obviously ordered it for me—and charged it to my room—just to wake me up and get me mad.

Later, I took a cab over to Candlestick Park for the first game that afternoon. As the taxi pulled up to the parking-lot entrance, National League umpire Eddie Montague blocked our way. He gave me a dirty look, but as mad as he was at me—and I understood that in my heart—I knew I couldn't back down. I told the driver, "Well, you have to get me in." He turned around and looked at me. I chuckled. "Run him over. Just get me *in* there." So he inched the cab forward and honked the horn, and finally Montague moved. But as we drove by, he gave me another dirty look. That was the general mentality during the strike: make it as tough as possible on the scabs.

Finally, the inevitable happened. On May 18—forty-five days into the season—the strike ended. The umpires got a new three-year agreement that raised base salaries and provided two-week in-season vacations and increases in per diem allowances. That was good news for me, too, because even though they wouldn't let me into the union, I was entitled to the same salary and benefits as union members. It wasn't a closed shop, so I enjoyed all the member benefits without having to pay dues. What sense did that make for the union? If I disliked somebody that much, and I was going to ostracize him whether he was in my union or not, I'd want him to at least have to pay his dues like everybody else. They never saw that logic. If there's a stupider example of cutting off your nose to spite your face, I haven't heard it.

The bad news for me was: now that the regular umpires were back, I was no longer a crew chief. In fact, I no longer had a "regular" crew. The eight replacement umpires became "swing" umps, filling in for two weeks at a time as veterans on different crews took their vacations. It wasn't the best situation, but at least it kept us in the league. One of the problems, of course, was that we weren't on any one crew long enough to be a part of it. When you added our "scab" baggage to that, there was virtually no chance of us being accepted. And although the new basic agreement stipulated that there were to be no recriminations, we were treated as outcasts anyway.

For example, since the veteran umpires had no forum against us on the field, they did what they could to disrupt us *off* the field. They practiced what the Amish call "shunning": they had a secret pact not to talk to or associate with us off the field, so they didn't travel with me, stay at my hotel, or eat with me. Other tactics included canceling my hotel and plane reservations; threatening me over the phone; and sending me ridiculous notes, like "Scabs shouldn't push their luck because shit happens to them."

Then there was their silly tactic of constantly bad-mouthing us in interviews. They knew their best weapon was words, so they used the press to run us down and remind us that we were dirt under their shoes:

Eddie Montague: "The new umpires prolonged the strike. They embarrassed us. . . . They weren't concerned about us and we're not concerned about them. . . . Let them take their own cabs and stay at different hotels and be lonely. . . . They'll never be accepted. And I mean never."

Don Denkinger: "I will not ride with them. I will not eat with them. I will not have idle conversation with them."

Billy Williams (to mild-mannered rookie ump Fred Brocklander): "If you were in Labor, you'd have a busted jaw now, and your nose would be on the other side of your face."

Gerry Crawford: "The only reason these guys got jobs is because we were on strike. On the field, I tolerate 'em. Off the field, I have nothing whatsoever to do with 'em."

The union umpires sang the same phony tune: "The replacement umps are the worst. They couldn't kiss our ass." Which was crap. First: we all knew that talent wasn't always the only criteria for making the majors. Second: what made these union umps so good? Didn't they start out in the minors like us? Blake Cullen told the media the real truth about the caliber of his four replacement umps (Steve Fields, Lanny Harris, Fred Brocklander, and me) when he said: "I wouldn't rate them as the four worst in our league." He meant, "Yes, they have a lot to learn. But there are *veterans* in the league right now who aren't as good as these guys." Blake also understood that all this "planted" media hype was designed to apply extra pressure to us in the hopes that we would either resign or be fired for low ratings. So he had the good sense to state publicly that the league would not drop any of us. He said, "These guys have too much guts to quit. And you can forget about the ratings. There are just too many roadblocks for them to mean much right now."

Meantime, some of the striking umpires went out of their way to single me out to the press and lie about me. One was Richie Garcia, whom I'd met back in 1972. Garcia and I were friendly then; I saw him a lot when I worked in Florida. We all went out for beers together, and Richie would sometimes invite us to his home. Yet now that he was an American League umpire and I had crossed the picket line, there he was lying to the press that I had run up gambling debts betting on football and basketball and asking why I hadn't been investigated.

First: there *were* no gambling debts—football, basketball, or otherwise. Second: the league investigated me *thoroughly*. The commissioner's office had former FBI agents on staff whose main job it was to check out gambling allegations about prospective major league umpires. They came to my hometown and checked me out with a fine-tooth comb and found absolutely nothing. And Barney Deary had already investigated the same false rumor and told the major leagues he'd found no wrongdoing. Third: what did the Puerto Rican thing have to do with anything? Obviously, if that had been anything serious, I never would have been asked to sign a major league contract in the first place. Last: who the hell was Richie Garcia to mouth off about my gambling? He used to go to the dog track with me in Florida and bet the dogs himself. He liked gambling more than I did, yet I never told the press that Richie Garcia gambled. The reason he lied about me was because he hated my guts for being a scab, and this was a way to keep the issue alive. If my reputation got smeared along the way, so what?

After four months of Garcia's phony allegations, I heard that the commissioner—Bowie Kuhn then—had ordered Lee MacPhail to get word to Garcia to shut his mouth about Dave Pallone and gambling debts. Then, on August 2, Blake Cullen sent this memo to all National League umpires: "National League umpires are hereby instructed to refrain from making uncomplimentary, personal remarks about other umpires to reporters. These remarks will be met with severe disciplinary action including fines and suspension." But there were no fines and no suspensions for any National League umpires, and it took so long to shut them up that it almost didn't matter anymore.

During that season some veterans tried to stick it to us in childish ways that no one in the league office was ever likely to find out about. Dick Stello used to do it to me whenever I worked on his crew. One time he came into the dressing room and said pointedly to Paul Runge, "This is not a full crew. This is just a three-man crew." I stood up and said, "Hey. See that door? It says 'Exit.' If you don't wanna work with me, go out the fuckin' door. But I'm part of this crew, and this is *my* dressing room, too, and if you don't like it, go home. I'm stayin' here and workin'. I ain't goin' *nowhere.*" Guys like Stello didn't have the balls to confront me directly. And it always seemed to surprise them that I had the balls to stand up for myself and give *them* a hard time. Why was that?

I was prepared for rough treatment, but two things really surprised me. One was that these grown men—the veteran umpires—were so angry with us that they put their personal resentment ahead of the game itself. The other was their ability to hold a grudge for so damn long. I lasted ten years in the league; so did the grudge. That told me something I didn't want to know about human nature—or maybe just human nature in baseball.

The union umpires did whatever they could to try to discourage us. It made me ashamed, at times, to be associated with them—which was ironic, since that was *their* point to *us*. But they carried it a step further; they also wanted us to know: "You're scum. We hate your guts." They demonstrated that to me constantly in the clubhouse, where their little cruelties ranged from the petty—like refusing to look at or talk to me, or walk out onto the field with me—to the vicious. For example, one day in June, when I came back to San Francisco to work for a couple of weeks with Bob Engel's crew, I sat at my stall to open my equipment trunk, and there was the word "scab" scrawled in red across the top. I pulled everything out of the trunk: my shin-guard straps were slashed, my hat was shredded, and there was a padlock on the bars of my mask. *Now* it seems funny, but when it happened I went through the roof. I knew immediately who

had done it. I had just come from working on Lee Weyer's crew in L.A., where, as usual, I had left the dressing
room ahead of the veterans so I didn't have to listen to
them talking to each other as if I wasn't in the room. It
was the last game of the series, my equipment was intact
when I left, and they had plenty of time to mess with it
before the trunk was sent to San Francisco.

So I turned to Engel—who wasn't thrilled to see me,
either, but who wasn't antagonistic like the others—and
I said, "Jesus Christ, this is terrible." And he said,
"You're right." So I said, "I ain't working this game—
I have no equipment. Get someone else to work the
plate." Well, that was no good. Number one: working
the plate was the toughest job on the field, so nobody
wanted to do it when they didn't have to. Number two:
they always wanted me to have my turn behind the plate
because there were more chances for me to make mistakes. So Dick Stello—whom I would have a big run-in
with the next time I worked on this crew—gave me his
mask. Stello was a disagreeable guy and a staunch union
supporter, so he didn't offer his mask graciously to help
me out. He offered it because there was no way in hell
he would work the plate for a scab.

I have to admit that this got to me. I thought: *"Did
I do the wrong thing? Do I really need this shit? Maybe I
should just walk away from it and do something else."* I
reflected on why all these guys who used to be my
friends—Crawford, Garcia, Steve Palermo, Frank Pulli,
John McSherry—were now abandoning me. It was tough.
McSherry and I had been close. When my mother died, he
was the first one to call—and now he wouldn't even talk
to me. I understood that they probably felt I had betrayed
them and now it was their turn to betray me. I thought,
"Maybe I would have done the same thing." But looking
at my mangled equipment, I realized that no, I *wouldn't*
have done the same thing. I would not have lied about
anyone; I would not have threatened anyone; I would
never have sabotaged equipment. I probably would have
ostracized them a while, but I couldn't have kept it up.
That thought made me decide, "I'm staying. They're
never gonna get me out of this league."

But the real problem wasn't so much the personal animosity off the field as the petty bullshit that spilled *onto* the field. The ostracism there was relentless:

1. They wouldn't look at me or talk to me the entire game.
2. If there was a conference over a controversy and I came over to the group, they'd either ignore me or walk away.
3. Whenever I worked an NBC *Game of the Week*, and NBC asked my crew chief for the names of his crew, he'd name the two other veterans and leave me out.
4. Veterans—like Gerry Crawford, for one—would warn the younger umpires not to talk to or be seen in the same room with me, or they too would be ostracized. At first I blamed the younger guys for being gutless. But then I realized that the veterans had no right to put these guys in that situation, and I sympathized with them. They never got to know me. But I didn't think anyone should have to go through what I was going through.
5. If I was working the plate and I called a ball on a checked swing, and the catcher asked for an appeal to another umpire, that umpire would either ignore me or automatically reverse my call. It was so obvious after a while that batters got madder than me. They'd say, "Tell your partner that sucks." I'd go, "*You* tell 'em. They don't know I'm here."

Sometimes they did things totally unrelated to the game of baseball. For example, normally all four umpires stood together for the national anthem. *Now* you'd see the three guys standing together on one side of home plate and me on the other side. And if *I* had the plate, they'd leave me standing there alone while they went and stood together out on the field. After three weeks of that I said, "Screw this. I ain't takin' it." From then on, whenever I was working the bases and they wanted to make me look like an asshole by letting me stand alone at the plate, I *left* before the start of the anthem. I ran out to my position and deliberately stood alone. I don't know if the public ever knew that, because the only report I ever saw on it was in *Sports Illustrated*, and it was totally erroneous. It said: "On another occasion, the four umpires were gathered around home plate when one of the veterans clapped his hands as if to end the discussion and send everyone to his position. Rookie Dave Pallone immediately turned and ran out toward second base. The others remained at home plate." The report mistakenly assumed that those other umpires had made a fool out of *me*, whereas *I* was actually showing *them* up. I did it to get the message across to the fans, to the media, and, most of all, to baseball, that they were ostracizing me and it was wrong. The league was aware it was happening, but they did nothing about it. So I kept it up: "Can you see it *now?*" But no one from the league office ever called me about it—and I certainly wasn't going to cry about it to them— so nothing changed.

Aside from the emotional isolation, the worst result of the ostracism my first year was the effect it had on the quality of umpiring. If anyone says the quality didn't suffer, they're full of shit. It hurt the replacement umpire; it hurt the crew as a whole; it hurt the ballclubs, who relied on us for professional performance; and, most of all, it hurt baseball. I tried my best to foresee problems and head them off before they happened. For example, every time I joined a new crew, I went directly to the crew chief and made this introduction: "I understand how you feel and I don't have any problems with that. I will listen to anything you've got to say to me. If there's something I'm supposed to do, all you have to do is tell me. I will not cause you any problems as long as you don't cause me any problems. All I expect is to be treated as a professional on the field."

It didn't help. I can remember the first time I worked with Bruce Froemming—a guy I was destined to have trouble with my entire career. He came strutting into the dressing room, looked at me, and said, "Pallone, you and I had our differences in '72 when you were in the minors. I didn't like you then and I don't like you now.

I expect you to do your job and stay away from me." And I said, "Hey, I respect you for your opinion. You just make sure you do the same for me." I would soon learn that Froemming's remark was typical of his ability to hold a grudge.

So for one reason or another, the union umpires' resentment leaked into the game and made difficult situations even more difficult. Some examples:

I had home plate in a Sunday afternoon, Cubs-Reds game at Cincinnati. In the eighth inning I called Cubs batter Larry Biittner out on strikes and he threw his bat against the stands. I said, "That's a hundred dollars," because we were supposed to fine them for throwing equipment. He gave me a hard time, so I ran him. Here came Cubs manager Herman Franks to argue with me. As soon as he cleared the dugout, I said to him, "You can't come out here." He kept coming, so I threw him out before he could say a word. He exploded on me. He had a sewer for a mouth; for five minutes he cursed me like a New York cabbie. Then I said, "Why don't you stay out here a little longer, so it will cost you *more* money?" And I kept waiting for my fellow umpires to bail me out. Normally, a crew would rush to protect a rookie in any kind of controversy. But not one of my crew helped me out. They *wanted* me to yell and scream and say something I'd regret.

Franks cursed so much, the only thing I remember him saying was, "You can't throw his ass out, you son-of-a-bitch Italian pizza vendor!" If I hadn't already been so goddamn angry, I probably would have laughed at that, because it was a bona fide classic. Instead, we went literally nose to nose—and his nose came to my chin. The result was that, as we argued, the bill of my cap kept poking his forehead: rat-a-tat-tat. It made him crazier. Finally, I lost it and called him a motherfucker—a terrible word that I had never used before on the baseball field. Needless to say, this got Franks enraged.

I felt so guilty about calling him that awful name that I reported it to the league. Unknown to me, the TV replay had clearly shown that word escaping my lips between pecks of my cap to his head, so the league would have found out even if I hadn't put it in my report. Chub Feeney reprimanded me and fined me one hundred dollars. He grimaced when he saw the replay: "Did you *really* say that word to Herman Franks?" I wanted to say, "Never mind that. Where the hell were my crewmates when I needed them? They could have stopped the whole thing before it got that far. They should be fined for deliberately doing nothing." But I thought it was better to try to handle the problems myself. I didn't want anyone to say, "There's Pallone, the crybaby who runs to Chub when he can't take the heat."

Another incident in '79: I had home plate for a Reds-Pirates game on Bob Engel's crew again, with Paul Runge and Dick Stello. Lee Lacy was on first for the Pirates, and the count on the batter was three balls, one strike. On the pitch, Lacy started to steal and I called ball four. But for some reason Reds catcher Johnny Bench threw down to second. The ball beat Lacy, so Dick Stello called him out. It was strange; it was ball four, yet neither Johnny Bench, Lee Lacy, nor Dick Stello knew the count. What the hell were they doing out there—watching TV?

Lacy got up, confused, and started to walk away from the base. Reds shortstop Dave Concepcion tagged him, and Stello called him out again. I yelled, "That was ball four," and all of a sudden Stello realized he had made a mistake. So he decided to leave Lacy on second base— *safe* now. That brought Reds manager John McNamara out like a rocket, yelling at Stello, "Hey, wait a minute! He's gotta be out! He can't be safe!" He argued vociferously with Stello: "He came off the bag and my guy tagged him out! He's gotta be out!"

Stello got together with Engel and Runge. I came out from behind the plate and told Engel that it was ball four. Runge said, "The man came off the base. There's no automatic time out. He's gotta be out." Stello said, "Yeah, but he wouldn't have come off the bag if I didn't call him out in the first place. So we have to leave him on second. He has to be safe." Engel said, "I agree with Paul," and called Lacy out, and McNamara left the field satisfied.

Now Chuck Tanner jumped out of the dugout and

started another argument. He yelled at Stello, "He only came off the bag because you called him *out*. It was ball four. Ask your home plate umpire." Stello wouldn't look at me, so I went back to the plate because no one was interested in my opinion. I said to Johnny Bench, "You knew it was ball four. You never questioned the call. Why the hell did you throw it?" Bench shrugged. "I don't know. I just did it. Instinct, I guess."

To make a long story longer, the argument went in ever-widening circles. Tanner stuck to his contention that the runner was safe because Stello made a mistake. Engel said, "Hey, it's your player's responsibility to know the count, too. He can't rely on the umpire for that. Same thing for your coaches. Although he's entitled to second base on ball four, once he reaches the base and steps off, he's relinquished the base." About twenty minutes into it—a ridiculously long time—Tanner lost his temper. He said, "Jesus Christ, it's a simple call. It's ball four and you made the mistake of calling him out at second base, so he's gotta be safe." But Tanner was *wrong*. Even if it was ball four (and it *was*), and even if Stello screwed up the call (and he *did*), there was no automatic time out, and that was that.

Again, the umpires got together—but the others still didn't want my opinion, so I retreated back to home plate. That's what I meant when I said ostracism on the field hurt the game. I could have ended the argument in ten seconds, because I was the one who called ball four. Instead, it was twenty-five minutes and counting. The impasse was that Engel and Runge (who, ironically, would eventually become the only two union umpires to fully accept me on their crew and befriend me when I really needed it) agreed that McNamara was right and Lacy was out, while Stello still insisted it was *our* fault and we had to award him second base.

After *thirty-two* incredible minutes of this nonsense, it started to drizzle, and Tanner was still arguing, and players were sitting on the bases waiting for the game to start again. Finally, I got disgusted. Being the obnoxious person I was, and having the nerve to actually think that I shouldn't mind my own business anymore because this *was* my business, I came out from behind the plate again and said, "Lookit, why don't we make a fuckin' decision? He should be called out and that's it." Tanner said, "I don't have to listen to *you.*" I said, "Fine. We'll stay here *another* thirty minutes." If Tanner had said that to me three years down the road, I'd have been in his face. But it wouldn't have been right at this time, because I was just a rookie.

After Tanner protested the game and we got it under way again, I went behind the plate and told Johnny Bench, "This was all *your* fault. If you hadn't thrown down to second, everything would've been fine." He said, "Yeah, I know." And I said, "Well, because of that, I'm sending two baseballs down to the clubhouse tomorrow for you to autograph for me." Johnny Bench rarely autographed baseballs for the umpires, so I saw my opportunity and took it.

After the game, the umpires were in the dressing room and the phone rang next to my locker. Dick Stello picked it up and started talking to Pete Peterson. He said plainly for me to hear, "Yeah, well if it wasn't for some of the incompetent people we work with, I wouldn't have made that mistake." Now, my whole first year it was standard operating procedure for the veteran umpires to conduct conversations as if I wasn't in the room; that was part of their "shunning" routine—and I tolerated it. But this was different. This was Stello blaming me for his own mistake, and I wasn't going to tolerate that.

When he hung up, I said, "Hey, if you don't know how to count, that's *your* problem. The count was three and one. You should've known what it was. If you don't, you can't blame me."

He said, "I wasn't talking to you."

"Look," I said, "you wanna ignore me in the clubhouse, fine. You wanna forget the count on the field, that's fine, too. But I called the pitch exactly the same way I always call it. It's not my fault you can't understand what's happening."

He said, "Fuck you. I knew what the count was."

"If you knew what the fucking count was," I said, "you wouldn't have gotten into the situation you were in, and we wouldn't have had a thirty-two-minute argument over the count you didn't forget. Seems to me you're the one at fault, not me. And you oughta be man enough to admit it.''

That was it; the argument stopped. He gave me a surly look and ignored me again. The point was, what Dick Stello did was immature and stupid and typical of the abusive ostracism I had to deal with. He had no business saying what he did on the phone. If he really believed it, he should have kept it to himself while I was in the room. Why didn't he? No guts. Dick Stello is dead now; I realize that he can't defend himself. But there were witnesses to this, and I want it known that I thought it was a cowardly thing to do at my expense—and at the *game's* expense.

One humorous note came out of that game. The next day, I walked into the Cincinnati clubhouse, went right over to Bench, handed him two baseballs, and said, ''Johnny, remember I asked you yesterday to sign these two balls for me?'' He looked at me like I was talking Chinese and left me standing there holding these two baseballs, looking foolish. After a few long seconds, he said, ''Oh, yeah. I had to think about it. I lost track of the *count* again.''

I remember one other light moment for me in '79—the only time that whole season when I felt there was *some* poetic justice in the universe. I had been to the National League office, so I decided to stop off at the American Airlines office in the same building to say hello to the young girl there who always handled my reservations. We had become friends, and she liked to talk to me about baseball. She told me that she'd had a talk with an umpire named Bruce Froemming recently, and he really made her mad. I asked, ''What happened?''

She said that when she realized Froemming was an umpire, she mentioned she knew me and that I was a real nice guy. Froemming said, ''I know Pallone. He's a scab. He doesn't belong in the major leagues. How can you like that guy?'' She was offended. ''If he didn't like you,'' she told me, ''he could have kept it to himself.''

I wasn't there, so I don't know exactly what he said, but knowing Froemming, I believed her—and I agreed.

A few days later I got a phone call from Blake Cullen, who said that when Bruce Froemming was in Chicago a few days before, he went to the airport and found his reservation canceled and the plane completely full, so he missed his flight—which Froemming blamed on me. "Do you know anything about this?" Cullen asked. I said I didn't and Cullen said, "I didn't think you had anything to do with it." I said, "Shit, I wish I *had* thought of it," and I could hear Cullen laughing.

The next time I saw my friend at the American Airlines office, I asked her, "Did you do that?" She said, "All I can tell you is, wait until he tries to get on his *next* flight." I laughed. "What are you saying? You canceled *all* his reservations?" She smiled mysteriously and shrugged. Yes, it was wrong—but it was ironic and funny, too, and I needed a good laugh. Besides, if anyone ever deserved a "whammy," it was definitely Bruce Froemming. In my mind: Justice Served.

Froemming was part of an old guard of veteran umpires who were narrow-minded, arrogant, and selfish. Yes, some of the older men were great guys, but I had to wade through all that old-guard resistance to find them. Some of the younger umpires were more sophisticated, more educated, more intelligent. They understood that life was too short for stupid feuds. They mostly adhered to the veterans' code, but they made it clear they thought it was petty and vindictive and (to use a term I heard a lot back then) counterproductive. That was an understatement.

I blame baseball for that. It was indecisive and short-sighted in its handling of the ostracism issue. No one can tell me that the abuses weren't obvious. Here were professional umpires trying to show up fellow umpires before, during, and after games, sabotaging the team performance that you needed to be effective at that level— all because they wanted to make a point about scabs. Here were guys being hung out to dry in arguments and fights; guys being ignored on appeal calls; guys left to stand alone for the national anthem on national TV—and the *owners* weren't watching, the *league* wasn't watching? How could the commissioner not have known about it? How could the league presidents not have known? Where were the fines and suspensions to send the message: "Don't mess with the game. Keep your personal grudges off the field"? It never happened. As far as I'm concerned, baseball's lack of balls sabotaged *itself*. The big loser was the game.

One argument was, "Well, the league can't make somebody like someone else, or eat with someone, or travel with someone." That was true, but why couldn't the league have clamped down on that crap before it poisoned the atmosphere? Didn't they have the option of saying, "There's no room for this attitude in professional baseball. You'll do it or you'll work someplace else"? How is it that the league had bulletins and regulations for which jacket you could or couldn't wear, but they couldn't get four umpires to stand together at home plate for the national anthem? How could the league enforce regulations about hats and shirts and shoes—silly regulations that affected only how you *looked*—but not develop any rules about professionalism, unity, and camaraderie that affected the outcome of a baseball game? I'm still waiting for someone to explain that to me.

It was the same thing when I suggested, "Why not put two replacement umpires on the same crew? That way, at least we'll have someone else to talk to and rely on when we need help." To their credit, the American League eventually tried that, but the National League stood pat. In my opinion, the union pressured both leagues not to use two replacement umpires on the same crew. The union didn't want two scabs to comfort each other because, if they did, it would make their jobs easier. I believe that, in this instance too, the union *and* the league were willing to sacrifice the quality of baseball.

I survived ten years of this because I believed in my heart, "What goes around comes around." I always thought that something would happen to the worst offenders—the ignorant bigots and arrogant jerks who couldn't just live and let live—that would cause them to reevaluate themselves. But I also survived because the other side of me said, "They can shove their ostracism up their ass."

I remember an old Dick Gregory joke about a "Negro" in the sixties who walked into a restaurant in Mississippi, sat down, and ordered fried chicken. Two bigots started giving him a hard time. The first one said, "Boy, we don't *serve* Negroes in here." The Negro smiled politely and said, "That's all right. I don't eat Negroes *anywhere.*" When the waitress finally brought the chicken, the second bigot came over and said, "I'm warnin' you, boy. Whatever you do to that chicken, we're gonna to do you." The Negro thought it over a second and put down his knife and fork. "Y'all line up," he said. And he *kissed* it.

I thought of that during the brunt of all the ostracism I got my first year in major league baseball. And in the end, I figured, "If that's the level of their maturity, then fuck them. From here on in, they can all line up and kiss it."

9

SCOTT

The 1979 season ended early for me—just after Labor Day—because the regular umpires had all taken their vacations and the replacement umps had nobody to replace. So they sent us home for the last few weeks and I collected my pay for doing nothing. I felt good, because I had survived a very tough year. And although people resented my being there, I felt I was qualified and that I did my job well, and I let everyone know it.

I was also happy with the way I stood up for myself all year. I remember visiting my dad early in the season at his factory, and he showed me a newspaper photo his coworkers had posted for his benefit. It was a picture of me yelling at Herman Franks, which they had captioned: "Like Father, Like Son." My dad was considered a tough manager at work because he yelled a lot, so this was kind of a tribute to him. He didn't show it, but I know it made him proud of me—and that made *me* proud of me. On another visit, I asked his advice about the ostracism. I said, "Jesus, these guys are getting worse instead of better. Are they ever gonna let up?" He said, "It takes time, but they always accept the new people. The thing you have to remember is that no one lost their job, no one was kicked out. That'll help heal the wounds quicker." I hoped he was right.

Once the off-season started, my dominant thought was, "My major league career is under way, so half my life is complete. Now I have to try to complete the other half.'' During the season, my personal life had taken a back seat to baseball again. I made some friends on the road, but I spent almost all my free time alone killing time before games by taking two-hour lunches, going to afternoon movies, lying by the pool, playing ''hacker'' golf, shopping in malls. At night, I sought company for conversation in hotel bars or clubs. I was twenty-seven and still incredibly lonely.

I never stopped wanting to be myself, but I didn't know how to be that yet. I was still combating my emotional feelings about my sexuality. It wasn't so much that I didn't know what I was as that I didn't know how to go about rectifying it. I had no gay friends, so I wasn't invited to gay parties. And although I knew there were gay bars, I couldn't bring myself to find out where they were. So I went to straight bars, where I was too afraid of exposure to be forward with anyone. I'd just nurse a Chivas on the rocks and talk to people at the bar, not necessarily to pick someone up but just to talk. Once in a while I'd see an attractive man and I'd think, ''Boy, I would like to find out what that guy's about,'' and I'd start a conversation. Even though I was a master at knowing what to say to people in bars, I was still a novice in getting a man to leave with me.

I'm not saying it's any easier for straight people to meet someone worth being with in a bar. I think there are as many lonely men and women in the straight world as there are in the gay world, because, like the song says, we're always looking for love in all the wrong places. But the reason we're out there seeking, and going to all the wrong places, is that we have no other place to go. Meeting someone decent under these circumstances is a luxury.

The only sex I had had since my encounter with José in Puerto Rico was in my own imagination. And the usual loneliness of a long baseball season was intensified in '79 by the brutal ostracism. So now, although sexual release was always on my mind, something else was, too. I was constantly searching the faces in stadium crowds and restaurants and bars for that special person who might come into my life. And I looked for any edge I could get in meeting new people. For example, I found that being introduced as "Dave Pallone, National League umpire" got a positive response, because people thought I had an interesting, prestigious job. So I started drawing more attention to myself that way, hoping I could hold people's initial interest in me longer. I was uncomfortable with it, because it was so immodest. But that's how desperate I was; I was willing to try anything to tip the scales in my favor.

It didn't work anyway. I still didn't meet that someone special. But after the season ended, I finally had enough money to rent my very first apartment—in Waltham, Massachusetts, a suburb of Boston. I thought that having my own place might help me in my personal life, especially if I did meet someone special. Now we wouldn't have to sneak around; we could just go back to *my* place. For the most part, though, I knew that everything would remain the same—unless something unexpected happened.

In late November, something unexpected *did* happen. Roger and Elaine Rossler, friends of mine in Waltham, invited me to a post-Thanksgiving gathering at their home. I was center stage immediately, because everybody wanted to know about my first year in major league baseball: "What it was like to work during the strike?" "How did you handle everything that happened to you?" After about an hour of that, a group of us were drinking toasts and talking in the kitchen. I chatted with another friend's son, Doug, who was now a sophomore at a college in Rhode Island, and he told me he had invited his classmate Scott up for the day. Scott was out visiting mutual friends in town, Doug said, but he was on his way back so they could take off for the evening.

I was sitting on a sink counter when a startlingly handsome young man walked in the kitchen door. His good looks absorbed the room, and he was so radiant he practically glowed with warmth. The physical attraction was overwhelming; I was excited just to be near him. I thought, "Who *is* this person? How do I find out about him?" In greeting the others, he made eye contact with me and I felt his eyes saying: "Wow, who are *you?*" I almost couldn't swallow.

He held out his hand to me and said, "Hi. I'm Scott," and his smile hit me like a truck. I said, "I'm Dave Pallone," and we shook hands firmly. Doug said, "You guys never met before, right?" I said, "Why? Should we have?" Doug said, "I thought I introduced you guys one time when he was here." I said, "Nope. I would've remembered that"—and we all made small talk about college. Then Doug said they had to leave for a local tavern. Scott looked at me and said, "Yeah, we're gonna go have a few beers. Why don't you come down and meet us?" I said, "Well, maybe a little later." As he opened the door to leave, he looked back at me. "Okay," he said almost teasingly, "but we expect you to be there."

I stayed at the Rosslers' for another hour, and then I went to the tavern, ten miles away. Inside, I found Doug and Scott standing at the bar with a group of people they knew. Everyone was interested in sports there, so the conversation turned to baseball again: "We saw pictures of that big fight you had with Herman Franks. That was great." "What's gonna happen next season?" "Did you get to meet Pete Rose?" I'm only human, so I did enjoy being the star of the conversation again. But after a while, it did get old. In this instance, though, I didn't care; Scott was asking some of the questions, and I was holding his interest. I thought, "Great. He likes baseball, too."

Eventually Scott and I started talking more privately at the bar. We talked about my job some more until I switched the subject: "What do you go to school for?" He said, "I'm not sure yet. I just started taking some telecommunications courses." I said, "What else are you interested in at school?" He said, "Sports. I play basketball." I said that basketball was a pretty tough sport, and he said I was right but that he loved the finesse it took to be really good at it. That attitude really impressed me.

After a while Scott started talking about his father, a successful criminal lawyer. He told me how he loved his dad but that they argued whenever Scott was home. "He's always telling me that I need to get serious about something. He wants me to get my life straightened out and pick a career. But I'm only twenty-one. I just want to enjoy myself right now.'' I said, ''I know what you mean. My father and I used to argue about the same thing.'' And I told him what my father had said when he heard I wanted to be an umpire. Scott laughed sympathetically, and I knew we were connecting.

Now Scott started revealing things about his family: they lived in Maine; his mother used to be a fashion model; his dad played football for Harvard, graduated at the top of his Harvard Law class, and set high standards for Scott and his older sister; he loved his parents very much but was feeling the strong need to be independent; he liked sports and jazz and he wanted to learn how to cook; he also loved boating, because his family owned a sailboat, although his sister could sail it better than him. I think he was so comfortable talking to me about his family because, even though I was only twenty-eight, he related to me as an *adult,* not a college peer. I had that openness about me; strangers always used me as a listening ear.

Scott went a little deeper into his relationship with his father. He said, ''Once in a while I like to have a few drinks, but my dad is so well known I can't afford to get him in trouble. We argue about that a lot. We disagree on so many things that I always feel better when I go back to school.'' I said, ''There isn't anyone in this room who hasn't felt that way. Whenever our parents tell us something, we always feel they're trying to hinder us, but they're really trying to help us. Your father probably has your best interests at heart, especially about drinking. When you drink and drive, something terrible can easily happen to you.''

When a bunch of us finally sat down at a table, Scott chose to sit next to me. I liked being physically close to him; at six feet, he had a slim, athletic build, straight blond hair, and green, accepting eyes. And I liked the way he spoke to me. He had a personable, disarming quality that said, ''We can tell each other anything.'' I had more than one urge to embrace him. And I thought how lucky it would be if he were gay. But if he turned out to be straight—which he appeared to be—that would be fine, too. I was still looking for that close buddy I never had.

We talked for almost two hours until I got tired. Then I said, "Lookit, Scott, if you ever come to the Boston area you should give me a call. I'll give you my number, and if you ever need anyone to talk to, I would enjoy it very much." He said, "I would really like that. I don't know that many people in Boston, and I like the city. That would be great." I said, "You're welcome to come. And if you need a place to stay, you have an open door." We shook hands and I patted him on the shoulder and I left.

On my drive home, I felt nervously excited. I was thinking, "Maybe there's hope for me yet. Maybe the person I'm looking for is out there after all." (I think most people, gay or straight, go through this at one time or another when they're lonely and distraught: "Is there *anybody* in this world for me?") I thought about the possibility that Scott might be that special person for me, and I wondered if I had missed any signals. The way he walked, talked, even shook hands told me only that he was "butch"—macho or masculine—like me. I hoped desperately that he would call and I would get the chance to find out if we could be more than friends.

Two weeks later, back in Waltham, I got a phone call from Scott at college. He said he was coming to Boston over the weekend and would I be around? I said absolutely, and I asked him if he needed a place to stay. He said he might, but he wasn't sure. He would have to call and let me know when he got in town on Friday night. I had plans to play cards Friday night, but I canceled and waited for Scott's call. It came at nine, and I gave him directions to my apartment. When he arrived, he had a big smile on his face that told me he was just as happy to see me as I was to see him.

He came in and I asked him what brought him to Boston. He said, "No particular reason—I just thought I'd come up." I said, "Are you meeting friends here?" He said, "Oh, I've got some friends in the city. Maybe I'll see them over the weekend. I'm not sure." That told me that he may have planned all along to spend the weekend with me. It lifted my hopes, but I didn't want to assume too much. That was one reason I had him stop at my apartment first. I wanted him to see—in case he *was* straight and this *was* just a friendship—that even though it was a one-bedroom apartment, I had a couch in the living room where he could sleep.

I decided we should get something to eat, so we went to Watertown Square for pizza and conversation. I remember thinking while he talked that if I could have molded a lover, Scott would be him. He was unusually handsome; we had sports in common; he was energetic, feisty, and bright; he had a warm, exuberant personality that wouldn't quit. After dinner I commented that he was welcome to stay at my apartment if he wanted to. He said, "Yeah, I think I will. That way I won't have to worry about where I'm going to stay over the weekend."

First, though, we hit a couple of bars. I noticed that he was very good at talking to girls. I thought, "Either he knows his way around women because he's a ladies' man or he just has a charming way with *everyone*." I was an expert at putting up a front with women, but I couldn't tell if that's what Scott was doing. So while we drank beer and talked, my mind was working: "What's his real story? Will we end up in bed together?" But I couldn't show him that. At this point I knew only one thing for sure: he definitely enjoyed my company.

We stayed at the last bar until closing at two o'clock. We had gotten along great; he didn't find me boring, and vice versa, which was important. But I still didn't know what he was thinking. Was he disappointed he didn't get laid? If so, who was he interested in—a girl, or me? Or did he just feel he had a nice night and he didn't care? My impression was that he had had a nice night and that was all there was to it. On the drive home, I didn't hear anything like, "I'm pissed because I didn't pick up that broad at the bar," or anything like that. It was more like, "We had a great time. I'm glad I came up. This should be a fun weekend."

When we got back to the apartment, I asked him if he was hungry and he said yes, so I made two sandwiches.

Afterward, I turned on the radio and we sat on the couch and talked some more. Eventually I sat on the floor, leaning against the couch. I always liked doing that; it wasn't a calculated "move." And it didn't seem awkward; it was almost like we were college buddies having a bull session. It got late, and we were tired and relaxed. I felt there was a possibility something might happen—but now I needed to know.

Because of my position below him, I had to keep looking back and up. So I said, "My neck is killing me looking up like this. Why don't you come down here?" I moved the coffee table back a little and he sat next to me, leaning against the couch, and we continued talking. Finally, I said, "It's almost four o'clock. We should try to get some sleep. I'll get sheets and a blanket for you, so you can make up the couch." As I got up, I tapped his leg lightly. When he grinned back at me, I laughed and ruffled his hair. As I walked away, I thought, "I don't want him to sleep out here tonight. I want him to sleep inside with me."

When I returned with the sheets and blanket, Scott was lying flat-out on the floor with his eyes closed and his hands folded behind his head. I noticed that he'd moved the coffee table further away. "What're you gonna do," I teased, "sleep on the floor?" He said, "No. I'm just resting my eyes." I sat down next to him, and I said, "We really should get some sleep. We might want to do something during the day tomorrow." He opened his eyes and nodded at me, and, instinctively, I leaned over and gently kissed his forehead. "I just couldn't resist that," I said. He gave me his dazzling smile and said, "That's okay. It's hard for me to resist *you.*" My heart was racing; I said, "I think we really should sleep in *my* bed tonight." He nodded. "I think we should, too." Then we fell into an embrace and kissed for the first time. When we kissed, I saw only *him* in my mind. Five minutes later, we went to my room.

We made love in the way that two people new to each other make love. (I know that some heterosexuals believe that all gay men play "masculine" and "feminine" sex roles. But neither Scott nor I had any awareness or interest in playing roles like that. To me—then and now—the only roles are that you're both human beings and you both want to love each other.) We were so sensitive to each other that I knew I was feeling something with Scott I never felt before. And all of a sudden I had something else I never had before: somebody I could spend a whole night with, and hold, and wake up with.

At the time I didn't compare this to what I'd felt with José, but later I realized that with José it was strictly sex. He was not anyone I could have fallen in love with. He lived in a different world; he wasn't someone who could ever be part of me. He was just passing through my life. And José and I didn't spend any time getting to know each other; he didn't even stay the night. So there wasn't the fantastic afterglow that I had waking up the next morning with Scott, feeling so at ease and fulfilled, and seeing that he was obviously happy to be here, and knowing that we could do it all over again and have the same feelings again. It was an emotional completeness I didn't feel with José. It was more than lust; it was also *acceptance*. Everyone is "accepted" *during* sex, because we get lost in our own arousal. But this was acceptance the *next day*—along with affection, comfort, joy. It was everything everyone dreams about with a lover, male *or* female.

Up till now, I still believed that the standard scenario for two men making love was that they got drunk together and fell on the bed and woke up the next morning and denied it ever happened. I didn't know if that would happen with Scott. I didn't *think* it would, but it could have. He could have gotten up and been nervous about it and said, "I have to leave now." He didn't. It was new and wonderful to me to get up and prepare scrambled eggs for two and come back in the bedroom to announce, "Breakfast is ready," and see Scott lying down barechested with his hands behind his head—exactly like the night before—giving me that amazing smile. I leaned over and kissed him and said affectionately, "How come you always have that shit-eating grin on your face?" His smile broadened. "I don't always have it," he said. "Only when I'm happy."

During breakfast I said, "You know, from the first time I saw you, I wanted to be with you." Scott said, "I'm here because I wanted to be with *you*. I didn't come to Boston for any other reason." That lit me up inside. I understood now that he knew what he was doing all along. So I said, "I hope we have the chance to see each other a lot more. I hope this isn't going to be just a couple of days." He said, "I hope so, too."

We got dressed and went into the city to walk around. We walked through Boston Common; I did some Christmas shopping at Faneuil Hall; late in the day we had a snack at the Oyster House. Over a couple of beers, we started talking about us. "Lookit, I have a problem," I said. "I have to be very careful about this type of situation. I'm at a point where I can't jeopardize my career. By the same token, I have this desire to be with you. I don't know whether this is just a fantasy that I'm fulfilling or if this is the real thing. But right now, I feel like I really have some feelings for you. How do you feel? Are you just fulfilling a fantasy, or do you have some real feelings for me, too?" He looked serious. "I've had my fantasy before," he said. "But nothing like this."

I took that to mean yes, he'd had sex with men before, but never as fulfilling as with me. I didn't probe him, because I didn't want to ruin it; *I* wanted to be the important person in his life now, not anyone else he had in the past. I said, "Well, we have to make a promise to ourselves that we will somehow see each other as often as we can." Scott agreed: "I have to go to school and I have basketball, so I can't get to Boston every weekend. But I *can* and *will* get there." I told him my time was my own now, so I could visit him at school if he liked. He said he lived in a dorm, so I'd have to get a hotel room—but it sounded great.

Saturday night we went out to dinner. Afterward, instead of going to a bar, we spent the night at my house holding each other and watching TV. It was a lazy, soothing night of just being together and enjoying each other's comfort and warmth. I was feeling: "This is the real me. All that emptiness I felt until now wasn't because it was wrong to feel the way I did about men. It was because the right person never came along." I knew that what I felt was right for me. Scott and I were loving each other, taking care of each other—the same as if we had been heterosexual lovers. And we didn't discuss, "Are we going to be gay for the rest of our lives?" That wasn't important at the time. This was our first weekend; we didn't want to get heavy about how our lives were hurting at the time. We just wanted to enjoy what we had.

Scott left before noon on Sunday to return to school. He gave me his number and we said goodbye with the intention of seeing each other often over the winter. When he was back in Rhode Island, we talked on the phone several times a week. I knew that he was special to me, because not a day went by when I didn't think of him. I had never had anyone who meant so much to me before. It was a feeling of nervous excitement and exhilaration, because here was a person I'd just met, and yet I could feel my whole life shifting under me.

Two weekends later, I visited Scott for the first time in Rhode Island. I stayed at a quaint bed-and-breakfast inn, and he drove over and we spent the weekend there together. We went downhill skiing both days and hung around the hotel at night. It was like a cocoon away from reality for both of us. We grew together that weekend, because we both accepted that we wanted to be with each other. The chemistry was there: we were physically attracted, we had no personality conflicts, and we shared a lot of the same interests.

In January I told Scott that I would be leaving for Florida at the end of February to prepare for spring training. I wanted to invite him to stay with me at my condo in Clearwater, but I didn't want him to get turned off by feeling forced into a heavy-duty relationship at twenty-one. I said, "I would like you to come down for spring break, if you can. It would give us a chance to spend the better part of a week together." I was pleasantly surprised when he didn't resist. "I'd love to go." He brightened. "That would be great."

Until I left in February, we saw each other every other weekend, him coming to Boston and me going to Rhode

Island. In March he came down to Clearwater to stay with me over spring break. It was an extraordinary week for me, because I was able to do things with Scott I had never done with anyone else before, like go to the beach on my off-days, go to dinner every night, and go parasailing. On one of my days off, Scott and I went to Disney World in Orlando. It was wonderful to be at this big playground for kids and to feel like a couple of teenagers in love.

We saw many openly gay couples and we kidded around about that. "See?" he said. "It's not that big a deal." I said, "It is if you're an umpire. It's a myth that nobody recognizes us. I could be in a room with two hundred people and no one would know me except one little guy. And he'd say, 'Oh, yeah, that's Dave Pallone, the umpire.' That's all it takes to ruin a career." It took a while, but Scott eventually understood that I had to be more wary in public than gays who weren't in the public eye.

Next, we went on rides together like a couple of best pals. We went on the Space Mountain ride and the roller coaster that zoomed through a tunnel with electric stars twinkling overhead. I'll never forget sitting in the first car of that ride when it shot straight up toward the stars and then dove straight down. I closed my eyes the rest of the ride and held on to Scott's leg. When it stopped, he laughed at me: "How could you be so scared?" I said, "I wasn't scared." "No?" he said. "Then tell me everything you saw." I said, "I saw *nothing*. That's why I wasn't scared."

Little moments like that helped me understand how far I'd come. Here I was at Disney World with a person I was falling in love with, acting like a million other people in love, laughing, teasing, making fun of myself, being scared like a kid, and holding on to someone for dear life. The great thing was that I *had* someone to hold on to. Maybe most people take that for granted; but to me it was a drastic change in my life.

This was all new to both of us. I was older than Scott, yet I was more immature than him about it. In a way, I was living through him what I missed in my younger years—all those years when I had no one. I imagined what it would have been like if I were still Scott's age. I was greedy for the attention, the affection, the *fun* of being in love. I wanted it all and I wanted it *now*. But Scott gave me some mature advice: "Take things slow." And that's why our relationship grew. One of his best qualities was that he was mature for his age. He had a better perspective—with less experience—than I did. I discovered new qualities in him every day that week. From looks to sensitivity to independence to generosity, he was my ideal mate. I couldn't have asked for a more perfect match.

As the week progressed and we went to dinner together every night, I realized that this was how I wanted to live my life. I was falling in love with the person I wanted to fall in love with—and it happened to be a man. I didn't believe that my love for Scott was any different than the love of, say, the couple sitting next to us. The only difference was that they were a man and a woman and we were two men. The feelings were exactly the same: a sense of self-esteem and self-worth, a shared admiration, a heightened interest in someone else's needs, a constant desire to please and laugh and hug and kiss and touch. Most of all, there was the distinct feeling that I was sitting across the table from someone who was a part of my life, not just someone to eat dinner with. I think that's how everybody's love develops, whether it's between two women, or two men, or a man and a woman—same process, different genders.

My fondest memories of our week together in Florida are probably the same kind of memories that millions of heterosexual couples have. I remember most vividly our midnight walks, hand in hand, along the deserted beach. We talked about simple things, like how nice it was to finally *have* someone to walk the beach with at midnight. Sometimes we pushed each other, kidding around, or wrestled, or embraced. I remember saying to Scott at the end of that week, "This is what I dreamed about for years—that I would be walking along a beach someday with the person I love." What human being hasn't dreamed something like that?

The downside—which we both hated but understood—

was that during the day we had to hide our real affection.
And we couldn't share each other with the most important people in our lives—our parents or relatives or any
of our friends. I kept saying, "That's wrong, wrong,
wrong." Yet I didn't have enough courage to tell anyone.
I never gave them the benefit of the doubt because I was
too insecure. I was too scared to lose their love and support. It was another sad irony: I had enough guts for any
confrontation in my baseball world, yet no guts to tell
the truth when it counted in my private life, where so
much more was at stake.

That one week together served as a physical and emotional outlet for both of us. That's why I felt secure
enough to say to Scott, "I would like to get to know you
better. I want to have a relationship with you. How would
you feel about that?" He said, "I never thought I would
have a relationship with another man. It's been so great
with you, I'd really like to."

When he left, I felt I had really lost something important. I didn't know when I was going to see him again,
because I had the baseball season coming up and he had
school. Once the 1980 season got under way, I sent Scott
my schedule and I suggested places where we could
meet—Cincinnati, Philadelphia, New York, maybe one
trip out to the West Coast. Finally I had a day off, so I
flew to Boston, and Scott and I took the shuttle together
to New York. We stayed at the Essex House, where there
were no other umpires. I got him tickets for the weekend
games, and it was fun to see him in the stands and to
meet him outside afterward. I had never had that pleasure
before.

During those first tentative months, I never stopped to
consider how to conduct my first gay relationship. Scott
was new to this, too, so I figured we would both teach
each other as we went along. We never held hands, embraced, or kissed in public. That was a given. It wasn't
such a big deal, because it wasn't my style—or his, either—to do those things in public anyway. Yes, we did
have impulses—maybe after a run in the park or while
watching a movie—to spontaneously show our affection
for each other, but we never did it. Most of the time,

heterosexuals don't have this problem. They don't have to think: "What if someone I know *sees* me?"

Although I hid from the public the fact that Scott was my lover, I wasn't hiding it from myself. That was my first big step toward having a serious relationship. But it was difficult for us to have our relationship while I went through all the ostracism again in 1980. It was hard to be away from Scott when I needed him most, but he couldn't visit me as often as I wanted him to, and my hectic schedule wouldn't permit me to go see him whenever I had the urge. On the other hand, the great irony of all the ostracism was that whenever Scott did come to see me on the road, my fellow umpires never knew what I was doing, because they always stayed at a different hotel. This benefit was crucial; it permitted us much freer access to each other throughout the whole first year of our relationship.

But I was still afraid of being exposed, we played it overcautious anyway. When he visited me during the season, if we ran into a player or manager I knew, I would introduce Scott as my friend—and from then on try to avoid running into that same person again. It was perfectly natural to be with a friend, because everybody had friends on the road; but because we were gay, we couldn't be as open as we wanted to. We had to avoid *any* suspicion, period. We had to go up to my hotel room separately (I reserved rooms with two beds for appearances); sometimes we sat apart in airplanes; and I wouldn't always meet Scott at the gate after my ballgames. I knew that if people saw me with the same man in three or four different cities, they might start to talk.

We saw each other about a dozen times during the season, mostly on the road. Boston was an American League city, so I never had games there. But any time I had a day off and could get free, I would fly to Boston to be with Scott. He might have fooled around on me at college; to this day I still don't know. I didn't *care* what he did when I wasn't there; I trusted him and I trusted our relationship. We never seriously discussed being monogamous anyway. I told him in Florida, "If you ever have an affair with someone and you want to tell me, that's fine. But personally I'd rather not know.'' In my mind he was growing, like me, in our relationship, but I knew it would be asking for trouble if I tried to throw a lasso around a handsome young man to keep him from finding out whatever he needed to find out. I just kept praying that whenever I got back, he would be there.

We didn't seek out the gay world; we didn't know where it was, and we didn't want to know. One time I said, ''I would like to see what a gay bar is like. Maybe we could find one in Rhode Island somewhere.'' But then I changed my mind, because I realized I couldn't chance it. ''Forget it,'' I said. ''What do we need it for anyway? We have each other.'' We never discussed it again.

It turned out, though, that I was my own worst enemy in 1980. During the baseball season, I had two sexual encounters with strangers on the road. The first one happened six weeks after I had last seen Scott. I was approached by a young man in my hotel's bar in New York, and after several drinks he said, ''Why don't we go up to my room for a nightcap?'' I should have been satisfied with Scott; but I was traveling constantly, I was still being ostracized and harassed on my job, I was *more* lonely on the road now than before I met Scott, and I couldn't be absolutely certain he would be home when I got back. Maybe it was the need for company and the increasing need for a sexual outlet; I didn't know. I *did* know that the same thing happened to heterosexuals all the time. It was called a one-night stand.

I learned over the years that some gay men in relationships too often become their own worst enemies—like I did then. It seems we're never satisfied with what we have; we always want what we don't have. When we have a secure relationship, we're still out there looking for someone who might be better. We're always trying to boost our egos to see if we're handsome enough for the next young guy who might come into the room. Maybe it's because, as homosexuals, our options in finding the ''right'' partner are so limited. Maybe it's because most homosexuals have to hide their real feelings for so long, it takes longer for us to feel safe and secure with someone we love. Whatever the reason, I think gay men find it harder than heterosexual men to stay monogamous.

My second encounter in '80 was spontaneous combustion, too. I was walking through Water Tower Place in Chicago when I noticed a young man cruising me: following me on the escalator and into stores, checking me out by running his eyes up and down my body. I found it intriguing, ego-boosting, exciting. I was vulnerable, because I was still learning about myself. For the first time I was starting to come out a little as a single, gay man. I was recognizing eye contact from other men a lot more; I was curious to know how much easier things *could* get now that I knew what to look for; and I had to really battle my hormones when I was away from Scott. Plus, I still had my sexual fantasies.

He followed me into Marshall Field's and stood next to me while I selected clothes. He said, "What do you think of this shirt?" Pretty soon, we were exchanging small talk: "What's your name?" "What do you do?" "Where do you live?" While we were walking through the mall together, he asked me to his home in Chicago. I didn't feel that going with him would make me "promiscuous," because, Jesus, hadn't I been *celibate* almost my whole adult life? Wasn't I entitled to fulfill a fantasy, like anyone else? That was enough to convince me to go ahead. But afterward was a different story. Reality drilled holes in my rationale; I felt awkward, uneasy, guilty. I knew when I left that house that I would never do this again as long as Scott and I were seeing each other.

And I never did.

10

"HOW CAN YOU SOAR LIKE AN EAGLE WHEN YOU WORK WITH TURKEYS?"

Once I survived 1979 intact, I felt my career was finally under way. I thought, "It will be so much easier from now on." I had the security cushion of one more year on my contract, and I'd proved to myself—and anyone else willing to evaluate me fairly—that I could be a very good umpire in the major leagues. More important, I had Scott in my life. For the first time as an adult, my professional and private lives were spinning together in harmony.

Yet the rest of my baseball career was to be a nonstop roller-coaster ride of peaks and valleys. Consistently over the next nine years, I grew smarter, less temperamental, and more proficient—yet I had the feeling that nobody noticed. Sometimes when things were humming along perfectly, I was lulled into thinking, "This is great. This is what I always dreamed it would be." But then, all of a sudden, the scab issue would rear up and jolt me back to reality again: "Nothing's changed." It was like battling a nagging illness. One day the symptoms would disappear and I'd feel strong enough to lift a car; the next day I'd feel like someone ran me over with that car.

I didn't know it then, but my career was speeding toward 1988 like a heat-seeking missile to a fire: it had "explosion" written all over it. Along the way, though, I found out enough about myself, and proved enough to myself, to survive the blast. But was surviving a blessing or a curse?

Spring training in 1980 was very rough. Not only didn't the ostracism disappear, it intensified—at least for me. The union umpires continued to treat me like a thorn in their sides, so they were a constant pain in my ass. Since this was my first major league spring training, now I had to make the rounds with union umpires from *both* leagues. I caught flak from somebody else every day, especially because of how outspoken I had been over the past year with the press. In '79, the media had always wanted to talk about the scab issue, and word got around that Dave Pallone would talk. I *did;* I gave them what they wanted in spades. Practically every week I was quoted someplace—and I didn't pull any punches. This newspaper statement was typical:

It's not that bad if they don't drink with me or eat with me or travel with me. But everybody should make sure we walk on the field as a crew. Communication is an integral part of umpiring. Everybody should help everybody else with problems that occur on the field. Our job is to see that things run smoothly. But if you have one man you don't want to talk to, things can't possibly run that smoothly. The league office or the commissioner's office should fine umpires who don't act professional just because they don't like us. If they keep it up, they should be fined again and warned that the next time they'll be fired.

Needless to say, the union umps considered me Public Scab Number One. During spring training, they wouldn't enter the dressing room while I was there, or else I'd come in and everybody would clear out. On the field, they continued to ignore the shit out of me in the same old ways. I never asked or expected them to be my friends. I only wanted them to respect me as an umpire and be professional on the field. But they never did. I was disappointed, because I had thought all the nonsense might stop.

If I hadn't had Scott to talk to, I would have gone nuts. He encouraged me: "Take things slow and turn the other cheek because they can't keep it up forever." And I'd say, "Maybe it'll take another year or two before they decide they're going to accept me. But what they don't understand is, I'm stronger than them. If they push me, I'll push back twice as hard.'' The union umpires weren't very bright in the way they dealt with me. If they had handled me with kid gloves instead of pitchforks, they could have destroyed my resistance, because I would have been more inclined to appreciate their side. But the more they tried to stick it to me, the more I fought back: "I'll be as big an asshole to you as you are to me. *Bigger.*" Scott agreed that I couldn't afford to be weak. But he also pointed out, "You have to try to understand how *they* feel." And I did. I just wished that they could possibly appreciate *my* side, too. But they had tunnel vision; they saw only what they wanted to, and they tried to shove that down my throat.

Toward the end of spring training, I learned that I had been selected to replace a retiring umpire on a regular crew for the 1980 season. This unexpected promotion told me that the league was pleased with my work and had high hopes for my future, because they made me a permanent member of a crew instead of keeping me a vacation umpire, like the guys I came up with. The other good news was that I wouldn't have to work with the Dick Stellos and Bruce Froemmings for one whole year.

My crew chief was Eddie Vargo, a longtime veteran and solid union man. When I met him, I distrusted him immediately. How could you trust a man who never looked you in the eye and greeted you with the wishy-washy handshake of a jellyfish? Yet Vargo was considered a very strong, obstinate umpire who took no shit. If somebody yelled at him, he didn't just stand there and pretend not to hear it. He went after people, just like I did. In that way, he was an "umpire's umpire." I have to admit, I admired his aggressiveness. And the fact is, throughout the 1980 season I never once saw the man miss a play on the bases or have a bad game behind the plate. At the end of the year I told him flat-out, "I know this won't mean anything coming from me, but I want you to know I think you're the best umpire I've ever seen. You did *everything* right this year."

Vargo didn't treat me as awfully as I had expected.

When he was in my presence, he was silent but cordial. Once in a blue moon he would say, "Good job, Dave"— but so low you could hardly hear it. For the most part he left me alone to do my job. And it was easier to work with the same crew over an entire season. They didn't associate with me or go out of their way to help me, but it wasn't the same tension as last year, because I didn't have to constantly prove myself to new guys. When the same people are around you long enough, if you're a decent human being they find that out—even if they don't want to.

But then the paradoxes popped up, as usual. I soon learned, for example, that Eddie Vargo was two-faced. He refused to talk to or be seen with me off the field— except in an airplane. He was deathly afraid of flying, so he would plead with me, "Dave, sit next to me," and he would talk to me the whole flight. At first I thought it was his way of showing me acceptance. I was wrong; he was just using me to help him make it through the flight. As far as I know, he never told a soul in baseball that he talked to me.

On the field, I started out less patient in arguments than I'd anticipated. I was sick and tired of all the undeserved abuse, and it clouded my judgment sometimes. Like the game we had in Cincinnati early in the year when I was at first base, Vargo was at home, and Dave Concepcion was batting. Concepcion and I were about to begin our long feud, which as far as I'm concerned will last forever. He was a miserable guy, a complainer, one of those pain-in-the-ass bullshit artists who whined at every called strike as if it were a ball. He would try to show you up—like Rodney Scott did in '79—by throwing a tantrum for the fans. He was a no-class individual; he always had a bug up his ass. In some ways I liked seeing him do poorly—though at this point I wasn't trying to help that along.

In this game, Concepcion had two strikes on him when he suckered at a slider in the dirt. He tried to check his swing, but he went through, and I called him out on the appeal. He cried like hell to Vargo, and then Reds manager John McNamara started yelling from the dugout.

Concepcion stalked away like a two-year-old, pouting and banging the bat. And McNamara kept screaming at me. So I looked at him sternly to shut him up. I couldn't understand getting all this flak over an obvious call. The only thing I could attribute it to was that I was still considered a scab, and to some people that meant I could never be right.

The rest of the 1980 season was unexpectedly smooth for me. I know I did a good job, because players and managers started to tell me so. For example, Houston manager Bill Virdon made it a point to tell me during my last series with the Astros that I'd done a great job for them that year. Dallas Green and Chuck Tanner told me the same thing. I thought I was on my way and that once the word got back to the league, they would certainly want me back.

Naturally, that hope was premature. Less than two months after the season ended, the roof fell in. I was visiting a minor league umpire friend of mine in Waltham and we got to talking about Pat McKernan, so we called him up to say hello. Pat asked me a strange question: "How did you get along with Chub Feeney this year?" I said, "I got along with him okay. Why?" He said, "I was just wondering." And that was it. A week later Blake Cullen called me and said, "Dave, I'm afraid I have some bad news for you. The league is not going to renew your contract." I said, "What do you mean? Why not?" He said, "Your ratings were too low. So we decided not to renew." I said, "Jesus Christ, my ratings should've been terrific."

I got so damn mad, I hung up, showered, went to the airport and grabbed the next shuttle to New York. (One of Blake's secretaries later informed me that after he'd phoned me, he slammed the door to his office and started throwing things around. I learned also that he'd argued with Chub Feeney on my behalf for weeks before the decision was made. In fact, Blake was supposed to have told me about the decision immediately after the season ended, but he kept trying to convince Feeney not to go through with it.)

The meeting at the National League office was between

me, Cullen, and Feeney. I spoke first: "Blake called me this morning and told me I'm being fired." I could tell by the expression on Feeney's face that he was surprised I'd just found out this morning. I said, "I don't understand what the hell is going on." Feeney pulled out a file, puffed his big cigar, and said, "We have your rating sheets here and they show that you dropped to the bottom of the league."

"That's impossible," I said. "I had a great year."

"The ratings don't say that."

"Let me see them."

He said no, the ratings were secret and he didn't show them to anyone. Then he started flipping through the sheets in my file. "Here's an average of three. Here's a two. Here's an eight, but that cancels out the two. We take the best one and the worst one and throw them out, and then average the rest."

I said, "Mr. Feeney, those ratings are worthless and you know it. They gotta be biased."

"That's the system we use."

"Well, it's never been explained to me. Who does the ratings?"

"The clubs do."

What did that mean? I could only speculate. Obviously, this rating system was pure and simple nonsense. First: the ratings were *not* supposed to be private. They were supposed to be sent to the union so that every umpire would know his ranking. Since I couldn't be in the union, I never saw my ratings and I never knew my ranking. Second: the league never once explained how the ratings were done or what their criteria were. For argument's sake, say I *was* the lowest-rated umpire that year. So what? As far as I knew, or the union knew, or even the league itself knew, there was no written or implied policy that the lowest-rated umpire would automatically be fired every year. What sense would that make anyway? They'd constantly be firing a rookie umpire every year, because, as everybody knows, it takes years of on-the-job training to really develop.

Another fatal flaw was that apparently managers and general managers rated each umpire in categories, like

Home Plate Calls, Base Work, Positioning, Appearance, and Disposition. Isn't that ridiculous? Say you have a run-in with a particular team during the season—a common occurrence—on anything from a missed call, to a manager's ejection, to a balk. And say your call costs that team a game. The name of the baseball business is winning. Today's Manager of the Year is tomorrow's has-been. And general managers change jobs almost as often as managers and movie producers. So if a manager or general manager disagrees with your work—or just doesn't like you personally—is he going to give you an unbiased rating or will he take his revenge on your ratings sheet? It was idiotic; baseball was asking the student to rate the teacher who'd just flunked him.

As I understood it, we were also rated by our supervisors. But what if your supervisor was a union man and he resented you for crossing the picket line during the strike? Was he more likely to say, "I have to be professional about this" or "I'll take care of this guy myself"? In the National Football League, officials are graded by retired officials who assign numerical grades for every call, along with detailed explanations. Those are reviewed with the game films to determine each official's actual performance level in every game. At the end of the year, the highest-rated officials get the playoffs and the Super Bowl. How does that compare with baseball's system, where you can't get a playoff until you have six years in the league, or a World Series until you have seven—and even then, assignments are based on an arbitrary rotation, not ratings or skill? In other words, baseball had no rationale for using the ratings for *any-thing,* never mind for firing someone.

I looked Feeney in the eye. "Mr. Feeney," I said, frustrated, "if you can look me in the eye and tell me that I was a worse umpire than Paul Pryor this year, I'll walk out of here right now." (In my mind Pryor's work had declined noticeably in 1979 and 1980.)

Feeney puffed his cigar and avoided my eyes. Then, out of the blue, he said, "There's a possibility something might happen."

"A possibility? What does that mean?"

"I'm not promising anything, but we'll look into it further."

I couldn't figure it out; why the sudden change of tune? I said, "What are you telling me? I'm *not* fired, or I *am* fired?"

Feeney looked at me without expression. "I'm saying we won't make our final decision today."

"Thank you," I said. "That's all I can ask." And I got up and left.

When I was back in Boston, I phoned Pat McKernan and asked why he'd asked me a week ago if I'd gotten along with Feeney that year. Pat said, "I heard some rumblings that Chub didn't like your umpiring and was thinking about getting rid of you." That's when it struck me that I really *was* on the verge of losing my job. If, in fact, ratings had nothing to do with why they wanted me out, what chance did I have against that kind of prejudice? I could see the union's hand in this. For two years, they had considered me their biggest enemy. Of Lanny Harris, Fred Brocklander, Steve Fields, and myself, there was no question that I had been the most aggressive. I was the one constantly badgering the union umpires when they tried to stick it to me. And I was the one speaking openly to the press about their childish tactics. They failed to intimidate me into meekness either on or off the field, so now they were trying another ploy to run me out.

It almost worked. By the end of that season, I'd finally felt I had it all: a great career and a fulfilling personal life. Then, all of sudden, I was losing one of them. It seemed like there would never be an end to that cycle, and that I would always be missing 50 percent of my life. Fortunately, Scott was there to console me. He kept me reasonably calm. When I told him what had happened, he came up for the weekend to be with me. That's when I found out for the first time how sympathetic he could be. I was crying on the couch—not sobbing, but with tears rolling down my face—and I said, "All these years I put into it and they fired me for no reason. I cannot believe this is happening. I don't understand why." Scott said, "I have no idea what you're going through. I've never been through it. But I can understand how people can be so mean.''

He held me in his arms and told me, ''You have to let them know that you're not going to take this sitting down. You're a good umpire and they know it. It has something to do with the union. You'll get your job back; you wait and see.''

Although Scott couldn't really do anything, he was there for me emotionally and physically. If that sounds trite, just consider that even though I was twenty-nine, nobody like Scott had ever been there for me in a crisis before. He was my security blanket; he was someone I could lean on. That was new to me; I could sleep with Scott and hold him and have the comfort of his company beside me. Family, relatives and friends can give you the security of letting you know that they love you, but they can't be a part of you the way a lover can. Having someone there, physically, brought me the comfort of feeling that at least this part of my life was in order, even if my career was in turmoil. It gave me the emotional stabilizer I needed to survive the crisis.

Over the next three weeks, Scott came up one weekend and I went down to his college one weekend, and we talked on the phone in between. We had both learned that summer how much we missed each other, and we were growing closer. Not only was the sex more meaningful and fun, but our conversations became more intimate. We discussed our life-styles and how we intended to improve them over the next year. I asked him if he had ever had a relationship like this before and he said no, but that it didn't matter, because he knew what he was feeling. I told him that I wanted him to become more important in my life because I had grown to love him. He said he felt the same way, and that my understanding of his problems with his father had made him feel closer to me than to anyone else he'd ever known. But the most important thing to me then was realizing that I was the true me when I was with Scott. And I knew during this period of uncertainty about my career that I could be comfortable living with him for the rest of my life.

I don't want it to sound like it was easy sledding; it

wasn't. Having to hide our feelings in public hurt us; having to keep it from family and friends hurt us; my travel schedule hurt us. But Scott was mature about it—in some ways more mature than me. When we had our little spats—like if he said he couldn't come see me one weekend because he had to study, and I'd rant and rave at him—all he had to do to get back on my good side the next time he saw me was smile at me and say, "I'll bet you're glad to see me *now.*" That warm smile would always melt away the disagreement. So I kidded him about it all the time. I'd say, "You think that as long as you smile, you can get anything you want from me. It's your way of wrapping me around your little finger." And he'd say, "I know. It works great, doesn't it?" In this way he handled my anger with grace, and I always got past it.

As for baseball during that long wait for the league to make a decision, Scott agreed that I should hire a lawyer. So I went to see Bob Woolf, one of the country's leading sports attorneys, and I later consulted with at least five other attorneys. The consensus was that I had a discrimination suit based on the scab issue. But if I went to court I would have to subpoena the ratings, and I didn't see how I could prevent the league from altering them first. Also, I had no union to back me up, and I couldn't expect support from other umpires, because they weren't talking to me. So would it be worth it?

I decided it was. If they fired me, I would sue their ass and let a jury decide. Yet, in my heart, I kept hoping that something would happen behind the scenes first. Finally it did. Just before Thanksgiving, Blake Cullen called, enthusiastic. He said, "Dave, good news. We're keeping you." He explained that Andy Olson had retired and they needed another umpire, so Feeney decided to hire me in 1981 as a vacation umpire—which meant that I had to work in Triple A until the veteran umps started taking their vacations. I would be on probation for the season, and if my ratings didn't improve, they would not renew my contract. It was obviously a demotion, but I was ecstatic anyway. For the second time in what was becoming a pretty strange career, I'd been fired and then rehired. I didn't know Chub Feeney's real reason for changing his mind; I just knew it beat the hell out of going to court.

In 1980 Scott and I didn't really know that much about each other. When he was there for me during my firing/ rehiring ordeal, I realized how badly I needed his care and compassion. Plus, I found I loved him as much for his sensitivity as for his other qualities: his physical beauty, his sense of humor, his frankness, and, of course, his shit-eating grin. At the same time, he learned that although I was older, I was just as vulnerable to insta- bility as him. As a college kid, he always had problems— with his studies, his friends, his family—but they weren't traumatic like mine. So for a time he probably thought I was indestructible because of what I went through in baseball. But when he saw me in despair that my whole career was going down the drain, he realized our lives were on the same level. That bonded us closer than be- fore.

Through January and February of 1981, Scott and I spent as much leisure time together as possible, strength- ening our hold on each other. He still had school, but we managed some ski trips to Maine and Vermont. I remem- ber trying to improve as a skier while Scott glided ef- fortlessly—as he did in everything in his life—teasing me whenever I fell: "I thought all umpires were jocks." And I'd say, "I thought all basketball players understood fi- nesse." He'd laugh—"Maybe someday you'll be as good as me"—and he'd ski away. That may seem insignificant, but I still remember those little moments vividly, because we weren't just skiing and teasing; we were in the pro- cess of becoming a *couple*.

At the end of March, Scott spent spring break with me in Clearwater again. In between my baseball games, we fell into the same routine as before: sun, swimming, parasailing, late-night walks along the beach. It was an- other relaxed, eight-day respite of fun and love. We still didn't talk about so-called gay issues; that wasn't part of our lives then. In fact, at the time I really wasn't inter- ested in gay issues, which may be why I'm still a little naive about some of the issues today. Our serious talks centered on our emotional needs.

At the same time, we carried our physical relationship an important step further. I asked Scott more about his sexuality for the first time: "How old were you when you had your first sexual affair with a man?" Some gays are never truthful about that. They'll talk about their first *adult* affair, but not what happened when they were younger. Scott said that when he was young he explored occasionally with boys, but that his honest-to-God first time was when he was eighteen, with someone he knew at college. He said they went to see a basketball game, got drunk afterward, and ended up in bed together. He kidded me: "Isn't that the way you always used to think it happened? We should call it the Dave Pallone Method."

Scott admitted that he'd also had sex with girls and enjoyed it, but that being with me made him feel like a whole person, which had never happened with a girl. He knew he was gay when he was with me, and he realized he needed to develop that side of him until he was totally comfortable with it. He said he was always hiding that side of himself at college, especially as a jock. He was afraid—and I found this ironic—of being ostracized. This was a key reason why he understood how I felt in my double life in baseball.

The night of this discussion, when Scott and I made love, we had intercourse for the first time. I had never done it and I *wouldn't* do it—until then. And I only did it then because Scott wanted to and I didn't want to disappoint him. I had resisted it in the past because the only images I had of it came from cheap porno films I'd seen at parties in which men had anal intercourse with women. It looked violent to me—like a rape. And the people in those films always looked so sleazy; they never showed any sensitivity or emotion. Plus, the way it was depicted made it look unnatural. I told myself, "I could never do this."

Yet when Scott and I first did it, not only didn't it feel unnatural, but it suddenly seemed like the most natural thing in the world. When you have sex with someone you love, whatever you do becomes another way of expressing your love. It made Scott and me feel more fulfilled, more like we were part of each other, because we were physically one. We both felt like "normal" human beings loving each other. No one was being hurt, or humiliated, or forced to do anything against his will. It was perfectly natural, because we were taking care of and pleasing each other. Isn't that how heterosexual lovers feel during intercourse?

I am aware, though, that our society has a taboo against anal intercourse—sodomy—as "unnatural" or "abnormal," especially if it's between men. But do men sodomize women? Damned right they do. And do they talk about it? Damned right they do. Is *that* unnatural or abnormal? Not if you go by them. Obviously, when sodomy involves a man and a woman, the culture relaxes its view of the taboo. So isn't it hypocrisy for heterosexuals to condemn something as unacceptable that they themselves do?

I am also aware that some people believe that God has commanded against sexual intercourse between men. I have always believed in God, but I don't accept that He would ever say that. As far as I'm concerned, God's word is "Love everyone." He makes no specific exceptions as to how you show your love. The idea that intercourse between men is wrong is a heterosexual idea. My own belief is that God wants me to love people and to be loved, period. If the way I show that love doesn't hurt anyone, and it makes us happy, then it has to be right.

As April rolled around, I was feeling euphoric, because both my personal and professional lives were finally running on the same track. It seemed like my dreams for both were coming true. But when the regular season started, I was working off my probation in the Pacific Coast League—a tough adjustment after two years in The Bigs. Suddenly, though, Blake Cullen rescued me. He called to tell me that the players were preparing to strike and that he was bringing me up to the majors in May rather than June because some of the umpires were taking their vacations early. When I got to the majors, the players' strike began, so I ended up with a six-week paid vacation. That was a great bonus; in fact, I always believed that Blake brought me up in time for the vacation to repay me for the injustice of my demotion.

The strike dragged on for six weeks, so Scott and I saw each other frequently for the first time during a baseball season. We alternated between him coming to Boston and me going to see him at school and, once school was out, in his hometown of Portland, Maine. There I would always take a motel room, although I did visit Scott twice at his parents' house. They knew we were friends, but they had no idea he was spending nights with me at the motel. Fortunately, they allowed him his independence at home, so he didn't have to make up an excuse for not coming home every night.

It seemed to me that Scott's mother and father were very nice people. They were very cordial to me and interested in my career. His father talked with me about my tribulations in baseball, and he concluded, "You could be a good influence on Scott. He needs to know that things don't always come easy." He made it clear that while he loved his son, he thought Scott was too much of a rebel because he always insisted on doing things his own way. I told him, "Just because a person wants to do things his own way, that doesn't mean he's a rebel. It just means he's independent. And isn't that one reason why *you're* so successful in life?" He didn't agree, but I made my point.

When Scott and I were in Boston, we went golfing, or to Revere Beach or the Cape for some sun, or just for walks around the city. At times it felt like we were living together. In fact, we discussed that, too. We knew it was impossible at the moment, that we needed our separate lives. Neither of us was ready to come out publicly with the truth yet; we agreed that it would cause more trouble for the people we loved than it was worth. Yet we did want to live together in the same house someday. So we decided to see how it went through '81, and then we'd discuss it again.

Once the strike ended, the regular season began in early July with the All-Star Game. Because of my probation, I felt I had to prove myself all over again, which seemed unfair. But I was relieved that apparently no one knew I had been fired and rehired. That would really have added ammunition to the veterans' arsenal. On the other hand, I ran into the same old resistance right away. And since I had to migrate again from crew to crew, I regressed back to feeling like a perpetual outsider. Although I kept improving on the field, I always had the feeling it didn't matter to anyone but me. Yet I kept telling myself, "It's been three years already since I crossed the picket line. How long can people hold a grudge?"

One memorable incident in 1981 answered that question emphatically for the whole year. I was working home plate in a Pirates-Giants game at Candlestick Park with crew chief Nick Colosi, Eric Gregg, and Steve Fields, another "scab" like me. Colosi was a meek, frail-looking veteran in the Froemming/Stello mold who had had a heart attack the year before. I knew from the first time we met that he would find some way to bust my balls. In this game he did. Early in the game, the Giants had men on base when the batter got a base hit, sending Jack Clark chugging for home. The play was close; Clark beat the throw, but I didn't see him step on the plate. There was no tag, so I waited. As Clark celebrated with teammates near the batting circle, the catcher turned to me and said, "He missed the plate," and then he stepped on home for an appeal. *Then* I called Clark out. It was a terrible call. I missed it completely, but I didn't know it at the time.

Jesus, were the Giants pissed. I remember arguing with their manager, Frank Robinson, when all of a sudden I got bumped hard from behind. I turned around and there were four Giants, every one of them a suspect— especially Jack Clark. But there was nothing I could do about it. I couldn't throw four guys out for something I didn't see. Meantime, while Giants went wild all around me, not one umpire came to my aid. I had to argue with everyone myself and calm them down one at a time.

Once I accomplished that, Pirates manager Chuck Tanner got into it. He said to me, "I want to know why the hell Jack Clark isn't out of the game. For chrissake, he came up behind you and *bumped* you."

I said, "You see those other three umpires out there? Not one of 'em came to my rescue. I turned around and I had four guys behind me. I don't know who the fuck hit me. Those guys should've been in here to tell me, so I could throw him out. They saw it, just like you did."

Tanner said, "Jesus Christ, it's not *my* problem you guys can't work together."

"It *is* your problem. Because now I can't throw *anyone* out, can I? Why don't you get on the phone and call the league office and tell them what's going on? I'm being hung out to dry here."

Wouldn't you know it: later in the game Jack Clark got a hit to drive in the winning run. The Pirates were irate—and with good reason. It had only happened because of the ostracism. Normally, if you were at your position and somebody bumped your partner from behind, and he couldn't see who it was, you'd rush in and throw the guy out *for* him. Well, that didn't happen here. The fact was, whether I missed the call or not, Jack Clark should have been thrown out of the game. If he hadn't been in the game, he wouldn't have driven in the winning run. So this was a clear case where the umpires—especially Colosi as crew chief—deliberately sabotaged a ball game by letting a fellow umpire fend for himself.

When we got into our dressing room after the game, I was ready to kill someone. All of a sudden there was a knock at the door, and in came a Giants executive named Ralph Nelson, who also happened to be Nick Colosi's friend. He sat down next to Colosi and they talked about the Jack Clark play. I heard Nelson remark—loud enough for everyone in the room to hear—that he saw the replay upstairs and that I had blown the call. I turned around and faced him: "You got something to say?"

He looked at me. "I have nothing to say to you."

"Who the fuck are you anyway to come into this dressing room and tell me what I did wrong?"

Colossi jumped in. "He's here to visit me. Why don't you mind your own fuckin' business!"

I said, "This *is* my fuckin' business! And this guy's got no business talking about my calls. If he has something to say to me, have him say it to my face." I turned to Nelson again: "You're not even supposed to be in this room. I want you outta here right now or I'll have your ass *thrown* out."

Colosi got steamed. "He's *my* guest, Pallone."

"Then tell your guest to get the fuck out."

Colosi yelled, "Go fuck yourself."

I completely lost control; I said, "Why don't you get the fuck out of the game and go have another heart attack!" And I picked up my stool and threw it at his head. He ducked, and the stool smashed a hole in the door. Colosi didn't come after me; he didn't even look at me. He just grabbed his stuff, and then he and Nelson stormed out together.

My blood was still boiling, so I turned to Eric Gregg: "And where the hell were *you* out there? Why didn't you help me? You could've at least told me who hit me." He said, "I didn't see it." I said, "Bullshit, you didn't see it. Who do you think you're kidding?" Now I went after Steve Fields. I said, "You're supposed to be on my side and you let me hang out there? You're an asshole, too. How could you ever do that?" Fields was scared shitless, because he didn't want to antagonize the union umpires (he ended up getting fired at the end of the season anyway, and as far as I was concerned, he deserved it).

I was so mad that when I got back to my hotel, I called Chub Feeney and told him what had happened and that Ralph Nelson had no goddamn business being in there. Feeney agreed and said he would take care of it. (He did: he wrote Nelson a letter telling him he was no longer permitted in the umpires' dressing room.) The next day, I was at the airport waiting to fly to my next assignment when I happened to see a newspaper picture of the Jack Clark play. There was Clark's foot right in the middle of home plate. I said aloud to myself, "Boy, I missed the shit out of that one."

Shortly after that, I was in New York at the league office when I ran into Chub Feeney in the hall. He showed me the same picture of Jack Clark with his foot in the middle of home plate. He said, "What were you looking at when you called this play?" I said, "I honestly don't know. Obviously not his foot." Then he said something

Even umpires were kids once.

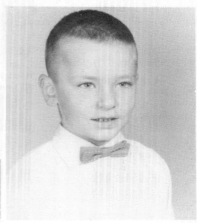

Me, Mickey, and Carmine in my grandparents' living room, the day of my mother's sister's wedding. Notice how cool I am in my white "jock" socks.

Me and my parents in front of our house the day I graduated from Watertown High in 1969. School took its toll on me; I've already got the sour look of an overworked umpire.

July 1979. Be honest: who looks more like an "Italian pizza vendor" here—me or overheated Cubs manager Herman Franks? (The Cincinnati Enquirer)

Shea Stadium, Mets vs. Houston, 1980. Eddie Vargo looks on as I give Mets manager Joe Torre (hands in pockets) the heave-ho for cursing me for calling Elliott Maddox (21) out on an attempted steal. OK, I admit it; the real reason I'm running Torre is because he looks so blasé. (*Nury Hernandez*/New York Post)

Expos vs. Phillies, 1980, Montreal. LEFT TO RIGHT: Expos outfielder Rowland Office, first baseman Warren Cromartie, and manager Dick Williams argue my "no-catch" call on Andre Dawson (not pictured). Williams is hot-dogging for the crowd; Cromartie *orders* a hot dog; Office looks like he's already out to lunch. I'm probably saying, "Hey, I don't *want* mustard on mine, Dick. OK?" (*Joseph McLaughlin*, Philadelphia Bulletin)

Three Rivers Stadium, Pittsburgh, 1980. I love this shot. I'm in perfect position to call this attempted steal by San Diego's Gene Richards. I hold off until the play is over, and it's a good thing, because the ball gets by Bill Madlock and Richards is safe. (The Pittsburgh Press)

Pete Rose and Phillies manager Pat Corrales try to argue me out of a strike-three call against Rose in 1982. Rose is insisting. "I tipped it!" but the call stood. Satch Davidson looks on silently, agreeing with me, of course.

One of my lighter moments in the New Orleans Superdome in 1983. The year before, I surprised the Philly Phanatic by "shooting" him with a starter's gun. He liked it so much, he asked me to do it again. There were a lot of fans I would have liked to pull this on, but I didn't want to give them any ideas.

My proudest moment to that time: posing for the crew picture before the fiftieth All-Star Game in Chicago's Comiskey Park, July 1983. LEFT TO RIGHT: John Shulock, Ted Hendry, George Maloney, Harry Wendlestedt, Jim Quick, me. (*Richard Collins*)

Looks like a simple ejection, right? But why am I laughing? Well, I had just thrown out Pirates catcher Tony Pena when manager Chuck Tanner came out to argue. But it was all for show, because he knew I was right. Calmly, he said, "Dave, you gotta throw me out so I look good in front of my players." I laughed and accommodated him. On his way off the field Chuck said, "Thank you." (*Marlene Karas*)

A "hang this in your den" shot with Ted Turner before a 1984 Braves game at Atlanta Fulton County Stadium. LEFT TO RIGHT: Me, Paul Runge, Turner, Bob Engel, Randy Marsh.

The Lighter Side #2. Famous manager and Italian food-hound Tommy Lasorda cracks everybody up with one of his outrageous pasta jokes. LEFT TO RIGHT: Dodgers catcher Mike Scioscia, me, unknown player, Lasorda, Bob Engel (thinking, "Oh, *reeeally*?"), second baseman Steve Sax. (*Phil Velasquez/ Chicago Sun-Times*)

Former U.S. Attorney General Ed Meese and I pose with one of the honored guests at the V.I.P. reception before the spina bifida affair in 1987.

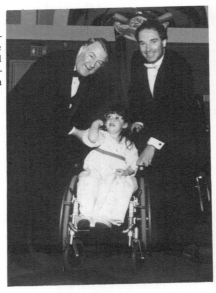

Before Game 2 of the 1987 championship series between St. Louis and San Francisco at Busch Stadium. LEFT TO RIGHT: Giants manager Roger Craig, Eric Gregg, Jim Quick, John Kibler, Eddie Montague (in shirt), me, Cardinals manager Whitey Herzog, Bob Engel. (*Jim Herren Photography*)

The start of the infamous Pete Rose shoving incident, April 30, 1988. Pete and I are trying to make our "points" simultaneously. A few seconds later, he lost control and ignited a controversy that people still talk about. (*AP/Wide World Photos*)

Eric Gregg and Reds coach Tony Perez try to lead Rose to the dugout after he gave me his forearm shove. Rose is screaming, "You touched me! You touched me!!" Do you see any marks on his face? I didn't, either—at the time. (*AP/Wide World Photos*)

I like this photo; this was when I was really enjoying the game.

The game after the Pete Rose incident. Just before game time, I'm watching stadium security take down the FIRE PALLONE sign. I'm thinking about the death threat, too. (*Dale Omari*/Sports Illustrated) unexpected: "I don't want you to think that this is the only criterion for keeping your job." I looked at him, surprised. "Thanks. I'm glad it isn't."

A final note to the Jack Clark story: I later learned that the next crew into San Francisco found out it was me who put the hole in the door, so one of them circled it with a Magic Market and wrote over it: "A Scab Did This." When I heard about that, I thought about the famous World War II graffiti "Kilroy Was Here." I figured "Screw 'em. At least they know I'm *here*." And then I decided I could play their game, too. I bought a bumper sticker and stuck it on the inside lid of my equipment trunk so that when I opened it before a game, the other umps could see it plainly. It said: "How Can You Soar Like an Eagle When You Work with Turkeys?"

11

FOOTPRINTS
IN THE SAND

Early that off-season, I found out from Blake Cullen that
I had jumped from the worst-rated umpire out of twenty-
eight in 1980 to the fourteenth best in 1981. That was the
greatest "phantom" achievement of my career. How
could I possibly have improved so dramatically in one
literally *short* year, especially without making any special changes? What did I do better than last year—whisk
the plate with more authority? It was just another note of
absurdity in a totally absurd system. If I had any doubts
about that, they were put to rest by something Blake told
me. He said that on one of the ratings sheets, a team had
rated me a zero for Appearance while rating John Mc-
Sherry a ten. That was amusing, since I was a notorious
stickler on appearance, while McSherry weighed over
three hundred pounds. I remarked to Blake, "And with
this system they can make and break careers?"

Not long after this conversation, I received a letter from
Chub Feeney confirming that my work had improved significantly in 1981 and that I was being rehired for 1982.
No mention of probation or any criteria for future improvement—just "sincerely yours" and that was it. Even
though I knew this system was a joke, I wasn't about to
look a gift horse in the mouth. I had gotten my reprieve,
and now I was determined to make the league sorry it
ever had doubted me. How? By making 1982 a banner
year—the absolute best of my career.

That was my attitude on Sunday, February 14, 1982—Valentine's Day—with spring training right around the bend. Although Scott had come up to Boston for the weekend, he had to return to grad school that afternoon. But we'd talked at length on Saturday about his upcoming spring visit to Florida. It would be our third vacation there together, and we were really looking forward to it. We were at a point now where our relationship was on automatic pilot; we felt we were on a straight course toward happiness. But then fate turned on me again. That day should have been the start of the happiest, most hopeful year of my life. Instead, it was the start of the *worst*.

Sunday night, I went over to a friend's house to play cards, and I stayed out late. When I got back to my apartment at about three A.M., I crawled into bed. But there were messages on my answering machine, so I replayed them. One was from my cousin: "Dave, this is Jenny. Please call me as soon as you can." I thought it was too late to call, so I went to sleep. But the phone jolted me awake at three-thirty; it was Jenny again. I said, "I got your message, but I got in too late to call." She said, "Dave, I have some terrible news. Your father died." I said, "No. *What?*" "Yes," she said. "He was in Atlantic City." I said, "Wait a minute—*what?* What are you saying?" She said, "I'm at Aunt Mary's house. Why don't you come down here?"

My father's sister, Mary, lived in Watertown on the same street where I grew up. I got dressed and drove over there. I couldn't believe it; Jenny had mentioned Atlantic City, but I had seen my father three days earlier and he never said anything about going to Atlantic City. It just couldn't be true. But when I got there, they explained that he was in Atlantic City on a junket with some friends, and that he died of a massive heart attack while throwing dice at the craps table in the Sands Hotel. I immediately thought about my brother, who was still living at home and very close to my dad, and my sister, who'd just moved back home that day. I would have to tell them both.

Early Monday morning I went to my father's house and

prepared to break the news to my sister and brother. We couldn't have the funeral until my dad's body was flown back from New Jersey. In the meantime I had to make all the funeral arrangements, including selecting my father's coffin. It was not easy. I was confused, anxious, sad, hurt. But I knew I would have to be strong for my brother, my sister, and my uncle Dom—my dad's brother. Dom was the closest person to my dad; he would be devastated.

Monday night, I called Scott and told him what had happened. He wanted to come up immediately to be with me, but I told him to wait until the funeral. On Thursday he came to the funeral, even though he had to stay in the background. I saw him in the church when we followed the casket out after the service, and again at the burial, which gave me strength. It was a military burial—my dad had fought overseas in World War II. I was still shocked, but I held all my emotions in until a soldier handed me the folded flag. Then I broke down in front of everyone for the first time.

At the house afterward, I snuck outside with Scott and we hugged each other. I told him how much it meant to me that he was here, and he said, "I'll always be here when you need me." That was an important thing for me to hear. We couldn't spend any time together now, but I knew he would be back Friday night for the weekend. I was going to need all the compassion he had.

He came back up the next night and I had the great comfort of falling asleep in his arms. Saturday morning, I brought Scott with me to the cemetery. He had never met my father (if my dad had met Scott too many times, he would have been too hard to explain), and I wanted him with me when I said my last goodbye. I told Scott, "Four people I loved are lying here: my mother's parents and my mother and father. It's so difficult when you lose a member of your family. You always think you can prepare yourself, but each time it happens it gets worse. Especially if they were young, like my parents. My mother was only fifty-one." He said he didn't think he could cope with losing a parent. I said, "I hope you never have to go through it. I hope you and everyone in your family live long lives.''

Then I kneeled to speak my heart silently to my parents: ''Mom, Dad, this is Scott. I wish you could have known him because I love him very much. He is such a good human being and he's made me so happy. I hope that, somehow, you will know that I'm going to be all right, because, with Scott, my life is very good. I miss you both and I love you. I always will.''

In two of the three most trying times of my life to date—when I lost my job and now my father's death—Scott was there for me to provide that special comfort no one else could give. And he was my listening ear in spring training, which was a time when I thought more about my dad. I told Scott then that I had so many regrets about my dad. I regretted all the times I didn't tell him I loved him; and all the chances he had to see me work, but either he didn't want to come or I didn't invite him; and all the times it would have been nice to see him in the stands, or take a weekend vacation with him on the road, or just tell him what was in my heart. I remembered the time I gave that poor kid a dollar in the Dominican and I wrote my dad a letter about it, and he wrote me back in the only letter he ever sent me: ''I'm glad you got to see that part of the world. Now maybe you can understand better how tough it was for me growing up in the Depression.'' Maybe he was trying to get closer to me, and I missed the chance again—like that time when I was a kid and he asked me to walk with him to Watertown Square.

And Scott would say, ''I've never been through a family death before. I don't know what to tell you, other than you can't relive the past. You have to think about all the *good* memories you have of your father, and cherish those.'' And I'd say, ''Yes, but the sad thing is that all the good times I had with my dad were when I was young.'' My grief caused Scott to talk about his own hopes for getting closer to his father. When he finished school, he said, he would have a long talk with his dad and see if they could find more common ground. ''I don't know why,'' I told him, ''but as you get older you start to think about life passing you by and how you let all these petty things get in the way of what really matters. and you realize you have to come to grips with the fact that if you let each day go by without trying to get closer to your family, there'll be a time where the opportunity is lost forever. That's what happened to me. Don't let it happen to you.''

I remember that we drifted into a talk about kids. I said how much I loved kids and would love to have my own someday. He said it would be great to have kids, but how could you have them if you weren't married to a woman? I said I didn't think I'd ever have a child with a woman, so maybe I would have to adopt. I remember saying that if I ever did have a kid, I wouldn't let him get away from me to the point where he couldn't tell me his problems. I admitted that my biggest regret was never giving my parents the chance to know who I really was. I said, ''I learned a hard lesson too late. If I could address gay people now, I'd say, 'Never hide your feelings. It doesn't do anybody any good. You cheat yourself out of too much.' ''

(I have so much respect for young gay people today who go to their parents and tell the truth. They show so much maturity and inner strength. It's got to be one of the hardest things to do in life, but the benefit is that they don't have to live a lie; they don't have to live a double life. If you live a lie, you're a completely lost soul. What I believe now is that if a mother, a father, or a friend withdraws their love and turns their back on you because you were honest with them, they never loved you to begin with. Not to understand is okay; to withdraw love is unforgivable. Unfortunately for me, I was never ready to take that chance, because I was so young and lonely, and I didn't think I could afford to lose the love of people already close to me. I'm sure people reading this will say, ''I know exactly what you mean. I didn't know anybody else felt the same way.'' Well, *most* gay people feel this way. The important thing is to *change* that feeling into: ''I'm going to live the truth from now on, no matter what it costs.'')

* * *

The entire 1982 regular season was tinged by the loss of my father. It felt so much like 1973, after my mother died, that it was like déjà vu. But this time I couldn't quit—and I had Scott to help me through it. Yet throughout the season my mind wandered constantly to thoughts about my dad. I'd be standing at second base in Dodger Stadium, or in the outfield at Wrigley Field, and the national anthem would play and I would look into the bleachers and remember the times that my dad and I went to games together. I kept blaming myself, over and over, for never getting closer to him—and this added an extra dimension of pain to my season. Maybe that's why whenever the stupid scab incidents came up that year, I really blew my top.

I started the season working again on Eddie Vargo's crew along with Satch Davidson and Terry Tata, another hard-ass union ump with a blind grudge. Did things change much? Not until Tata was switched off the crew halfway through the season and was replaced by Eric Gregg. One little anecdote tells all you need to know about Terry Tata. In Chicago, before a Phillies-Cubs game, the clubhouse man got Tata's uniform socks mixed up with mine because they were practically identical. So, without looking closely, I slipped them on over my freshly laundered "sanitaries." But when I went to put on my shoes, I realized, "Terry, these are your socks." I took them off, but Tata growled, "What the hell are you doing with my goddamn socks?" I said, "Hey, our socks are almost identical. It's no big deal." He said, "It *is* a big deal." And when I held out his socks, he yanked them away and tossed them into the laundry bag. "These can't be my socks," he sneered. "Mine are *clean.*"

Since Vargo and Davidson had already worked with me one full year, and Gregg and I went all the way back to umpire school, I expected them to loosen up a little around me, especially off the field. But it didn't happen. For example, they still made a big deal out of riding with me in the same car. In 1979, the league had allowed us to rent a crew car in the three cities where the ballpark was farthest from the airport—Houston, San Francisco, and Montreal. But since no one would let me drive or ride in the car, I rented my own car and charged it to the league. They let me get away with it in '79, paying twice instead of once. But in 1980, they wanted me to pay for my car. I said, "No way. Why should I have to pay if they won't let me ride in the car the league rents for the *whole* crew?"

Blake Cullen then issued an ultimatum: "One crew, one car," and either everybody would use it or nobody would. Well, the other umpires were so offended by this, they declined use of the crew car and rented another one, paying for it themselves. That left me with the crew car. But I got smarter; I cut a deal with National Car Rental for free use of a car in *every* city in exchange for game tickets. So I didn't need anybody's car anymore—and those guys still had to rent a car in every other city.

Luckily, the '82 season wasn't all gloom and doom. Some humor did soften my isolation. For example, Houston Astros pitcher Joe Niekro befriended me, and occasionally we had a beer together and traded war stories. We didn't know each other very well, but he had a relaxed openness that put me at ease. He saw things for what they were, and he liked to turn them upside down for a laugh. That's why I enjoyed talking to him, especially that year. His friendly humor helped me forget my troubles.

Early in the season in Chicago, we ran into each other in a hotel lobby, and he had two dozen golf balls that someone had given him as a gift. He asked if I would like a dozen and I said yes, but that I was on my way out for the night. I asked if he could bring them to the ballpark tomorrow and give them to me there. No problem, he said, and we went our separate ways. The next day, Niekro gave me the golf balls all right—but not the usual way. He sent them out to me a couple at a time with different players throughout the game. And he not only gave me *my* dozen, he sent *his* dozen, too.

It was a very cold day, so I was wearing my jacket, but after a few innings I had no place left to stuff those goddamn golf balls. Yet players kept coming up with them: "Special delivery from Joe" and "Joe says these are the balls you ordered." After four innings, I had golf balls sticking out of my pants pockets and bulging from my jacket like extra-large eggs. Plus, my hands were frozen because I had no place to warm them up—and Joe Niekro was in the dugout in a parka and wool cap, waving a putter at me.

A short time after that, I was in San Francisco getting ready for a Houston-Giants game when there was a loud knock on the door. I opened it, and two burly men in suits stepped in, looking grim. One of them said, "We'd like to speak to Dave Pallone." I said, "That's me." They showed me badges: FBI. The second guy said, "Mr. Pallone, we have a warrant for your arrest," and he whipped out these heavy handcuffs, spun me around, cuffed my hands, and started reading me my rights: "You have the right to remain silent. Anything you say can and will be used against you in a court of law. You have the right to an attorney—"

"Wait a minute," I said. "What're you doing?"

"We're arresting you for trafficking in prostitutes."

"*What?* What are you talking about? You can't be serious!"

"We're serious," one of them said. "Is ten to twenty in the federal pen serious enough for you?"

I said, "This is crazy. I don't understand the charge."

"The charge is simple. You brought prostitutes across state lines from Mexico."

"Mexico?" I said. "I haven't been to Mexico in four years." It was like bad TV; *they had the wrong guy.* "Look," I pleaded, "you have the wrong guy. You can't be looking for me."

"You're right," one of them said, spinning me around again. "We already *found* you."

Vargo, Davidson, and Gregg saw all this—but they couldn't believe their eyes. Vargo went apeshit. "Hold it," he said. "What the hell is going on here?" But they started walking me out. I was nervous now; I didn't know where they were taking me. I said, "This is ridiculous. I didn't do this."

One of them said, "Mr. Pallone, we read you your rights. We told you that anything that you say can be held against you in a court of law."

"Are you crazy?" I said. "I don't even know what you're talking about. Prostitutes. Mexico—this is *nuts.*" Despite my protests, they led me all the way up the runway. I started to worry: "Jesus, what happens when this hits the papers? My career is ruined."

As we approached the exit, there was Joe Niekro laughing his ass off. Then the FBI agents cracked up, too—and unlocked the cuffs. Finally, I realized I'd been had. "You gotta be shittin' me," I said to Niekro. He laughed so hard, he collapsed against the wall.

During '82, my schedule didn't allow for Scott and me to see each other as often as we wanted. We were in a groove, so that was the only flaw in our relationship. Most of our communicating was done on the phone, but we also sent cards with sentimental love notes. I could write pretty much what I wanted to, but he couldn't send an "I miss you, I love you" card because my mail went to the National League office while I was away, and sometimes mail was opened inadvertently. For a while, I got smart and had him send his cards to the ballparks. But I had to be careful, because someone might read it there, too.

The constant separation was one of the hardest things about our relationship. Yet I always thought it helped, because I believed the old adage "Absence makes the heart grow fonder." I remember, though, that during his last road visit that year, Scott was upset about my travel schedule. He said, "I understand that travel is part of your job, but it's tough for me to accept that you're so far away all the time. The only time we have together is during spring break, and even then we don't see each other that often." We didn't fight about it; I just said, "That's the way my job is. You just have to realize that you're the most important person in my life right now and that nothing will come between us." I told him that next year I would arrange for him to visit me much more often. "Meantime," I said, "we have to learn to savor the time we do have together during the season." It was interesting: this time *I* was the mature voice of wisdom.

When Scott visited that year, we didn't have to hide so much. We didn't run into the same players over and over again. People I knew met Scott a couple of times, but the meetings were spaced so far apart that nobody remembered him from before. Even if they had remembered, everyone saw friends on the road, so it wouldn't necessarily occur to anyone that he was my lover. In one way, it was more enjoyable being on the road together than being at home. Even though we always had to hide our true relationship, nobody knew us on the street like they did in our hometowns.

In October I took Scott to two games of the World Series (Milwaukee versus St. Louis). He loved baseball, and it was his first World Series. I remember him telling me that he couldn't wait for me to work my first major event. I said, "I'll be eligible for the All-Star Game next year. If I get it, we'll be there together." And I made that a secret goal: Scott and I together at my first All-Star Game. One day, I hoped, he would also join me when I finally achieved my ultimate baseball goal: working a World Series. I felt so good with Scott during that week in October. *Everything* seemed possible for us then.

Just before Thanksgiving, I visited Scott and some of his friends in Portland. The day after Thanksgiving, Scott drove back with me to Waltham to spend the next few days with me there. I had to make an appearance at a party that night without him, so he arranged to go to a couple of parties across town. At dinner I told him, "I will try to meet you later. Call me at my party and either I'll meet you where you are or I'll just come by and pick you up."

He gave me that grin of his and said, "I didn't bring enough shirts to wear. Okay if I wear one of your jerseys tonight?" Naturally, I said yes. It was a little game he liked to play with me. Every so often he'd say, "I didn't bring enough shirts. Can I wear one of yours?" Then he'd go into my closet and put on one of my brand-new shirts. And I'd always say, "Hey, c'mon, I haven't even worn that shirt yet." He'd say, "Well, I wanted to break it in for you." That was his teasing sense of humor; he knew how important my clothes were to me, and that's why he always put on something new. He really got a kick out of my protests. He was like a little kid that way, which is something that endeared him to me even more.

So I showered and got dressed and came back into the living room, where I found Scott wearing my new black Polo jersey. "Looks better on me than it does on you, right?" he said. I said, "No, it looks better on me. It just looks *newer* on you." We both laughed and hugged and said goodbye. Then I left for my party. Two hours later, Scott called me at the party to tell me where he was. It was way on the other side of the city, and I was exhausted from all the traveling the last few days, so I said, "I'm really tired, Scott. But I'll try to pick you up. If I don't make it before your party ends, call me when it's over and I'll come get you then."

About an hour later I hadn't heard from Scott, so I got in my car and started toward his party. I came to this corner where if I turned right, I'd go to the party, and if I turned left, I'd go home. I was so weary behind the wheel, I turned left and headed home. I watched TV for a while, waiting for a call—but it never came. At two-fifteen, I thought, "The party's gotta be over, and the bars are closed. Where the hell is he?" Finally, I couldn't stay awake any longer, so I went to bed.

I was sound asleep, when I suddenly bolted awake for no reason and looked at the clock. It was exactly three A.M. I thought, "Jesus, Scott's never stayed out this late when I was home." But I fell asleep again. Exactly fifteen minutes later, my phone rang. It was Randy, one of the guys Scott was out with that night. He said, "Dave, I'm at the police station." I thought, "What now? What kind of trouble are they in?" I said, "What happened?" There was a pause; Randy started sobbing. A chill shot up my spine. I said, "Tell me."

He could barely talk. "Oh, God," he said.

"Randy," I said, scared now. "Is it Scott?"

"Yes."

"Jesus Christ. Tell me."

"We were in an accident. He's in the hospital. It's bad."

I froze; I couldn't get a breath. Somehow I managed to ask the name of the hospital, and when he told me I rushed over there. A policeman at the hospital told me what had happened. According to his report, Randy, another friend, and Scott had left a party in Randy's car at one A.M., heading for another party. While they were stopped at an intersection light, Scott spotted a phone booth across the road and decided to call me. When the light changed, Randy started his turn out of the intersection for the phone booth when, all of a sudden, they were struck on the passenger side by a van running the light. The driver, a drunken teenager, was cut and shaken up but otherwise unhurt. Scott was seated by the passenger door; he was still alive—but only barely. His parents had been notified in Maine; they were driving down early that morning.

I was allowed to see Scott briefly in intensive care. As far as I knew, I was the first person to see him. His head was bandaged, his right arm and right leg were in casts, and he was vaguely conscious. I broke down; I had to leave the room. I remember a nurse finding me in another room and consoling me. Then I got up the courage to go back in. I stood by Scott's bed and took his free hand in mine. I leaned over and whispered, "Scott, this is Dave. Can you hear me? I'm here." And as God is my witness, he squeezed my hand. His eyes were swollen shut; he didn't move a muscle, but he squeezed my hand. He knew I was there.

That was the last time he heard anybody. That morning, before his parents arrived, Scott died. I left the hospital to be by myself. My first thought was, "I've just lost the most important person in my life. What do I do now?" I was angry with God. I thought, "How could this be? How could you take him away at such a young age?" I had now lost everyone dear to me, and I didn't know if I could come through this. I didn't know where to go to find the strength, and I had no gay friends to turn to.

But I did go to Scott's wake and funeral in Maine. At the wake, I went up to the casket, looked at Scott, and said a brief prayer: "I will always be with you. I will never forget you." On my way out, I gave my condolences to Scott's parents and sister, and it was all I could do to keep myself from embracing them and sharing their grief, and telling them that Scott meant as much to me as he did to them. But I just walked away like everyone else and tried not to draw attention to myself.

At the church the next day, I sat alone in a back pew—like Scott had done nine months earlier at my father's funeral. During the service, I blocked everything out except my own thoughts. I talked to God: "I know you have a purpose for everything. But I cannot understand the purpose for this. Why did you take him? Help me understand, so I can accept this." It was incredibly hard to contain my emotions. That's what I'd been doing my whole life—I hid my personal life, and now, when I loved someone so much, I couldn't even show how I really felt at his funeral.

I had never felt the charade of my double life as sharply as I did right then. I felt cheated not only of Scott's love but also of my own grief. It nauseated me; I resented it. And when I got back to my apartment in Waltham, the feeling increased. I opened my drawer and pulled out the only picture I had of Scott and myself in Florida, and I thought, "How stupid, how absurd. He was my lover and the most important person in my life for three years, and I couldn't even leave a picture of him out in my own house."

I was despondent at home, so I decided to visit the only place where I could find comfort at that time—my parents' graves. I kneeled beside them and said, "I've had too much death to deal with. Help me understand this. Why would God, knowing all my problems with baseball, take away the only person in the world that I loved, the only stabilizing force in my life?"

There were no answers, of course—only pain and a void. Anyone who has ever lost a loved one knows that awful feeling, and how long it takes to stop—if it ever does. It was so depressing that when I left the gravesite, I knew I would never return. And I never have.

In February 1983, I could not find any enthusiasm for baseball, which was approaching fast. I couldn't bear to think of being in Clearwater for the first time in four years without Scott. Everything there would remind me of him and torture me. But I had no choice. I knew I would have to go, and I knew I would have to handle it somehow.

I tried to tell myself that the only way to defeat fear was to face it. So I guess I thought if I just fiddled with my baseball gear, that might be the first small step to dealing with what lay ahead. I dug out my equipment trunk and opened it up, and the first thing I saw was the printed card I'd pasted next to the bumper sticker on the inside lid. I'd bought it in June, so I could refer to it whenever I needed inspiration. It was an anonymous fable entitled "Footprints." I sat down and read it to myself:

One night a man had a dream.

He dreamed he was walking along the beach with the Lord.

Across the sky flashed the scenes from his life.

For each scene, he noticed two sets of footprints in the sand, one belonging to him and the other to the Lord.

When the last scene of his life flashed before him, he looked back at the footprints in the sand.

He noticed that many times along the path of his life, there was only one set of footprints.

He also noticed that it happened at the very lowest and saddest times in his life. This really bothered him, and he questioned the Lord about it.

"Lord," he said, "you said that once I decided to follow you, you would walk with me all the way. But I have noticed that during the most troublesome times of my life, there is only one set of footprints. I don't understand why, when I needed you most, you would leave me."

The Lord replied, "My precious, precious child. I love you and I would never leave you. During your times of trial and suffering, when you see only one set of footprints, it was then that I carried you."

I sat there, aching and lonely again, and I told myself, "That's not good enough anymore. You can't always rely on God to carry you through. From now on, you have to carry yourself."

12

LOVE
YOUR ENEMIES

When I went to spring training in 1983, I thought it would be just what I needed to escape my depression and pain. I was wrong; I was depressed as hell. Everything in Florida—my condo, the beach, the restaurants, baseball—reminded me of the vacations Scott and I spent together there. Now he was gone, and so were the feelings that were changing my life. I just couldn't understand why both my dad and Scott had to be taken from me the same year like that—so suddenly and so violently.

Losing Scott made me realize I was not prepared to suffer through another year of ostracism. I didn't think I had the strength to handle it. When it started up again the first week of spring training, I was a phone call away from quitting. But I rationalized my way through it. I've always believed the old adage "God works in strange ways and does everything for a reason." So I kept telling myself, "Maybe there's a reason for this, and someday I'll find out what it is." Another rationalization was: "Scott's up there saying, 'Life goes on, Dave. Be strong; keep fighting.' " I figured if I quit, Scott would haunt me for the rest of my life: "You dumb jock. Quitting means giving in to those asshole umpires, which is what they want you to do. Have the courage of your convictions."

I tried to, but I just couldn't get my mind on baseball. It was like a job I was dreading. I'd been assigned to Bob

Engel's crew with Paul Runge and Jim Quick; and even though I'd worked with Engel and Runge before, and liked them, I expected them to ostracize me like everybody else. Over the past three years, Scott had always been there to talk to me and bolster me through it. But now, even before I got on my own crew for the regular season, I had to face so many different guys—the Crawfords, the Tatas, the Stellos, the Garcias, the Palermos— without support. Where would I get the emotional stamina to face that crap alone again?

I remember calling an old friend, Father Piermarini, a priest at St. Anthony's Church in Webster, Massachusetts. I'd met him, ironically, through Steve Palermo when I was in the minors, and I talked to him sometimes when I needed spiritual advice. I knew I could trust him, so I told him about my double life and the pain of losing Scott. I said, "I can't go through this anymore without him. I can't take the hate and the shunning anymore." He said, "You are a good person, David. Don't doubt yourself and don't doubt God. There are some words from Matthew that might help you: 'Be ye perfect, even as your Father which is in Heaven is perfect.' And: 'Love your enemies. Bless them that curse you. Do good to them that hate you. And pray for them which despitefully use you, and persecute you.' "

At the start of the regular season I kept those words in mind, but I still lacked enthusiasm. So much was missing inside me, yet I told myself to hang in there and focus on the positive: "I'm working with Engel and Runge. Maybe things will change with them."

My earliest memory of working with Bob Engel, a witty, fair-minded man who liked to listen yet never let his guard down, was the time in '79 in San Francisco when Lee Weyer's crew padlocked my mask and I commented that it was terrible, and Engel said I was right. It wasn't a major breakthrough, but I never forgot that he was cordial to me when almost nobody else was, and that he thought the union umpires were carrying their grudge too far. It sent me a message that I stored in my memory: "Bob Engel is a human being."

So was Paul Runge—a suave, analytical man who

missed his calling as a lawyer. My first memory of him was a '79 game in Cincinnati when I called George Foster out on a half-swing from first base. After the game Runge came over to me in the dressing room and said, "Great call on Foster." That meant a lot because, as president of the Major League Umpires' Association, Runge had almost a duty to ignore and despise me. Yet here he was defying his union's secret pact by not only talking to me but complimenting me. And I remember that during the early part of the strike, when the league directed union umps to call us "the new umpires" instead of "scabs," and a lot of them popped off emotionally to the press about what assholes we were, it was just like Runge to rationally defend the use of the word "scab." He told the media: "I looked it up in Webster's and one of the definitions is 'a worker who replaces a union worker during a strike.' So they *are* scabs." He was the only union umpire who could say "scab" without making it sound like "war criminal."

I don't remember where we opened the '83 season, but I did give Engel my introductory speech. I expected the usual hardass response: "Just do your job and stay out of our way." Instead, Engel said, "I think you do good work and I expect you to continue doing it. I don't know if the crew will associate with you, but I can tell you that I don't like all this ostracism crap. The job is tough enough without having friction in the locker room. I've talked to Paul and Jim about it, and we all hope it stops." To me, that little speech was like the Declaration of Independence. For the first time in my career, instead of hostility I sensed a chance for acceptance.

I remember the first incident that really broke the ice between Engel, Runge, and me. They didn't associate with me off the field yet, and although they treated me in a friendly and professional manner in the locker room, they hadn't quite come around the corner, because as word got around that they were cordial to me, they caught flak from the hard-core union umps. Guys like Bruce Froemming and John Kibler called them to say, "What the hell are you doing? God damn it, you're a union man. You can't talk to that scab." But Engel and Runge were their own men. It had been four years since the strike, and they were fed up with the aggravation and the problems.

At the end of May, although they weren't flying with me, or staying at my hotel, or eating meals with me, the atmosphere in our locker room was fun and relaxed. Engel and Runge treated me like one of the regular crew—and Jim Quick, a mellow, congenial guy back then, followed their lead. In fact, they'd already started needling me about my habit of sending flowers to the league secretaries when they did small favors for me. I enjoyed that teasing—and it gave me an idea. When we worked in Atlanta the first time, I decided to buy a rose for each guy on the crew and leave it on his locker room stool before the first game. It would be my way of saying, "Thanks for accepting me." I thought it was the right idea at the right time.

I got too busy before the game, so I ended up buying the roses the next day. But when I got into the locker room, there was a rose sitting on top of *my* stool. When Engel arrived, I showed him the rose. "That's funny," I said, laughing. "I was gonna do the same thing for you guys, but you beat me to it." Engel said, "Don't look at me. I didn't do it. Maybe it was Paul." When Runge showed up, he admitted to it. "I just did it to bust your balls," he said amused. "Don't get a big head about it. I didn't buy the damn thing; I stole it." What a fantastic turnaround after four terrible years of cold shoulders and malicious remarks.

The camaraderie continued all season, cementing our relationship. They saw that I was not only a likable person in the locker room but also a solid, reliable umpire on the field. They opened up, I think, because they saw the real me, not the fabricated Asshole Scab the union made me out to be. And I saw so much more in them worthy of my respect. They kidded instead of fought among themselves; they liked and respected each other; they handled themselves professionally at all times on the field (from the very first game, they stood *with* me for the national anthem, and they were there for me in controversies); and they were intelligent men with a wide range of outside interests, like finance, real estate, and family. Best of all, they included me in their ribbing and practical joking. For example, when Engel and Runge realized that I vented frustration by complaining, they rode me mercilessly about it. Twice I came into the locker room and found a padlock in my hat—their way of reminding me of what I *used* to complain about. One time in L.A. there was a dent in the wall, and when I came into our dressing room I saw that somebody had written over the dent: "Dave Pallone's Been Here." Well, it wasn't a repeat of the Colosi incident; the writing was Runge's funny scrawl.

Engel had a very dry wit; he was a master at antagonizing sarcastically. He used that sarcasm to instigate all the "trouble" in our locker room. For example, if Runge talked about another umpire whose work he admired, Engel would go, "Well, that isn't what *Dave* thinks" or "That's not what *Dave* said you think." Then Runge would give me the evil eye. Or I'd complain about a player who pissed me off and Engel would give me his favorite dig in a low, sarcastic drawl: "Oh, *reeeally,* David"— and it would totally defuse my anger.

They were always pulling my strings because I was so goddamn gullible. One time, I asked the clubhouse man for an autographed baseball to give to some kids after the game, and Engel said, "David, how many autographed balls do you have today?" I fell for it. "What do you mean 'today'?" I snapped defensively. "I only got one." Engel mocked, "Oh, *reeeally,*" and cackled at me for an extra dig. I got such a kick out of hearing that tease that when we talked on the phone in the off-season, I would sometimes catch myself saying, "Oh, *reeeally,* Bob."

Engel and Runge knew that it was easy to get me upset, so they took full advantage of that. One way was to hide things on me—equipment, clothes, baseballs, towels, you name it. They knew I had an extensive hat collection at home, so one time before a TV *Game of the Week,* they told me that NBC had given the crew three new NBC-TV hats. I said, "What do you mean, three? Where's *my* hat?" Runge said, "Oh, you're not getting one." Naturally, that lit me up. I said, "You gotta be shittin' me. Why the hell not?" Engel said, "We asked them that, David. And they said, 'Pallone doesn't get a hat because he's a *scab*.' " They knew I would blow my top when I heard that. "*You* guys can call me a scab," I exploded, "but that guy has no goddamn business calling me a scab. He has no business coming into my dressing room and bad-mouthing me to my crew like that. That son of a bitch never—and I mean *never*—comes into my dressing room again." They didn't say a word.

I had home plate that game. That was significant because it was an NBC *Game of the Week*, and the home plate umpire had to watch the NBC man in the dugout for the signal to start every inning after the commercial break. The NBC man wore a towel around his neck, and when he removed the towel it meant the inning could start. I was really steamed at NBC; as far as I was concerned, their schedule could wait. So, in spots, I deliberately ignored their signals and they had to scramble like crazy to rearrange commercials.

After the game, while I got ready to shower, Runge said casually, "By the way, Dave. You know the hat that NBC didn't give you? It's under your towel." I couldn't believe it; they'd hidden it from the start. I said, "Jesus Christ. I liked it better when you guys weren't talking to me." And Engel cracked, "No problem, David. That can be arranged." As I headed to the shower, I warned, "You guys will pay for this. I'm gonna get you." Runge left shaking his head; Engel muttered, "Oh, *reeeally*," and followed him out. Getting dressed, I told myself, "I'll think up a way to get even with those guys on my walk back to the hotel." And I would have, too—if only I could have found my goddamn *shoes*.

The main reason I had so much respect for Bob Engel and Paul Runge wasn't because they kidded with me and treated me like a human being but because their priority was excellence as a crew on the field. They took tremendous pride in that, and they were smart enough to know that the crew couldn't be excellent if there was a wall between the members. So they had the intelligence and guts to treat me the way they wanted to, not the way they were expected to by other people.

One of the problems when nobody was talking to me was that I couldn't learn everything I needed to learn in order to improve my work. That's because a lot of learning in umpiring takes place on the job, where you pick up tips from the experienced vets. Obviously, I didn't have that opportunity my first four years, because nobody took me under their wing to give me advice. But Engel and Runge freely offered me suggestions and tips—"Position yourself this way on that call," "Here's an effective way to explain this rule to a player"—when they felt I needed them. And I always listened gratefully.

I really benefited from their advice during '83, especially when I slipped into another mysterious slump behind the plate. I totally lost the strike zone—just like when I was in Triple A. If you ever wanted to find an umpire who looked like he was missing pitches on purpose, that was me. I mean, guys were going, "How could he possibly miss that pitch? It was right down the tube." I didn't know; I was bewildered. Then Engel made suggestions about positioning, and Runge said I might do better calling pitches from one knee instead of in my usual squared-up crouch. Pretty soon I was seeing the ball better and getting my confidence back—and then I got my strike zone back, too. No question it would have gone on longer without their help.

Working with Engel and Runge taught me lessons about my on-field demeanor, too. My whole career, it was always an effort for me to control my temper and my mouth. Engel and Runge, on the other hand, were masters at calmly controlling explosive situations and earning the respect of players and managers. Engel did it by never losing his temper. I saw him throw people out that year with the manner of a parking-lot attendant politely giving directions: "You'll find plenty of spots in the clubhouse. You can park down there." And it worked. He used to say, "If you control your temper, they'll usually control theirs, too. It's a lot easier canning a cooperative player than a pissed-off one, right?" Of course, he was right. I saw him work that magic again and again.

Players, managers, even other umpires used to refer to veteran umpire Doug Harvey as "God"—some sarcastically, but most reverently. There were two reasons. The first was that he had a habit of calling everyone "son." He'd say, "You were out, Son" or "You're gone, Son." The other reason was that he had total control on the field. Managers used to look at their schedules and say, "God will be here next week. We better be on our best behavior." Well, the only other umpire I ever saw who had that kind of presence was Paul Runge—in fact, even more so than "God." It was most obvious in the precise way he explained controversial decisions. He had a special talent for always saying the right thing, and he knew how to be stern without raising his voice or getting upset or using foul language. He could point his finger at you or level a gaze, and that would end an argument before it began. Not many umpires had that power on the baseball field. I admired it; I thought it was something to strive for. So I tried to control my temper more than before.

Maybe it worked—because in June, I was awarded the 1983 All-Star Game in Chicago's Comiskey Park—my first major event in my first year of eligibility, and the fiftieth anniversary of the game. I was sky high; it was the first step toward my World Series goal. Jim Quick was selected too, so we figured we represented our crew. I expected it to be the proudest moment of my career. I guess I forgot that whenever things were going along smooth for me, something weird always happened. This was no exception.

We finished the first half of the year on the July Fourth weekend in Atlanta. We left the ballpark early after our last game to beat the crowd, and we drove back to the Airport Hilton. Since I wasn't flying to Chicago until the next morning, I decided to go out for a drink to relax. Bob Engel said he had left his reading glasses at the ballpark and asked me if I could get them on my way out. I said sure and I drove back to the ballpark. The crowd was still there, watching the fireworks, and the atmosphere made me think about how festive things would be in Chicago for the All-Star Game.

I retrieved Engel's glasses and then drove to a bar, where I had one scotch on the rocks. After an hour I was tired, so I left for the hotel. I was driving down Peachtree Street when, out of nowhere, a state trooper pulled me over. He asked me for my license and told me to get out of the car. I got out reluctantly and he said, "Sir, I am placing you under arrest." I said, "Why? What did I do?" He said, "Sir, you're drunk." I said, "What are you talking about? I haven't been drinking." He started reading me my rights, so I told him, "Officer, I'm Dave Pallone. I'm a National League umpire." I told him the name of the chief of security at the ballpark and suggested he call him to confirm that I had just been there and that I hadn't been drunk. It didn't work. He said, "You were weaving back and forth"—and then he cuffed me.

Joe Niekro popped into my mind. But then I realized, "No, it can't be. He isn't even here." When the officer put me in the back of the squad car, I got nervous. I said, "Lookit, this is a mistake. I haven't been drinking. I only had one drink. I have to be in Chicago tomorrow to work the All-Star Game." I was petrified that I might miss the game. He didn't care; he called a tow truck for my car and drove me to a police station.

At the station I got out, protesting. The trooper told me to calm down because I would have to take a Breathalyzer test. He said, "This will go a lot easier if you cooperate. You might as well stop worrying, because you won't pass the test. You'll be spending the night in jail." I couldn't believe it—this guy had already judged and sentenced me. Plus, I was worried because I had never taken this kind of test before. I didn't know how much alcohol one scotch on the rocks had put into my blood. It was a classic Dave Pallone Nightmare: ALL-STAR UMP FAILS BREATHALYZER TEST: JAILED IN ATLANTA FOR DRUNKEN DRIVING.

Inside, the trooper gave them my name and someone said, "Are you the umpire?" I said, "Yes. I umpired the game today. I am not drunk. I had one drink on the rocks, and it wasn't even a full drink." A sergeant said, "That's what they all say. Sorry, but you have to take the test."

So I took it. They told me that to be considered "under the influence" in Atlanta, my blood alcohol level had to be above .10. Well, when I blew into this thing it read .03. So the testing officer said, "Wait a minute. You must not have blown into this right. Do it again."

I did it again—and again it was .03. He turned around to the state trooper and said, "Man, he's not drunk. There's almost no alcohol in him. He's normal."

I said, "That's what I've been telling him. I had one drink all night. I don't know where he got his information. And I wasn't weaving on the road either."

The trooper said, "He didn't have his lights on. He must've been speeding." The other officer said, "You can get him for that if you want."

I said, "What? He didn't pull me over for that. He cuffed me for being under the influence. Which I proved I'm not. What's going on here?"

The trooper said, "I could write you a citation. But because we put you through all this trouble, I guess I won't. Just remember, I'm giving you a break." I probably had a lawsuit here, and I was so pissed I could have belted somebody, but I was thinking, "Here I have my first All-Star Game and I could end up in jail for something I didn't do. All I want is to get the hell back to the hotel, go to sleep, and catch that plane to Chicago tomorrow morning." So I pretended this guy was Chub Feeney calling me on the carpet for something so stupid, it wasn't worth a protest anymore. "Thanks for the break," I said. "I appreciate it very much."

The trooper drove me to the towing lot, where I would have the privilege of paying fifty dollars to get my car back. The kicker was when he said in this suddenly friendly tone, "So you're an umpire? Do you get to Atlanta a lot?" I said, "Yes. Quite a bit." He said, "I really like baseball." I said, "That's great." I just wanted him to hurry the hell up and get me to my car. Then he said, without a hint of remorse for the trouble he caused me, "Do you think the next time you come to town, if I called you, maybe you could get me some tickets?" I thought, "You gotta be shittin' me." But I knew that with my luck, I might say the wrong thing and end up back in jail for assaulting the dignity of a state trooper. So I just said, "Sure. I always stay at the Airport Hilton. Give me a call and I'll take care of you." I gave him my schedule, figuring if he ever did call I'd tell him I was leaving him tickets and then I'd stiff him.

The All-Star Game itself was a bittersweet experience. On the one hand, it was a thrill to be out there with about sixty thousand people in the ballpark and millions watching on TV. And for this one game, the union umps—George Maloney, Ted Hendry, Harry Wendelstedt, and of course Jim Quick—broke their code of silence and treated me and fellow "scab" John Shulock like we really belonged. The camaraderie was great; it was as though there had never been a strike. The downside was that when I first looked into the stands, I thought, "Scott would've been here." So during the national anthem I silently dedicated the game to him. I said, "Scott, you're not here physically, but you are here in my heart. I couldn't have accomplished this without your support. Thank you; I miss you and I still love you."

The period immediately following the All-Star Game was the best of my career to date. Engel and Runge seemed even more friendly and supportive; who knows, maybe my getting the All-Star Game provided them with extra justification for accepting me. Although I had never felt better about my career, something was still bothering me. While my relationship with the crew kept improving, along with my mechanics and technique, my temper was always simmering. Maybe it was the aftershock of losing both my dad and Scott, or maybe it was just my nature. Whatever the cause, my temper was put to one of the toughest tests I ever had on the field in a disgusting, unforgettable confrontation with Cincinnati shortstop Dave Concepcion. And I failed the test.

It was a July ballgame between the Reds and the Cubs at Wrigley Field. I was working second base, and Concepcion was on first with one out. He tried to steal; I called him out; he got up and left—never said a word. When the Cubs were batting, Reds manager Russ Nixon came to the mound to change pitchers. Concepcion strolled over to me and said, "Man, how come you called me out?'' I said, ''Davey, you *were* out.'' I didn't sense a big argument. I thought he was just asking about it, like ''What went wrong?'' Ballplayers did that a lot to establish a rapport with an umpire. All of a sudden, he got mad: ''I was safe, man.''

''Davey,'' I said, maintaining my cool, ''I'm not gonna discuss it with you now. The play is over, you were out, and that's all there is to it.''

''Well, you know where you come from anyway, man.''

''Excuse me?'' I said. ''What do you mean by that?''

''You know where you come from. You're a goddamn scab.''

''And you're gone. Get the fuck off the field.''

(People might think, ''How could he throw a player out for saying he's a scab?'' Many fans believe that players get thrown out only when they curse; that's not true. As I've said before, to me, the magic words were ''You are.'' And although ''scab'' wasn't a curse, I couldn't let a player get away with calling me that on the field. If I did, then everyone would have called me that. I wanted the respect that I'd earned. If I couldn't call a player a rookie or a bum or a jerk or a loser, why should they be free to call me names?)

Concepcion threw a fit. He yelled at me, ''You cock-sucker motherfucker!'' Then he cursed me in Spanish and made threatening gestures—but he pulled the typical coward's move of waiting for someone to hold him back before losing control. Once he was held, of course, he got even angrier. The closest thing I'd ever seen to this was the time when Joaquin Andujar tried to destroy me for calling an obvious balk.

Concepcion struggled and threatened and cursed, and I yelled back, ''I told you to get the fuck off this field.'' All of a sudden, he reared up and spat in my eye. I went absolutely crazy. I lost my cool and my hat, and I went after him. It took Engel and Runge and several players to keep us apart. The second that spittle hit my face, I was no longer an umpire. I was an ordinary human being who'd just been spat upon. And like everybody else, I instinctively wanted to fight for my integrity and my manhood. I wanted to rip Concepcion apart; I wanted blood.

I know one thing: if Engel and Runge hadn't been there to rescue me, it would have been a disaster. If I'd have been working with other umpires who were hoping I'd screw up, I would have ended up hitting Concepcion and either getting suspended and fined or fired. Just the kind of incident the union umpires dreamed about for a scab.

A few days afterward, Chub Feeney fined Concepcion and suspended him for a week. But Concepcion delayed the sentence by appealing. Three weeks later, we had the hearing in Feeney's office. Engel and Runge were there along with Feeney, myself, Concepcion's lawyer, a representative for the Players' Association, and a lawyer for the National League. Concepcion wasn't there, which pissed me off. In fact, I was pissed that there was a hearing at all, because they had the goddamn tapes. I remember Runge asking me beforehand, though, "Did you reread your report, so you know exactly what to say?" I said, "I don't need the report. I remember everything." I was being foolish and obstinate.

I sat down and described the incident, right down to Concepcion's spittle hitting me in the eye. Concepcion's lawyer asked me, "Which eye?" "What difference does it make?" I said. I thought that was stupid. The point wasn't which eye; the point was that he'd spit on an umpire. But the lawyer repeated the question, and it got under my skin. I said, "He hit me right here," and I pointed to my right eye. He said, "In your report, you said the *left* eye." That was correct; they'd unnerved me into screwing up.

I said, "All I know is it hit me in the face."

He said, "Does it bother you when someone calls you a scab?"

"Yes, it bothers me," I snapped. "What the hell does that have to do with anything? God damn it, Concepcion spit in my face and that's all that matters." I was extremely upset; everyone could see that there wasn't any point in continuing. That's when the league lawyer said, "I think we've had enough of this," and then Feeney concluded the hearing. It lasted about twenty minutes.

I knew when I left that I hadn't done well. That turned out to be true; for whatever reason, Feeney reduced Concepcion's suspension to three days. That was outrageous. Feeney had originally found Concepcion guilty enough to merit a week—and that was one of the longest suspensions he'd ever handed out. I couldn't understand the big retreat. I mean, being spat upon was the most demeaning thing that had ever happened to me. In my opinion, Concepcion should have been sentenced first to getting hit in the mouth by me. Then he should have been suspended for anywhere from a year to life. How can that kind of cowardly behavior be tolerated in professional baseball? In my opinion, if you spit in someone's face, especially in this kind of situation, you're not a man—and you don't belong in a civilized game. What would happen to a bus driver, or a teacher, or an executive if they spit on somebody? Three days off without pay? I doubt it. I think they'd lose their job—which is what they'd deserve.

The only positive thing I could see in the whole affair was that as long as Concepcion remained in the National League, I'd be seeing him again.

13

GOING IN AND COMING OUT

My relationship with Scott had lasted exactly three years, Thanksgiving to Thanksgiving. I knew I would never be able to replace our intimacy. No one else could ever be the first; others would have his look, some of his gestures, even his manner, but no one would ever have his touch with me; and no one else would ever be there for me in the toughest time of my life. But relations were so good in '83 between Engel, Runge, Quick, and myself, I began to feel that the void left by Scott was at least partially filled by their camaraderie. I remember telling myself, "Maybe *this* is what God intended. Maybe He took Scott from me only to replace his love with the other important things missing in my life: peace, harmony, and friendship on my job."

Although I accepted that possibility, my mind kept wandering to Scott throughout the season. I remember a Mets-Astros game in New York when the Mets had a runner on first with less than two out, and I started daydreaming at second base. I was recalling, vividly, some of the times in seasons past when Scott and I had met in New York. While I was in my crouch with my hands on my knees, the pitcher delivered to home plate. I put my head down when, all of a sudden, the runner took off and the catcher threw to second. I thought, "Oh, my God"— and I looked at the play *through my legs*. I couldn't really see the play upside down like that, so I just said, "Ahh

. . . *safe.*'' I was lucky; it was the right call. But Astros infielder Bill Doran knew what had happened. He shook his head and said, "Maybe you should stand on your head next time."

In the cities where Scott used to visit me regularly— New York, Cincinnati, Philadelphia, Chicago—I stayed in the same hotel where we used to stay together, and that would remind me of him. I would start regretting things—that we didn't spend more time together, that we never had a chance to be out in the open with our relationship, that we never lived together—and I'd feel mournful again, and sorry for myself. So I talked a lot, in my heart, to Scott. I told him it was times like this when I missed him most, and that although my crew had accepted me and my career was going so much better now, it wasn't enough. But I would always snap out of it by imagining what Scott would have said if he could have answered me: "You're acting like a two-year-old. You've been waiting all these years for this to happen, and now that it has, you won't let yourself enjoy it. You'll always remember me. I'll be there when you need me, whenever you think of me. But now it's time for you to go on with your life."

In May of '83, this process helped me get up enough courage to seek a substitute for Scott. It had been six months since he died; I had no one to talk to intimately, and I needed that void filled. I also knew I would never meet another Scott in someone's kitchen, so it was up to me now to go out and actively find someone. I hadn't pursued the gay world before, because I was too afraid to be recognized in gay bars. I was still worried about that—but now I needed to take the chance.

I decided to get started in Atlanta because I knew Atlanta had a big gay community. I just didn't know where it was. First I thought I'd look for a magazine or a book. I went to regular bookstores, but they had no gay-oriented material. Then I checked the phone book for "X-rated" bookstores and went to a couple of those. That's where I found men's magazines like *The Advocate,* which covered gay life in general, and, even more helpful, *Bob Damron's Address Book,* a guide to specific gay bars and clubs throughout the United States. I looked up Atlanta and found a listing for a bar called Backstreet at 845 Peachtree Street. Its description key indicated something like: "private club; men and women; dancing; young college types." It sounded perfect for my tastes.

So, Friday night after a game, I drove to Backstreet. It was situated off a large parking lot full of cars, but there weren't many people walking around. I thought that was a break, because it would make it easier for me to sneak to the bar unseen. But first I sat in the car a moment and reviewed my strategy one last time: "No one will know me here. But if I see a ballplayer I know, I'll try to hide and then leave. If he sees me first, I'll go talk to him because at that point neither of us has anything to hide anymore." Satisfied, I hurried nervously across the lot and ducked into the entrance, hoping nobody I knew saw me going in.

I went straight to the bar for a drink. Immediately I felt at home. I looked around me and, Jesus, it was a whole new world. I couldn't believe the size of the crowd. My first thought was, "I never knew there were so many gay people." Most gays wonder when they're growing up, "I can't be the only one, but how many others are there?" I was shocked and excited to see so many. It reassured me that I wasn't alone. And it gave me hope that I *could* eventually find someone else.

The first person I talked to was the bartender—a burly, friendly guy—because I wanted to have a contact in the place. (Whenever I went into straight bars, I tried to establish a rapport with the bartender, because he always knew the people who came in there better than anyone else.) Well, this guy took my order, and when he brought my Chivas on the rocks I asked him his name. He said, "They call me Peaches."

I asked, "Is it always this busy in here on Friday night?"

"Yeah, this is a popular place. You new in town?"

"Well, yes. I'm just visiting. Are there many other places in town to go to?"

"Yeah. There's a place called The Library." He described the clientele there, and then told me more about the regulars at Backstreet. Finally, I left the bar and cruised around the edge of the dance floor, watching people dance. It was reassuring to see so many different types of gays—butch types, effeminate guys, transvestites—talking, laughing, having a good time. I wasn't looking to pick anyone up; I was just trying to ease into the scene and enjoy myself. In fact, it occurred to me, "It's too bad Scott isn't alive. We would have had a lot of fun here. We could be out there dancing, like everyone else."

I think it's a standard heterosexual myth that all gays go to gay bars with only one thing in mind: to pick someone up and get laid. Well, it's wrong. "Gay" does not mean "slut." I'm not saying gays don't ever go into pickup bars looking for sexual encounters. They do. But that's why heterosexual men go to straight pickup bars, too—especially the type of people I associated with professionally. Most of them were baseball people—players, management, even league executives—and they all had their minds on getting laid. I think that basically, intentions are the same whether you're in a gay or straight bar. Both gay and heterosexual men visit bars for many different reasons: sometimes for company, sometimes for conversation, sometimes to escape loneliness, and yes, once in a while to try to score and relieve pent-up frustrations. What's the difference, then? Could this misperception about gays possibly be the close-minded view of heterosexuals who can't admit that in most ways they're just like us?

My purpose for being in Backstreet that night was to get a sense of gay nightlife in general. I was searching more for conversation and friendship than for sex. (I was also aware of the AIDS crisis then, which put a damper on the idea of casual sex. On the other hand, if I met the right person, I was prepared to abstain from intercourse or practice "safer sex.") My main interest was to meet someone who could be a listening ear, like Scott, when I needed to talk to someone about things that mattered to me. That was my thinking as I admired the strikingly handsome men in the bar, trying to imagine what *they* were thinking.

I remember looking for someone who physically resembled Scott. I saw several, but one in particular really interested me—an athletic-looking young man in a baseball hat, standing near me drinking a beer and watching the dance floor. I walked up to him and introduced myself. His name was Jeffrey, and once we started talking he reminded me even more of Scott in his easy manner and his sarcastic, playful sense of humor.

When he asked me who I was, I just said, "Dave." And when he asked me what I did, I said I was a traveling shoe salesman. I was not comfortable enough yet to risk being identified, even if he was a total stranger. But Jeffrey talked openly about himself: he was twenty-one; he went to college in Alabama; he played baseball; his parents were divorced. After about an hour, I got his phone number and we said goodbye. I told him I would call him next time through, and I meant it.

After my night at Backstreet I felt I'd finally crossed the line and entered the community of gays, where I felt more like the real me. It was a great relief, very satisfying—but still a little scary. I couldn't totally shake my fear of being found out and losing my job. And that's why I didn't go to another gay bar for the next three months. But something happened in July that helped to change my mind about this for the future. I had my first sexual encounter since Scott—with one of the world's most famous "heartthrob" movie stars.

One night after a game at Dodger Stadium, I went with some Hollywood friends—an actor, an actress, and a TV writer—to an exclusive party in Topanga. When I arrived around eleven P.M., there were about a hundred guests, mostly people in "the business," so I guess it was appropriate that I was introduced around as "Dave Pallone, National League umpire." I was always self-conscious about that, but it was a conversation starter, so I sometimes let it slide. I desperately wanted to meet new people, and this was one of those times.

The party was loaded with attractive people, but one man in particular caught my eye. He was in his late twenties, about six-two, slim, darkly handsome, with a sensual smile. Even from a distance he was magnetic and very masculine, though not "macho." People—especially

women—kept finding their way over to him, and he enjoyed being the center of attention. I thought, "Boy, is
he handsome. And he looks so familiar." But I had no
idea who he was.

Around midnight he was on the terrace, sipping champagne by himself. The physical attraction I felt for him
was the strongest I'd felt since the first time I saw Scott.
Naturally, I wondered if he could possibly be gay, but
there were no signs. I was wary of showing my feelings,
but after several glasses of champagne and my first Chivas, I walked up and said, "Hello, how are you? Are you
enjoying the party?"

He said, "Yes, I am."

"My name is Dave Pallone."

He smiled. "I'm Greg." We talked about the party and
how I came to be there. He said he was in the film industry and I told him I was an umpire. Since he was a
big Dodgers fan, he asked me about baseball. After a
few minutes we broke off and mingled with other guests.
As the party wore on, I got a little high on the scotch
and I noticed that Greg was feeling his champagne. I also
sensed from his long glances at me that he could be interested in the same thing I was—sneaking away and
leaving together. At about two A.M., he came over to say
goodbye to some people I was talking to. Then he said,
"Good night, Dave. I hope you have a good game tomorrow." I felt that was his way of saying he wanted me
to follow him out.

About two minutes later, I left. Fate was with me for
a change; when I got outside, there was Greg walking to
his BMW, which was two cars in front of mine. He
looked a little shaky, so I said, "Are you okay to drive?"

He saw it was me and he smiled. "I think so. I haven't
had that much to drink."

"Well, where do you have to go?"

"The Valley." Music to my ears; it was a long way.

"That's pretty far. If you want, you can leave your car
here and I can drive you to my hotel. I'm at the Bona-
venture."

"No, I'm okay. Thanks anyway."

"Lookit, you're more than welcome to sleep on the couch in my suite. It's a lot closer than the Valley."

He thought it over. "Yeah, it's a long drive. But I need to be home tomorrow. I have things to do."

"So do I. I have to umpire a ballgame. I'll make sure you get up early."

I guess that nailed it down, because he said, "Do you have any booze?"

"No champagne. But plenty of scotch."

"Let's go," he said, opening his door. And off we went in our separate cars.

We parked in the hotel garage and went up to my suite. I showed him the hide-a-bed couch in the living-room area. "This is your luxury bedroom," I said, and I fixed us two scotches. We sat around talking about the party again, and then I got tired. As I got up to go to my bedroom, I blurted, "I don't know how comfortable that couch is, but you're welcome to share my king-sized bed. It's definitely big enough for two."

He didn't hesitate. "Well, if you really don't mind, I'd like that." I couldn't believe this was going so smoothly. I was still high and still missing Scott terribly, yet this felt so right. Maybe it was because it had been so long.

We entered the bedroom and undressed on opposite sides of the bed. Without speaking, we climbed into bed together and I trembled with anxiety and anticipation—like a teenager. The next thing I knew, we were facing each other and his leg brushed mine, and we were kissing and embracing.

We slept until my ten A.M. wake-up call. I felt almost as good as the first time Scott and I slept together in my apartment. I wasn't confusing it with love; I was just happy to wake up with someone I liked again. I didn't know how much I had missed that until now. I ordered up breakfast—and aspirin—which we devoured near the window overlooking the pool. I mentioned the party again and how lucky it was that we were there together. I said, "I didn't expect to have a good time and look what happened." He said, "That's how I felt." Suddenly, I was struck again by how familiar he looked. I said, "What do you do for work?"

"You don't know?"

"Well, I think I do. But I'm embarrassed to say I'm not sure. Hey, I don't even know your last name. Which isn't fair, because you know who I am and what I do." I tapped him playfully on the shoulder. "So c'mon, fess up."

He looked down at his coffee. "I'm an actor just trying to make a living." A light bulb went off in my head. Then he named his last major film, and my jaw dropped open when I realized who he was. He said, "I had a pretty good role in that." What an understatement. I'd seen the movie; it was a blockbuster—and he had played the romantic lead.

"What a dummy I am," I said. "I hope you aren't mad that I didn't recognize you. But at least you know I didn't sleep with you because of who you are."

"It's actually kind of nice," he said with a little laugh. "But my ego just got shot to hell." We both laughed together—and I remember feeling impressed at his modesty.

After coffee, he said he was late getting started and really had to leave. I told him I would be back in L.A. in September and asked if I could call him then. He said, "Sure. It would be great to get together." He wrote his number on a breakfast napkin and off he went.

Since I was late getting packed and checking out, the first time I had to reflect on what had just happened was when I was standing out at second base in Dodger Stadium at the start of my next game. The first thought I had was that last night's experience was a turning point, because it was the first time I had really wanted to go to bed with anyone since Scott's death. In fact, I thought more about Scott during that game than about Greg. I still missed him, but now I accepted that I was capable of *feeling* something again, of being with another man.

In August I was in Atlanta for the second time, so I called Jeffrey—the college kid I'd met in Backstreet. I told him I was in town for three days and that I wasn't a shoe salesman but a professional umpire, and the reason I didn't tell him that at first was because I wanted to be sure we would see each other again. I said, "If you'd like to come to a game, you're welcome to. I can leave you tickets.'' He said that would be fun, so I left tickets for him and a few of his friends, and they came to the game. Afterward, I met them all at Backstreet. I was loose and relaxed there—Jeffrey and I talked and danced for hours, and I enjoyed talking to his friends as well. It was the first really ''social'' night I'd ever spent in a gay bar with all gay people, and it was great fun.

Finally, Jeffrey and I drove back to his house and I slept with him there. Again, although I liked Jeffrey, this wasn't a love match. In my mind, it was the first step of my return to the world of relationships by establishing contacts in cities where I worked. This way, I figured, if I didn't meet anyone else I could love, at least I could see people I liked.

In September I called Greg to tell him I would be back in L.A. for the coming weekend, and we arranged a meeting at his beach house Friday night after my game. That Friday, I remember, my adrenaline was really pumping. For one thing, the Dodgers were in the thick of the pennant race (they would eventually win their division), so every game was critical. And I was working home plate, which always gave me an inner high anyway—and especially down the stretch with a pennant on the line. Then there was my personal desire to prove myself to Dodgers manager Tommy Lasorda. On top of that, of course, was my anticipation of seeing Greg later on.

I was hoping for a quick, smooth game—no problems, no delays. Naturally, that didn't work out. The Dodgers had their ace, Fernando Valenzuela, on the mound, and he was mowing the Atlanta Braves down. But he was wearing Dodger-blue spikes with long white tongues flapping over the laces. Finally, the Braves complained that the tongues were a different color than his spikes and that they were distracting the batters. So I went over to Lasorda and said, ''Tommy, he's gotta take those shoes off.'' Valenzuela, who was temperamental to begin with, got pissed.

Lasorda said, ''Why's he gotta take his shoes off?'' I said, ''They've got long white tongues. They have to be the same color as the shoes.'' Lasorda said, ''Why the hell do they have to be the same goddamn color, can you tell me that? What the hell's the color got to do with it?'' He was trying to stall and get the upper hand. I said, ''Look, Tommy, you know the rule as well as I do. The shoes gotta go.'' Then Valenzuela spoke up in his broken English: ''I wear these shoes always.'' I said, ''I don't care if you sleep in those shoes. Either take 'em off or color in the tongues.'' Valenzuela gave me a hard time, so the crowd started to boo—and I was pissed at him for trying to show me up when he knew I was right.

Finally, he went into the dugout and colored the tongues with a Magic Marker, and then we resumed play. A few innings later, I called a ball that Valenzuela thought was a strike and he showed me up by throwing a fit for the crowd, which started booing me again. Well, it never took much to get Tommy Lasorda on my case, so this brought a barrage of abuse from him, too. I was ready to kill now; I turned around and yelled to Lasorda, ''You better knock that shit off, Tommy. I don't wanna hear another word.'' Tommy was shrewd; he loved to bait me. He didn't say another word; he just started mouthing curses silently, like a mime. ''That's it,'' I thought. ''I have to nail him.'' So I wheeled around, took a few steps toward the dugout, and threw his ass out of the game.

Predictably, he shot onto the field, yelling and screaming at me. I thought, ''Now I'll get him really good.'' Tommy came right up behind me, jawing away, and bumping me slightly with his big belly. Every time I turned away from him, I deliberately nudged his stomach with my elbow. ''You're hitting me,'' he complained. ''I'm not hitting you,'' I said, turning away again and hitting him with the other elbow. If we hadn't been so goddamn mad at each other, we would have been laughing our asses off at how childish we were.

Well, all this nonsense extended the game, which caused me to be late getting to Greg's. I was aggravated about that until I reached the address on my directions— a low-slung house overlooking the beach. I went to the side door and rang the bell, and there was Greg in a sweatshirt and jeans. He gave me a ''great to see you again'' smile that relieved my aggravation. He was as open and friendly as I remembered him, and more relaxed. We shook hands and he said he'd heard the score of the game and was glad the Dodgers won. "How good was Fernando tonight?" I told him what had happened and we had a good laugh over it.

He served me a scotch and we went from the kitchen into a beautiful, sunken living room with a stone fireplace and picture windows facing the ocean and the sky filled with blinking stars. I said, "I've always dreamed about owning a house like this someday. The view is right out of the movies"—and we got a laugh out of that, too. Then we sat on a black leather couch to talk.

"How long have you been an umpire?" he asked me.

"Professionally, about thirteen years. In the major leagues, just since 1979."

"It's an unusual job. Did you always want to be an umpire?"

"Well, since right after high school. What about you? Did you always want to be a matinee idol?"

He sipped his drink and flashed the grin that helped make him one of the sexiest "macho" movie stars of the 1980s. And I thought to myself, "That grin's for *me* tonight. Women, eat your hearts out."

"I don't know," he answered. "*Are* there matinee idols anymore?" I said sure there were and that I thought he was definitely at the top of the list.

He seemed genuinely embarrassed, so he switched the subject. "Dave," he said, looking serious now, "can I ask you something personal?"

I said, "Sure. As long as I get to do the same thing."

He nodded yes. Then he asked, "How long have you been out of the closet?"

"It depends on what you mean. If you mean am I openly gay, the answer is: I'm not."

"Then put it this way: how long have you been active?"

"What do you mean?"

"I mean, have you been with many people?"

"Not that many, no."

"Have you ever had a lover?"

"Well, I'm just now getting over the loss of my lover."
Those words stuck in my mouth. It was the first time I'd
ever acknowledged to anyone that Scott was my lover.
"He died in an auto accident last November."

His face turned grim. "I'm sorry," he said sincerely.

"That's okay. I didn't tell you that to put a damper on
our evening."

"How long were you together?"

"Three years. It was a lot of fun. He was a special
human being." Suddenly I had a flashback of Scott's face,
and my eyes started watering. But I recovered and com-
posed myself. "How about you? Anyone special?"

"No," he said flatly. "It's really difficult for me. I
have to keep up my image all the time."

"Me, too. And it gets to be an incredible drag. I can't
get used to the lies and the charade I have to put on in
front of everyone—family, friends, especially the people
in baseball. I do my best, but it's really tough."

"I know exactly what you mean. I'm dating women. I
have to be seen with them all the time—for display."
Short silence as he looked at me. "No wonder we get
along so well. We have so much in common."

He lay down on the couch and I caressed his chest. I
remember thinking that he would probably never get a
chance to come out of the closet in his profession, especially with his screen image. His secret might be
known in the film industry—like Rock Hudson's double
life was known—but if it ever reached the public, his
career would be over. That was true in my case, too, at
the time; but I envisioned a day when baseball could be
mature enough to accommodate gays in the ranks. I just
hoped it would be in my lifetime.

The next morning it was too hazy to catch rays on the
beach, so Greg cooked breakfast: omelettes made to order. A small gesture, sure; but I was touched by his
thoughtfulness. It showed me that he was not just another
wealthy, famous, shallow movie star but that he had some
class. I thought, "No wonder he's such a big star. All
these traits come through on screen, too."

Before I left, I told him that I had enjoyed our time
together more than any I had spent since I lost Scott. He

seemed touched by that. I said, "It sucks that I live in Boston, because I would love to spend more time getting to know you better." The season was almost over and I knew I wouldn't be back to L.A. until next year, so I asked if I could give him a call sometime soon. He said, "Sure. Please keep my number. It would be great to hear from you."

On my drive back to L.A., I fantasized how exciting it would be if I was Greg's full-time lover. But I knew it would never happen. Although we got along great and shared the common bond of a double life and were both in the "entertainment" business, our life-styles were different, and we lived too far apart to try to bridge those differences. I knew our paths would never cross again. Yet our encounters helped push along a change in me that had started when I went into my first gay bar in Atlanta. For the first time, I resented my job because of all the traveling. Any time I met someone nice—like Jeffrey or Greg—I couldn't develop a strong, healthy relationship, because I always had to move on to the next city, and I might not return for months. By the time I got back, that person might have forgotten me, decided it wouldn't work out, or found somebody else closer to home.

It was so obvious now: I felt too much like a whole human being again to slip back into my emotional jail cell. I told myself, "I must stay active. I have to go further into the gay world and take more chances to find the people I need." I realized I had to go to gay bars more often on the road during the season. And I also knew I had to take the biggest risk of all: I had to venture into the gay scene in the off-season in Boston, where people were much more likely to recognize me.

One Friday night in November of '83, I decided it was time to go to Buddies, the gay bar in Boston best known for the kind of clientele I sought: young businessmen and college types. But when I found the place, there was a long line outside. I thought that was ridiculous; I was willing to take a reasonable chance just going there, but I wasn't going to stand around outside where somebody I knew might coincidentally walk by and see me on line. I returned again Saturday night and, of course, the line was longer. It pissed me off, yet it also told me how popular the place was, which was even more of a lure. Sunday night, another long line—and I still wasn't ready to wait.

The following Friday night, I went again and saw the line and said, "Fuck it. I'm going in." So I stood in line, coat collar up, back hunched and turned away from the street to hide my face. When I finally got to the entrance downstairs and paid my money, I started talking with the doorman. I said: "Isn't there any way a person can get into this bar without having to wait in line? I don't mind paying, but don't you have a VIP list or anything like that?" He said, "Yeah. But you gotta know someone inside." I said, "Oh." Then he said, "Don't I know you?" I said, "No." And he said, "Do you have anything to do with sports?" I said, "No."

About five minutes later, I got in. While I was still walking around and getting my bearings, the doorman approached me and said, "I got something for you. Come into the other room." There were two large, connected rooms—one with a dance floor, one a sort of game room. I followed him through the game room to a back office, where he grabbed something off a desk and handed it to me. It was a temporary VIP pass with my name on it. He said, "I know who you are; I follow baseball. Now you won't ever have to wait in line again to come into this bar." And he said he'd make sure I got a permanent pass by next week. That's how he and I became friends—and we've been friends ever since.

In a way, it was a relief to be recognized for the first time in a gay bar. It made me a little less paranoid. And the VIP card made me feel like this was "my" place; it was a psychological enticement to keep coming back. Plus, the atmosphere suited me—a lot like Backstreet. So that first night I ordered a drink at the bar and then just walked around the dance floor to watch the crowd. One thing I noticed was that in gay bars, you didn't just walk in for the first time and start approaching people left and right. The regulars knew each other and were wary of strangers. A lot of gays are naturally uptight in bar situations, especially given the AIDS factor.

I saw a lot of people standing around waiting for other people to approach them. Some were just scared of the unknown. Some were afraid to go talk to a particular guy because they thought he was too handsome and he might turn them away. There was a real sensitivity to that—maybe even more so than among straight people. I never had those kinds of fears; I always had the knack of meeting people. But I decided to take my time before acting like my usual bold self.

I returned to Buddies almost every weekend, and I gradually accumulated friends as people got used to seeing me there. I did a lot of observing, and then, after seven or eight visits, I made my first "approach" to someone I didn't know. I'd been observing this handsome man standing alone, his body language saying, "Stay away." I watched him shoot down three different men, and I thought, "I have to give him a hard time." I decided to try something unusual, so I walked up to him acting like a mime trying to find a doorknob on a door in front of him. He said, "What're you doing?" I said, "I'm just trying to open this door to get inside to talk to you. It looks like there's a wall here." He laughed. "It's open," he said. "You can come in." Surprisingly, another friendship developed out of that, so it was worth the ingenuity it took to introduce myself.

That entire off-season I slowly adapted to the gay world off the field, if only in bars like Buddies. I wasn't sure I would meet the man of my dreams in a bar, but it was a start. You met one person and maybe saw him again at a party, and he introduced you to someone else, and you eventually established a little circle of friends outside the bar. But I was trying too hard then to find someone exactly like Scott, and no one measured up. When that got me depressed, I reminded myself of what Scott had said: "Life goes on"—and *I* went on. As for the conflict between my career and a love relationship, I saw the handwriting on the wall. Yet what choice did I have? Thanks to Bob Engel and Paul Runge, I was coming into my own as a major league umpire, and that was exciting—especially after all I'd gone through to get there. As lonely as I felt traveling, and as weary as I was of leading a double life, umpiring still made me happier than anything else. I wasn't ready to toss it away.

My worst enemy now wasn't the ostracism at work or not having a lover; it was my double life. My brain said, "You need umpiring," but my heart said, "You need to be the real you—*all the time.*" For the time being, though, I just had to live with it.

14

STEEL NUTS

From 1984 to 1986, the league let me stay with Engel and Runge, and I learned more about umpiring in those three years than during the previous five. I attributed that to their unselfish help as well as my obsessive need to prove myself worthy of it. But while I was developing into a solid umpire and earning respect, weird incidents with players kept undermining that respect. It was strange; my attention would be focused for a few weeks, then suddenly scattered. Or I'd be calm for a month and then, like in the minors, I'd detonate and do something I regretted. It was one test after another for a while; I needed steel nuts to get through it.

I couldn't figure it out. After five years of passing tests and improving steadily, why couldn't I find that groove of consistency? Looking back now, I can only guess that it was because I was always on the edge emotionally.

Who would have believed back in 1979 that by 1984 all the ostracism would still be going strong? But it was—and it was still getting under my skin. I thought I'd proved, without a doubt, that I deserved everyone's respect. But except for Engel and Runge, the umpires wouldn't give me my due—at least not publicly. And there were still the same old standard bearers for the union umps. Eddie Vargo, for example. At the tail end of '83, when my crew came to St. Louis for a series, Engel, Runge, and I went out for dinner at the Pasta House—a favorite umpires' restaurant, which I used to avoid for obvious reasons. When we walked in, I saw Eddie Vargo and Satch Davidson sitting at the bar, hanging around on their day off. Runge said hello to them and they started talking to him, but they ignored me. Here I'd worked with these guys for two years ('80 and '82), and they'd occasionally talked to me then, yet they didn't have the guts or the class to acknowledge me now. They didn't want anyone to see them talking to me, including the personnel of the Pasta House, because they were afraid someone might tell the other umpires who rotated through.

At the time there was a rumor that Vargo would retire at the end of the '83 season. I remember thinking, "How can he be so two-faced? What the hell would happen if he ever became one of my *bosses?*" Well, he did retire, and he did become a boss; in 1984 he became a supervisor of umpires. Then, during spring training in March, a strange decision by the league: they yanked me off of Engel's crew—even though I'd done well and the crew was highly regarded—and they paired me with two of the league's most narrow-minded, hard-core veterans, John Kibler and Bruce Froemming. I had to wonder about the rationale behind that switch—and who engineered it. Was it just coincidence that when Eddie Vargo became a supervisor, Dave Pallone got lifted from a crew of sympathetic umpires and added to a crew of hardass union sharks?

Then another switch. At the last minute—in the same mysterious way that Chub Feeney had reversed his decision to fire me back in 1980—I was suddenly reassigned to Engel's crew. I didn't try to understand it; I just felt like I'd been saved from the pit of hell. I was so happy that I impulsively phoned Paul Runge from Clearwater, and I said, "Paul, I just wanted you to know that this is the most excited I've ever been before a season. I'm looking forward to working with you guys more than I've ever looked forward to working with anybody."

We opened the regular season in Atlanta, and I remembered last year when Engel and Runge beat me to the punch by leaving that rose on my stool. So I ordered a big basket of flowers and sent it to Engel in the dressing room before the first game. The note I wrote said, "Thanks for taking this big burden off our hands." I signed it: "John Kibler & Bruce Froemming." Engel saw through it right away. "You son of a bitch," he said, chuckling. *"You* sent these flowers. *They* wouldn't have spent that kind of money."

It was a great, positive way to start the season. But then, in April, my second incident with Dave Concepcion set the negative back in motion again. In a Reds-Giants game at Candlestick Park, Engel worked the plate and I had first base. Concepcion took a half-swing, Engel asked me for help, and I said, "Yes, he swung." Concepcion threw his usual childish fit and sat down in the dugout. After the game, as everybody headed up the runway toward the dressing rooms, Concepcion happened to be walking near me. He said, "I'm gonna get you, Pallone. I'll be in this game longer than you, and I promise I'll get you."

It was such an obvious threat, we had to report it to the league. Feeney sent Concepcion a letter stating that any more threats would result in severe disciplinary action. It was appropriate for Feeney to send a letter about future incidents, but where was the "severe disciplinary action" for *that* incident? A player threatened to "get" an umpire; if that didn't merit immediate punishment, what the hell did? There was no question he should have been suspended and fined.

There was also no question that I still despised Dave Concepcion. I was surprised at how much. In fact, for five straight years after he spit on me, if I could have wished upon a star for somebody to fail every time he played a baseball game, Dave Concepcion would have been that guy. We had a feud; everyone knew it. And it did funny things to Concepcion's mind. Whenever I had his games, he thought I was sticking it to him. He was wrong; he stuck it to himself. I didn't have to lower myself to make calls against him for revenge. On the other hand, beginning in 1984, I did try to unnerve the man whenever possible. For example, I'd deliberately stand in his sight line. The sight line is the background a batter sees when the pitcher throws the ball. If I stood in a batter's sight line when the ball was released, he'd see it coming out of my body. Even when I wore a blue shirt, there would sometimes be enough reflection of light to cause a distraction. A slight movement on my part could do the same thing.

I remember this one time late in '84 when Eddie Montague worked a Reds game with us as a temporary replacement. He had home plate and I had second base, so before the game I told him about my feud with Concepcion. I said, "Don't ask me to move at second base when Concepcion is up, because I ain't movin'." Sure enough, in Concepcion's first at bat, he asked Montague to move me out of his sight line. Of course, Eddie didn't want to ask me. Concepcion got pissed off and started to wave at me, trying to "order" me to move. I stayed put. Pete Rose had just come over from the Expos to play with and manage the Reds, so he came out to ask me why I wouldn't move. I said, "Pete, this is a courtesy. It's not something I have to do. My position is where I'm standing. If he wants the courtesy of me moving, he has to ask me politely—which you know he doesn't do. I don't just move my body on a wave for *anybody*." Rose had a little smirk on his face, and he said, "Okay, Dave, *I'm* askin' you. Would you mind moving a little bit?" I said, "Pete, for you I'll move." So I moved a couple of steps to my left, out of Concepcion's sight line. It did him about as much good as his personality, because he struck out anyway.

Normally, when I worked second base and it was a steal situation, I stood just to the second-base side of the bag. Sometimes, depending on the shortstop's angle to me, he might not be able to see the runner on first. Again, I was under no obligation to move. But most players were decent people, so I would always do it. On the other hand, Dave Concepcion was the type of guy who'd go "Hey!" and just wave at me to move. I would ignore him. Since he was permanently mad at me—and vice versa—I never moved for him.

Although I didn't call anything against Concepcion that wasn't legal, I did other things that I knew would irk him, hoping it would affect his performance. For instance, if I was working second base and he was at shortstop, I would stare at him. I wouldn't say a word, but he hated people staring at him. He'd go, "Who you lookin' at?" I'd say, "I'm not lookin' at anybody." He'd go, "Don't look at me." I'd say, "Who the hell would *wanna* look at you?" Boom, he would erupt into an argument—and then try to make it look like I had started it. Which, in a way, you could say I did.

Then Rose would come out and say, "What the hell's goin' on?" And I'd say, "Hey, I ain't doin' shit. I'm just standing here minding my own business and he's getting pissed off that I'm looking at him." Rose would go, "Jesus Christ, I don't know what to do." And he'd tell Concepcion to play ball and forget it. But Concepcion was a mean-spirited, militant hothead who couldn't take advice any better than he took criticism—so he just got angrier.

I wasn't proud of my unprofessional attitude. But I'll be honest: if I could go back right now, I wouldn't change anything I did. I needed to let Concepcion know that his behavior was not only cowardly and disgusting but unforgivable—especially since he never had the courage, the good sense, or the manliness to apologize to me. That's why whenever I worked his games, I made sure he was aware of me. And I won that war. I unnerved him so much every year, he couldn't relax and play his game when I was around. If I worked the plate, for instance, he had it fixed in his mind that if a pitch was close, I'd call it a strike. His paranoia altered his perception, so he didn't seem to know what to swing at and what to let go. The great irony was that I didn't need to do anything to affect his game. I just had to be there.

I said earlier that I couldn't understand how adults—specifically the union umpires—could carry a grudge and act so childishly for so long, and here it looks like I did the same thing with Concepcion. I guess I did act a little childishly; I'm only human. But I think these were totally different situations. The union umpires allowed their grudge to affect players, teams, other umpires, and the outcome of games. My grudge against Concepcion hurt no one—not even him. He hurt himself. And as far as

I'm concerned, it couldn't have happened to a more de-
serving guy.

Concepcion had a vindictive side, too. He not only
didn't accept responsibility for his actions or try to make
amends, he also poisoned other players against me. The
best example was Dave Parker. A lot of people didn't
like or get along with Parker, but I always did—until he
joined the Reds. I think that when Parker arrived in '84,
Dave Concepcion must have told him something like
"Dave Pallone's an asshole," and Parker believed him.
So now Concepcion's grudge affected someone other than
him or me. Some players were naive; when they joined
militant teams, like the Reds of the mid-eighties, and
they talked to angry guys like Concepcion, they became
more militant themselves. That's what happened to Dave
Parker.

When he played for Pittsburgh, we got along great. He
never disputed my calls, either at bat or in the field. As
soon as he joined Cincinnati and talked to Concepcion,
he disputed everything. One game, I called him out at
first on a close play and he went into the dugout and
threw his helmet, screaming. That wasn't like the old
Dave Parker. When the inning ended, he started to strut
past me to his position in right. So I said, "What's goin'
on with you, anyway? Why are you acting like such an
asshole? We used to get along well. Now you come over
to the Reds and you're always giving me a hard time.
What is the problem?"

"The problem," he said, "is that I wasn't out on that
play."

"Bullshit. It doesn't matter whether you were out or
safe. You always think I'm wrong now. When you were
with Pittsburgh, you never thought I was wrong. I don't
want a feud with you, but if you want a war we'll have a
war. And I'll guarantee you, I'll win."

He said, "Hey, man, I'm not acting like an asshole."

I said, "Yes, you are. And it's because of that fuckin'
Concepcion. He tells you I'm a horeshit umpire because
of the problems that he and I have. Do you know *why* we
have problems?"

"No," he said, looking away. He obviously didn't know.

I said, "What would you do right now if I spit in your face? Tell me what you'd do to me."

"I'd break you in two and chew you up."

"You're damned right," I said. "That's what your friend Concepcion did to me. He spit in my face. If you think I'm gonna take that from anyone, you're crazy. And I'm not gonna let you be an asshole to me, because you were never that way before."

"I get your point," he said, and he walked out to his position—minus the strut. From then on, Parker stayed off my case. In my mind, this was not only a victory over ignorance; it was another Concepcion defeat.

Besides my aggressive confrontations in '84 with Concepcion, I experienced the strangest "non-confrontation" of my whole career. Here I was getting tougher, smarter, and better at picking my spot with hothead players, when all of a sudden: another attack of Vapor Lock of the Brain. It happened in Philadelphia with Mets utility player Rusty Staub. I was having a bad game behind the plate and my mind was wandering, so I kept missing pitches and losing concentration. Staub was a deliberate hitter. He had a very good sense of the strike zone, and he rarely got called out on strikes. Naturally, I called him out on strikes. He got right in my face and exploded on me: "How the fuck can you call that pitch a strike?"

He was screaming and waving his arms, which got the crowd riled up. But I let him dominate me completely and show me up like I'd never been shown up before. I was aware that he was humiliating me, yet I didn't even take my mask off—the ultimate sign of submission. For some reason, I felt meek; I was afraid of getting into an argument with him. So he ate me alive in front of everyone.

A couple of batters later, rookie Mike Fitzgerald came up and he started giving me a hard time, too. That's when I whipped off my mask. I said, "Your next word's your last. Now get your ass up there and hit, and don't give me any shit." But the damage was done; that's what happens when you let your guard down for one second in the major leagues. Afterward, Runge took me aside and said, "I don't know what happened to you, but you can't ever let anyone do that to you again." Of course, he was right.

Then there was a mid-season incident with Pete Rose—just before he took over the Reds—where having veteran umpires like Engel and Runge behind me really paid off. Unlike the crews I worked with before, they were always there to keep a small crisis from blowing up into a bigger one. It was a Mets-Expos game in New York, and I had home plate and Runge had first base. When I called Rose out on a checked swing, his eyes went wide. "I didn't swing," he insisted. "I can't believe you called me out on that." He was such an intensely motivated competitor, he couldn't stand anyone taking a strike away from him. Unlike a Dave Concepcion, he wasn't arguing just to put it to me. He was arguing because he couldn't accept failure. That's one reason why he was such a great player.

I said, "Pete, you're out. That's it. Let's go."

He said, "You just wanna show me up in front of all these people in New York." He was Pete Rose, a sure Hall of Famer, and he knew that a lot of umpires were impressed with that.

"Pete," I said calmly, "why do I wanna show you up? That has no bearing on anything. I don't care about showing you up."

"That's all you're doin'," he said—and he started clapping. That was terrible; it meant: "Good performance, ump."

I thought of the Staub incident and Runge's comment, and I knew Rose had to go. I said, "Pete, you're gone. The show's over." And I threw him out. It was significant at the time, because not every umpire had the guts to throw Pete Rose out in front of a full house in New York, especially at that stage of his career. Some would have backed down because they were timid; some because they were in awe of Rose; some because they avoided controversy in order to get high ratings. I did none of those—and it hurt me in my ratings. But it helped me gain the respect of the players, especially competitors like Pete Rose.

As soon as I ran Rose, Expos manager Bill Virdon rushed out to argue. Meantime, the Expos' trainer started mouthing off from the bench—and a trainer has no business saying *anything* during a game. But I couldn't see him; my back was turned. All of a sudden Runge approached Virdon, looking mean and pointing his finger. "You're losing control of this team, Virdon," he said sternly. "If you don't take control of it right now, I will." Immediately, everybody got quiet. It was like Runge had stuffed the whole Expos team in a Zip-loc bag and snapped it shut. I thought, "Jesus, how do you *get* that much power and respect?"

According to Engel and Runge, one way was to assert yourself more behind the plate, where an umpire could really command a ballgame. So I started concentrating more on working the plate and showing everyone that I really knew how to call a game. It was also important that people understood I made all the calls on everyone, rookies and vets alike. I remember one game in Philadelphia when I called two balks on Steve Carlton, one of the greatest pitchers of all time. Hardly anybody ever called a balk on him. Some umpires were afraid of him because he was a legend, like Rose, and he rarely said a word to anybody and always scowled. Another reason was that he took a deceptive step out of the stretch position, leaning all the way toward home and then suddenly throwing to first. A left-hander has to step directly toward first base on a throw-over, and there's a fine line in that step. The line is so fine, it's an umpire's judgment. If you're experienced, before you call a balk you draw an imaginary line where you think the pitcher's foot should land. But it's still difficult to know for sure. Most of the time Carlton got away with it.

In this particular game, I felt he stepped over that line both times. When I called the first balk, Phillies manager Paul Owens argued, "That wasn't a balk. Chrissakes, he does that all the time and it's never a balk." I said, "He's leaning so far toward home, he's practically a catcher. He can't do that." Carlton stepped off the mound and stared at me in disbelief. He was offended; he thought he *never* balked. I said, "You're leaning too far toward home. If you don't want me to call a balk, stop leaning that far." He scowled at me, returned to the mound, and—two innings later—deliberately did it again. Steve Carlton always did things his way, even if it cost him a balk. I admired that attitude. It was self-defeating at times, but it earned him tremendous respect.

Another unique thing about Carlton was that he didn't take advantage of the umpire; he knew how to use the umpire to his advantage. He had such perfect control with his pitches, he could work the corners better than any pitcher I ever saw. His first pitch would be over the middle of the plate. The next one would be about an inch off the outside corner to see if the umpire would call it a strike. If so, Carlton would throw the next one about two inches off the corner. He would consistently move the pitch out to see how far the umpire would let him go. As soon as the umpire called a ball, Carlton would throw another pitch to the same spot, just to be sure. Once he knew he couldn't go any further, he'd bring his pitches back in again. That's how he learned an umpire's strike zone. And he was smart enough to know that if he threw a hundred pitches and controlled ninety of them like that, he'd get more strikes called, because his control made our job easier.

Most fans know the expression "a pitcher's pitch." That's a pitch thrown so precisely to the outer boundary of an umpire's strike zone that no batter could ever hit it. If a pitcher can consistently throw to that location, an umpire can get away with calling a pitcher's pitch. That's why umpires often gave pitchers who controlled their location—like a Carlton, a Tom Seaver, a Don Sutton, an Orel Hershiser, a Dave Stewart, a Roger Clemens, a Bret Saberhagen—bigger strike zones. On the other hand, if a pitcher is constantly wild and then throws a pitcher's pitch by chance, he can't expect the umpire to call it. The key is *consistent* control.

If Steve Carlton was throwing his slider consistently two inches off the plate, there was no batter or umpire alive who could tell with certainty how far the ball was off the plate. If a fastball came in two inches outside, I didn't *know* it was two inches outside. I didn't have a measuring tape; how was I supposed to measure two inches? And needless to say, no fan in the stands or sitting home watching on TV—even with the miracle eye of instant replay—could judge two inches either. If I had a pitcher who threw ninety of one hundred pitches right around the plate, I'd have had to be *God* to know if those pitches were an inch or two off the plate. But I did know when a pitch was too close for a batter to let it go by.

My theory of a strike zone was this: The plate is seventeen inches wide, edge to edge. The baseball is two and a half inches in diameter. The rule reads that *any part of the ball touching any part of the plate* is considered in the strike zone—as long as it's also within the vertical zone (supposedly from the bottom of the letters to the top of the knees, although we all made our own strike zones—anywhere from the bottom of the knees to just above the waist). This means I had an extra five inches to work with on the corners, two and a half on each side. A *thread* of the baseball is part of the baseball. So if the pitcher threw the ball two inches outside, and a thread on that ball crossed the plane of the plate, I was still within my means. In fact, I had a half-inch leeway. Obviously, my eye couldn't pick up a thread on a baseball. Yet something told me, "It's close enough." Of course, there were exceptions to my theory. For example, I wouldn't give that kind of leeway on a curveball or a screwball that was too high coming in. Most of the time I gave it only on fastballs.

Starting in 1984, the smart pitchers found out I was a pitcher's umpire. They were the guys who would come to the ballpark and check out where I was. If it was a three-game series and I was working third base the first game, it wouldn't matter, because I wouldn't get to work the plate that series. But if I was at second base, the pitcher of the last game knew he would have me behind the plate. Sometimes they'd flick their hand at me to say, "It's me and you Wednesday night." They looked forward to having me call their games, because they knew that a pitcher's umpire gave more strikes.

Just as most good pitchers know their umpires, so do most good hitters. Disciplined hitters—Pete Rose, Keith

Hernandez, Tim Raines, Tony Gwynn among others—knew which umpires had which strike zones. If I was a manager and I needed a crucial hit, of all the players I ever saw I would call on either Hernandez or Gwynn. They were great contact hitters who could come through in the clutch—which took more than just raw ability. And Hernandez and Gwynn went out there every day and they wanted to know, "Who's umpiring?"

Since I called a lot of strikes, I had most of my problems with batters. I followed one guideline: "The more strikes you call, the quicker you get home." That meant: the more often a pitcher was around the plate, the faster the game moved. I also remembered something that Frank Pulli told me when I was in the minors: "If you call strikes, you only have to worry about the batter. If you call balls, you have to worry about the catcher, the pitcher, and the manager in the other dugout." It made sense. Although I felt the hitter was at a disadvantage because he didn't know what was coming, I thought the only way you were going to get a hit was by swinging the bat. By calling strikes, I made batters swing the bat.

People used to ask me if umpires gave "breaks" to veterans or stars. Maybe some did, but I never consciously called a strike a ball just to give the hitter a break because he was Johnny Bench or Pete Rose or Steve Garvey or Mike Schmidt. I did go out of my way, though, to help some hitters get to know my strike zone, if I knew they really cared. Take Keith Hernandez. After our one run-in in 1979, we got along pretty well. He might not have liked me, and he might have thought I was the worst umpire ever, but when I called that pitch on the outside part of the plate, 99 percent of the time he didn't say a word. He would nod as if to say, "Yes, that was a strike."

Sure, there were a few times when he thought the pitch was outside. But Keith was the type of hitter who wanted to know where those pitches were if he missed them. In spring training once, he swung at a terrible pitch that was up too high. He didn't ask me about it; he just headed for the dugout. Between innings, I yelled, "Keith!" and pointed to a spot on my chest to indicate, "Too high, in case you want to know." That was my way of showing him I respected him as a hitter, and that he could ask me in the future and I'd tell him what I thought.

While I developed my ability to control a ballgame, I also appreciated a pitcher's ability to do the same. I loved umping behind the plate for a control pitcher. Former Houston Astros star J. R. Richard ranked right up there with Steve Carlton and Nolan Ryan as the best I ever saw. He was probably the hardest thrower of them all, because he could throw a hundred miles an hour without effort. I remember a game when he threw a slider to Mike Schmidt. I called, "Strike—" and Schmidt was on his way back to the dugout before I said "—*three.*" I went over to the guy on the radar gun and asked him how fast the pitch was. He said ninety-five—and that was just a *slider.* That's unheard of for a slider; that's the speed of a Nolan Ryan *fastball.*

Speaking of Ryan: when he had his control, there was no one like him. He was absolutely awesome. The ball moved with such velocity and precision, you found yourself watching and almost forgetting your job. I had a game when Ryan pitched for Houston against the Mets, and he was blistering through the lineup. I thought he was going to pitch the game in thirty minutes. Mets pitcher Sid Fernandez came up to bat and Ryan got two quick strikes. Fernandez didn't move the bat off his shoulder. The next pitch was way too high, so I called, "Ball." But Fernandez had already turned and started back to the dugout. That made me look terrible. I yelled, "Fernandez! Where the hell are you goin'? The pitch was a ball." He looked at me over his shoulder and said, "I don't care. Just call me out." So I did. I was mad at him for showing me up, but I understood how he felt.

The most thrilling game I had in 1985—and also the most "stunning"—was another Astros-Mets game in Houston. The date was July 11—the day that Nolan Ryan became the first major league pitcher to achieve four thousand strikeouts in a career. Commissioner Pete Ueberroth was in the stands and I had home plate. I was excited as hell, because this was an opportunity to become part of baseball history (I had worked third base when Ryan broke Walter Johnson's strikeout record, which wasn't the same as calling the historic pitch from behind the plate). Well, the four thousandth strikeout was momentous—but, as it turned out, not as memorable as something that happened shortly before. The Mets had a runner on third with less than two outs when Ryan delivered one of his "expressballs." In other words, I didn't actually *see* the ball, but I knew it was a fastball because I saw its vapor trail—and also because the catcher missed it completely, and it hit me right in the cup.

I crumpled to my knees in excruciating pain, still watching the runner, because if he came home that would be my call. Luckily the ball didn't travel too far from the catcher, so the runner went back to third and I went back to my unbearable pain. A time out was called, and the trainers came out and loosened my belt and gave me smelling salts. Ryan was sorry for me, but also amused. After about fifteen minutes, Bob Engel leaned over and said, "You should leave. You can't work after that." I thought, "Jesus, he must think I'm dying." That was about the only excuse Engel would consider valid for missing a game. He was a stickler about working; he rarely missed one himself. But I said, "Absolutely not. There's no way I'm not gonna be behind the plate for Ryan's four thousandth strikeout."

Finally, I recovered enough to get up and walk to the Houston dugout. And there was my favorite practical joker, Joe Niekro. He said, "Nice stop, Dave. Did it break your cup?" I said, "No, it didn't break my cup." I opened my pants and reached down for the cup to prove it—and it *was* shattered. The ball had crushed a hole right in the center. Everyone in the dugout started laughing. I said, "Who's ever gonna believe this?" Meantime, I needed another cup. So someone brought me a steel one from the clubhouse, and Niekro remarked, "This one won't break, it'll just jingle. If we hear it in the dugout, we'll go get you the *cement* cup."

I went back to work again, and between innings I asked the guy on the radar gun how fast the pitch had been. He said, "It was ninety-four." I said, "Jesus Christ, I could probably sing *opera* now!" Shortly afterward, Ryan got his record strikeout and I thought, "This really is a record-setting day. I called Ryan's four thousandth strike-out, and, on top of that, I'm probably the only person on earth who knows what it feels like to get hit in the nuts by a Nolan Ryan fastball.'' In fact, thinking about it now, who else—still living—knows what it feels like to be hit in the nuts by *anything* going ninety-four miles an hour?

The next day, I handed my shattered cup to our club-house kid and said, ''Bring it to Ryan and tell him I want him to sign it.'' Ryan sent the cup back signed: ''Dave, I didn't know I could throw that hard. Good job. Nolan. P.S.: It took a lot of balls to save a run like that.''

(15)

"WHAT IS THE PROBLEM NOW?"

What really took a lot of balls were the chances I took *off* the field beginning in 1984, when I had my first sexual encounters with major league players. Until then, it had been unthinkable. There was too much jeopardy; I was way too scared to try it. And although I knew through rumors on the gay scene that there were quite a few gay major league players, we had no network or signaling system to identify each other on the field. Like me, other gays realized that revelation to the wrong people in the game could ruin their careers.

I had always been attracted to players. One reason was because they were in such peak physical condition. And they had the looks to go along with those incredible bodies; for some reason, baseball players are unusually good-looking. And they all seemed to be the masculine, butch types that I preferred. That was important to me also, because if I ever was involved with one of them, no one would ever suspect they were gay. The last thing I wanted—for obvious reasons—was to be involved with someone who drew attention to himself as gay.

It would have bothered me for another reason: I believe gays are born gay, but I don't believe we're born effeminate. If I'm with a friend today and I see a gay man who's extremely effeminate, I'll remark, "I think he goes home and practices." Effeminate behavior doesn't offend me; it confuses me. I think everybody should be what they really are and what they really feel, so I don't believe it's wrong for a man to be effeminate. I just think some gays take it too far. Similarly, I don't understand gay men who wear those leather outfits. I know it's part of gay life, just like it is in the straight world—but it makes me uncomfortable. Here are gay men dressed in leather hats, sleeveless leather vests, tight leather pants with open crotches, and spiked leather bracelets—but for what? Are they saying, "I'm tough, and I want to show it off"? Well, as far as I'm concerned, you don't have to wear leather to be tough. In the gay world, you have to be tough just to survive.

I have the same problem understanding gay men who are obviously trying to be effeminate. Maybe it's insecurity, or just their way of trying to attract the type of person they want to be with. Whatever it is, I think it invites ridicule and feeds the heterosexual stereotype of all gay men as "fags" or "queens." I know there are gays who insist that they're women trapped in men's bodies, and lesbians who say they're men trapped in women's bodies. No doubt there are instances where that's true. But I don't think it's true in most cases. So when I see a man acting like a woman, I always feel like I'm watching a woman. The thing is, if I wanted to be with a woman, I'd find a *real* one.

What attracts me about men is that they're *men*—like me. I am what God made me: a strong, healthy, male human being. I am my father's son, not my father's daughter trapped in a man's body. When I walk down the street, I want people to say, "There goes a handsome man," not "There goes a faggot." I want people to know I'm a man.

The nice thing about major league ballplayers is that, outwardly, they're all so butch, so masculine. I wasn't attracted to the big, muscular, macho types; I was interested in the smaller, "boy-next-door" types with more personality than swagger. They were everywhere—especially in the infield. But when Scott and I were going strong, I didn't need anyone else. I still looked, though; I always believed the adage "Just because you're on a diet, it doesn't mean you can't look at the menu." Even when

Scott was gone, I still held back. I knew that if I showed my interest to a player, I could be leaving myself open to anything from rumors to blackmail. Also, until the end of '84, I had no idea which players were gay. I heard things, but I'd never seen any players in a gay bar, or made a pass at any, or been approached myself. For two years after Scott's death, I stayed cautious. I didn't want one stupid mistake to cost me my career.

But, throughout 1984, my increasing loneliness made me more needy and vulnerable. I don't know; maybe I was open to more signals, because something finally happened. For a long time, I had been very attracted to this one player—Wes, a rising young star. He was the spitting image of Scott, including the dazzling smile; he exuded an aura of energy and confidence on the field that drew all eyes to him. Whenever I worked the bases in his games, I studied him. Often I caught him staring at me, too, but I didn't read anything into it then. We talked to each other on the field—mostly about the games, but sometimes about personal matters like good restaurants or buying property. He mentioned women a lot, and getting laid, and he was convincing. In fact, you could watch him on the field and talk to him all day long, and you'd never guess he was gay. Even *I* didn't know.

Although one time he did slip. We were talking about getting together for drinks after the game (we knew that we weren't supposed to fraternize, but it happened all the time in hotel bars, and none of us believed it made any difference on the field), and he said, "I know a great place in the city. Why don't you meet me there?" He gave me directions and started to say, "There are a lot of gays there"—but he caught himself and said "people" instead. But I knew, and I filed it.

I never planned on approaching him and crossing the line. But toward the end of '84, when I had a series in Houston, things changed spontaneously. During the first game Wes came out to the batting circle to get ready to lead off the next inning. I started a conversation and eventually asked him what he was doing that night. He said he had no plans, so we arranged to meet in the hotel bar to talk. We were both staying at the Shamrock Hilton, which had a great bar with a live band and friendly bartenders who remembered umpires from their last visit. I got ready quickly after the game and asked Paul Runge if he wanted to join me, but he was expecting a call from home. So I went down alone.

When I walked into the bar, it was half-full with guests and ballplayers. I sat at the bar with a couple of players and talked with them. When Wes walked in twenty minutes later, he joined us. We were talking about the ostracism. Wes was against it; he thought it was stupid. I told them I was lucky because I was working with Engel and Runge and they'd treated me so well. Wes said, "It figures. Those guys are great umpires; I love seeing them at our games because they're so fair." The more we talked, the more opinions we shared. After an hour I was feeling the scotch, so I ordered us each a B-52. Since Wes wasn't much of a drinker, the B-52 got him flying.

Pretty soon it was late, and Wes and I were the only ones left at the bar. There was no hint of what was about to happen. At that point, as far as I was concerned, it was just a relaxing, fun evening on the road. We left just before closing and headed to the elevators together to go back to our respective rooms, which were on different floors (as a matter of policy, players and umpires staying in the same hotel have rooms on different floors). We rode up silently, and all of a sudden I looked at him and got aroused. I thought, "Maybe he's another Greg." But I wasn't sure if I should take the chance.

On impulse, and a sense of a rare opportunity, I said, "How about another drink?"

"Sure," he said, without hesitation. "You have anything in *your* room?"

"Yeah," I said. "I have some beer on ice." So we let the elevator pass his floor to mine. I know now that he was thinking the same thing I was, because he knew it was safer to go to my floor, where we wouldn't be seen by other players.

We went into the living room of my suite and had a couple of beers. The more I looked at him, the more nervous I felt. But I wasn't sure what *he* wanted, and I didn't want to make a mistake I might regret. Usually, I know exactly what to say, but at this moment I didn't know how to get things going. Then, out of the blue, he said, "Shit, this is a big room," and he walked into the bedroom. When he didn't return, I thought, "Well, let's find out what's going on," and I followed him in. He was lying on the bed face down. That was enough for me—consequences be damned. "Are you awake?" I asked.

He said yes, so I sat down next to him and began rubbing his back. "Feels good," he said, removing his sweater. And then we fell into making love. The next two hours were wonderful; he was a relaxed, sensitive lover, and it was like we'd been together before. Afterward, when he was ready to go back to his room, I said, "I'm sorry this happened. Maybe it wasn't the right thing to do."

"Why?" he said. "I'm not sorry. I wanted to do this for a long time. I'm glad it finally happened. You should be, too."

"Well, that's good to hear. This probably shouldn't continue between us, but you're right—and I *am* glad it happened. You always turned me on. I just figured I couldn't make it known while we were both in baseball. I never thought this would happen during the season. I guess I never thought it would happen at all."

"I know what you mean," he said. "I want to be with men, but baseball gets in my way, too. At home I can sometimes be myself, but it's not that easy there, either."

"I've just started to be myself at home, and I'm happy about it. Tonight makes me want to keep going forward with my personal life, instead of backward."

We said our goodbyes and he left. I didn't sleep, thinking about what just happened: "Did I screw up? Should I have done this? I'd felt the drinks, but I wasn't drunk. How could I have let myself take that risk? But shit, just because we're player and umpire doesn't mean it's wrong. I know I can still be impartial on the field. The only thing I don't know is how *he* will react. Will he be fair with me? Will he still argue a call if he thinks I'm wrong? Will he expect special treatment just because we slept with each other—and will he be angry when he doesn't get it?"

In the game the next day, I found out. I was working third base and Wes was on first after a hit. The next batter singled to right and Wes slid into third, but I called him out. He got up and said, "Oh, shit! You gotta be kiddin' me! He missed the fuckin' tag!" That was just like him; he *never* thought he was out. I thought, "Well, that answers that. Things are back to normal."

I had only one other encounter with Wes—in August of 1985, when we had a series together in Philadelphia. One reason we didn't see each other in between was that I had met and gotten involved with a new lover—a man I hoped would be my second Scott. That meeting, too, was unexpected.

After the first encounter with Wes, I had spent more time in gay bars. I wasn't there every night of the week—though I was more apt to go to a bar than not, and more likely to talk with people and establish friendships. For the most part, outside of Boston, I was still lying about who I was and what I did for a living, and I wondered if that was one reason why I wasn't meeting the right person. Though I didn't go into these places thinking I'd necessarily meet a man I could spend the rest of my life with, I was more anxious now to find a steady lover again.

On the Sunday evening of Halloween weekend in 1984, I was in Buddies when I noticed this attractive young man across the room. I could tell he was new to the scene, because he was drinking nervously. I went over and started a conversation. He was too apprehensive to be outgoing, but he said his name was Rick, he was twenty-five, from Illinois, and working his way through grad school at Boston College. He was a handsome ski enthusiast with a fun sense of humor—another All-American kid. After a while, he admitted, "I've only been to a gay bar twice. I get real nervous because I'm not used to them yet."

We got a little drunk together and I finally said, "I just moved to a place in the city. Would you like to go over there?" He said, "Yes, let's go," so we went back to my new apartment—and we ended up in bed. The next day, before Rick left, I wrote down my name and phone number and said, "I would really like to get together with you again. I hope you will take the time to call me." I wanted to play it slow, but I definitely wanted to play it. When he left, I felt good about how things had gone and I sensed that I would be hearing from him soon. The only thing that bothered me—and it seemed minor at the time—was how uncertain he seemed about being gay.

Three days later I was talking on the phone when another call buzzed in. It was Rick. We talked for a moment and I said, "Would you like to get together tonight? Maybe take in a movie?" He said, "Yes, I'd like to." I said, "Okay, let me tell you again where I live." But he said, "You don't have to tell me. I know where it is." It was a good sign that he remembered.

He came over, and since the movie wouldn't start for about an hour, we went into my den to talk. He explained that he'd never been involved with a man before and was trying to find out more about his feelings. Then he looked me in the eyes and said, "Would you be interested in seeing me on a regular basis?" It was his way of reaching out. Little did he realize that I needed someone, too. I said, "Absolutely. You seem like the type of person I would like to get to know better. We'll just take it slow, so neither of us gets hurt."

There was something about Rick that was different from others I had met in the bars—maybe just that he seemed so open and vulnerable and sincere. Plus, I sensed he liked me for me, not for the prestige of my job. So over the next few weeks, we slowly spent more time together, on ski weekends and out for dinners and movies. Since he was living in Newton with roommates but worked as a store manager in the Copley Place mall next to where I lived, I gave him a key to my place and he started staying with me regularly. My attachment increased, because I'd never spent so much off-season time with anyone before.

Rick and I saw each other often until Christmas, when he had to go home. My Christmas present to him was a plane ticket home, because I thought it was really important for him to be with his family at Christmas, and he didn't have a lot of money for plane fare. He called me Christmas Eve and Christmas night from Illinois and told me that he missed me and wished he could be with me. That was the high point for me, because I hadn't felt so wanted and needed since Scott died. In fact, the night Rick returned after Christmas, we embraced and I blurted, "This reminds me so much of my time with Scott." I realized immediately that I had said the wrong thing. It could have been all over right there. But Rick said, "Don't worry, that's okay"—and I fell asleep in his arms. That's when I felt that maybe all would be right with my world again.

For New Year's, Rick and I went to Colorado together. When we came back, he had to go on a trip with some school friends. He called me twice during that trip and we really started to miss each other. When he came back to Boston, it was like we hadn't been together for ten years. He said, "I've never missed anyone this much. It's a little scary." We embraced and went right to bed. This was different from what I had with Scott, and it was only a few months old, but I felt that an important relationship was under way. Rick was still tentative, though, and didn't talk about himself very much, so I knew it would take time.

Then, just as the baseball season began in April of '85, one of Rick's sisters was killed in a tragic swimming accident. I was in Chicago when he called to tell me he had to go home. I felt helpless; this was when he needed me the most. But, like with Scott, our double lives prevented us from being together. That must have had an effect, because through April and May we didn't see each other as often as we could. And whenever we *were* together, Rick was distant. I asked him again and again, "Why are we drifting apart? We were so close. Don't you want that anymore?" He said, "I don't know whether I want to be with a man or a woman. I'm not sure I want a relationship with anyone now. I want to be alone for a while."

He said he wanted to just be friends for now, but I resisted and acted like a child. This was the first time I had ever been rejected in love, and I couldn't accept it. I would drag myself to see him at Buddies, and he'd try to be nice and buy me a beer, but I'd refuse it stubbornly.

I started thinking that he had used me to help him find out about himself, and I felt bitter. But that passed. Having been through the sexual confusion myself, and the loss of Scott, I realized that I should sympathize with Rick's situation. And I did.

In June I was in New York, and I knew that Rick was a big Bruce Springsteen fan, so I managed to land two tickets to one of his concerts at the Meadowlands. I invited Rick down and he came and we had a wonderful evening, even though he seemed distracted. Afterward, back at the hotel, I felt something coming. Sure enough, he told me flat-out, "David, I just can't handle the relationship anymore." I calmly asked him why. He said, "I don't know which way to go. I just know I'm not ready for this yet."

I was actually very relaxed about it. I said, "Well, okay, that's your prerogative. There's nothing I can do about that." I wanted to say, "Please reconsider what this means. If you walk away from me now, it really is the end." But I couldn't bear to prolong it with a discussion of the issues. So I walked him downstairs and saw him into a cab. He said, "I'm so glad you took it this way. If I had known you would take it so well, I would've told you a couple of days ago." I thought, "What difference would *that* have made?"

It was bizarre; one way or another, death kept stealing people out of my life when I needed them the most. I strongly believe that the death of Rick's sister had a lot to do with us breaking up. I don't think he was mentally prepared for a loss like that. He knew that Scott had died, so maybe he figured he couldn't handle the closeness along with the fear of another loss. Add to that the fact that he told me he wanted kids someday, and maybe it made some sense. I don't know; I never learned why he really shut me out. Maybe he never did, either.

So, all of a sudden, I lost another love of my life. Maybe it wasn't real love; maybe it was just my fantasy of love. But it was something I thought I wanted and needed; and even though our relationship lasted only eight months, losing it destroyed me inside. I thought I was about to regain emotional stability with Rick, and when it was suddenly over like that, it was like dropping back into the same instability I'd felt ten years before. Scott had been taken away from me abruptly, but there was an answer for why I'd never see him again: he was dead. With Rick, there was no answer. He quit—and just like that, I was back in the emotional void again.

Not long before our breakup, Rick and I had planned an off-season backpacking trip around Europe—so in October I went myself. We had mapped out the Paris portion of the trip, so I thought a lot about Rick there. I remembered him wanting to quit school after his sister died, and asking my advice. I told him, "If you're not getting anything out of school, there's no sense wasting your time and money. You can always go back." It was ironic; he had quit school and we planned this trip, because he was now free to travel. We had looked forward to it so much, it was hard to believe he wasn't there.

For two months I wandered through France, Italy, Germany, Switzerland, and Holland. In Amsterdam I decided to explore the gay scene, so I looked it up in a book called *Spartacus International Gay Guide*, and I went into a few of the bars. It was basically the same scene as in America—only I was so much more open and relaxed. Nobody knew me there; I could go into a gay bar the same as if I were going into a post office. I was comfortable enough to talk to a lot of people, though I didn't have any encounters. I just enjoyed being there and knowing that the next time I came back to Europe, I'd know what it was like.

But something else occurred to me while I made the rounds: "These people are having such a good time, and I'm having a good time. Why shouldn't I have a good time *all* the time? Why do I have to worry about who I am? Why don't I just *be* who I am?" When I considered the frustration of my masquerading, I felt more depressed about hiding my nature. So I thought more about where my life was headed. I had lost two lovers in two and a half years, and I was wondering if I was ever going to have another long-lasting relationship again. I decided, "I have to open up more avenues. I have to straighten out this loneliness, this charade I'm living."

I realized also that I had to start being more open and honest on the road whenever people asked me who I was. In other words: no more lies. People hate liars, no matter how innocent or necessary the lying is. When someone asks you what you do for a living and you say you sell shoes or work construction, and then they find out you're an umpire, they think, "Why'd you lie to me about *that?*" They can't understand it—and they're right. So I figured, "If you can't be true to yourself, how can you be true to somebody else?" I had to finally say, "Screw it. Be proud of who you are and what you are." I knew I would still worry about being exposed and losing my job, but I decided that would be secondary now: "I'm putting *me* first for a change."

One funny twist to my search for a new man to love was that, for some reason, in 1985 I suddenly had aggressive *female* admirers. Women had always found me very attractive—they'd approached me often for dates, especially in New York, Pittsburgh, and Philadelphia. At times I would go out with them for a drink, but I wasn't ever interested in anything more than that. It was never a problem—until one admirer in San Diego got carried away.

Every trip I made to San Diego in 1985, this one woman who had a crush on me would go to all my games and sit in the stands, smiling and waving at me. Before every game she'd wait for me at the umpires' entrance, and when I appeared she'd yell, "Hi, Dave! Hi, Dave!" She always brought her young son with her, so I would go over and talk to them. She was so nice to me, so happy to see me, even for just those few minutes. One time she found out my birthday was coming up, so she gave me a gift-wrapped bottle of amaretto. I didn't think too much about it. I just figured she was a nice person, a little lonely like me, with a crush on a "celebrity" she didn't know.

One Sunday afternoon in San Diego, Bob Engel, Paul Runge, Jim Quick, and their families were in the stadium parking lot after a game, anxiously awaiting my arrival. When I finally showed up, Quick said, "Dave, I didn't know you were *God.*" I laughed. "What're you talkin' about? C'mon, let's go.'' Then Jim's wife remarked, "That's great, Dave. Are you really God?" I didn't know what they meant, so I played along. "Okay," I said. "Yes, I am God." Engel grumbled, "Oh, *reeeally?*" and everyone cracked up. Then Quick's kids started chanting, "Dave is God! Dave is God!" and everyone else joined in—but I still had no idea what was going on. Then I noticed them staring at something behind me, so I turned around. There, on the fence by my car, was a big goddamn sign: "Dave Pallone Is a God."

The lady with the crush was standing right next to it. Her little boy hurried over to me and said, "Dave, my mom would really like to talk to you." So I went over there and took down the sign. I said, "You shouldn't have written that sign. It really embarrassed me." She said, "I know. I'm sorry. I just had to. I think you're so nice; I just really want to get to know you. Maybe we could have a drink sometime." I said, "Lookit, I'm gonna go over to Bennigan's for a little while. I'll meet you over there."

I met her there and we had a drink together. I couldn't bring myself to tell her the truth, so I just told her that I was flattered by her attention but I was engaged to be married, and it wouldn't be appropriate for me to see her anymore. She said, "Oh, yes, I understand completely. I won't try to bother you." But right after that she called me in New York and said, "I'm not trying to bother you, Dave. I just wanted you to know that I was thinking of you." She kept doing things like that the entire year. And she continued to show up at my games in San Diego.

My mistake was that I felt bad for her because (a) she was a fan; (b) she liked me so much; (c) she kept giving me nice little gifts; (d) her son seemed so devoted to her and to like me as much as she did. I felt so guilty, I used to leave them tickets for games—and that helped create a monster. Eventually, I had to ignore her. When I'd see her in the parking lot after games, I would switch my All-Star ring from my right hand to my left and turn it upside down so it looked like a wedding band. I would tell her, "I'm married now. I just cannot meet with you. My wife won't like it." I remember how sad she looked when that sunk in, and I thought, "Just my luck. Why can't some handsome young *man* be after me like this?"

Well, if this was all I had to worry about as I entered my eighth big-league season, I would have been a happy man. But, as it turned out, the 1986 season was the start of my downward spiral out of baseball. Through July, the season was almost totally free of controversy. As far as umpiring, it might have been my best overall season ever. I earned more respect and compliments from players and managers, because my work was steady, solid, often excellent. I was on target for my first playoff assignment, which was my next major goal. And my relationship with Engel and Runge was fantastic. (In the dressing room, they continued to razz me about my temper and play practical jokes; off the field, I'd accompany Engel and his wife to places like Tijuana for lobster and laughs, and I would go with Runge, his son, and his nephew to amusement parks all around the country. In other words, we were like family now.)

But beginning in August '86, for the next two years bizarre events, rumors, and lies would pile up to bury me—and I couldn't stop it. To this day I cannot explain why these things happened to me, but I do know they didn't happen by accident.

It started in late August, in Pittsburgh, when Bob Engel asked me in the dressing room, "Did Quick talk to you about what Montague told him?"

"No. What do you mean?"

"I guess Rose told Montague, and Montague told Quick, that you tried to pick up some guy in Flanagan's bar in Cincinnati."

That almost knocked me over. *"What?"* I said. "What the fuck are you talking about?"

"Calm down. Talk to Quick."

Jim was right there, so I asked him what the hell he'd heard. He repeated what Engel said, and added, "Then Montague asked me, 'Have you noticed anything about Pallone being gay?' I said"—and here Quick jabbed me kiddingly—" 'No. I've dropped the soap in the shower and I've never had any problem.' "

Quick chuckled and I said, "I don't know where they

got their information, but it's a fuckin' lie. It did not happen.'' I was angry, first of all, that such a rumor would start. Second, I knew that I did not do it. Third, I wanted to know who the hell started the rumor, so I could challenge him on it. I considered calling Rose for more information, but Engel talked me out of it. He said it wasn't the right thing to do, that I should let it die. I took his advice—but I had a bad feeling that it might *not* die.

A few days later we started our final West Coast trip of the year in San Francisco. When we arrived in the dressing room, Engel found something taped to his locker: an article from the *San Francisco Chronicle* about the AIDS epidemic in the city. The name of a gay activist had been crossed out and mine was handwritten above it. Engel showed it to me—and I went through the roof: ''Jesus Christ! Who the fuck did this?''

''It had to be Kibler's crew,'' Runge said. ''They were here last.''

''What a coincidence,'' I said. *''Froemming*'s on that crew. I believe he did it.'' Engel and Runge both agreed. I thought, ''That asshole Froemming. He doesn't have the guts to come right at me. He's always on my case behind my back. There has to be something I can do.'' I was so frustrated because for three years Engel and Runge had been telling me that Kibler and, especially, Froemming had been hammering them for associating with me. According to them, Froemming constantly took shots like, ''Don't you know that Pallone's gay? You ever see him with women? . . . He's egotistical. . . . He has too many friends. . . . He spends too much money on clothes. . . . He's a scab.'' Runge told me once, ''They used to think you didn't belong in the majors. Now they criticize everything about you *except* your umpiring.''

Next, when we were in Los Angeles, Runge came into the dressing room after the first game, irritated as hell. He told me that rumors about me being gay were flying around the league and he couldn't understand why. He'd defended me to the hilt, but he was disgusted that anyone believed it in the first place. He said, ''Bill Madlock told me today, 'I heard your buddy Pallone has a problem. Is it true?' I don't understand these guys.'' I said, ''How do you think *I* feel?'' Paul said, ''Just ignore it. The season's almost over. Don't worry about it.''

After our last West Coast series in San Diego, I returned to New York, where I'd recently moved. That's when the next strange event happened. I got a call from a somebody I didn't know named Kevin Hallinan. He said, ''Dave, I need to talk to you right away.''

I said, ''Wait a minute. Who is this again, please?''

''Kevin Hallinan. I'm head of security in the commissioner's office.''

Boy, that pissed me off. I was still steaming about the rumor, and now, for some reason, league security was on my case. I said, ''Yes? So?''

''Look, Dave, there's something very important I want to talk to you about.''

''Okay, talk to me. I'm listening.''

''It's league business. I don't think we should talk about it over the phone.'' He asked me to meet him—and I didn't want to, but I wasn't in the position to refuse. After I hung up, I thought, ''What is the problem *now?*''

I met Hallinan in a garden café at the Citicorp Building in Manhattan. He started off, ''Mr. Feeney asked me to talk to you personally about a rumor that's been going around the league.'' And he recounted the Flanagan's bar rumor that I'd heard. I was not thrilled that Feeney knew about it.

I said, ''And he believes the rumor?''

''No. He just wanted me to find out if you knew about it.''

Something that had just happened in San Diego popped into my head. Feeney had come into our dressing room before the crew left for New York, and when he saw me in my usual road outfit (sharp V-neck shirt and pressed, tailored slacks), he said sarcastically, ''What are *you* dressed up as?'' It struck me then as odd, but it didn't register. Now, listening to Hallinan, it registered: Feeney must have just heard the rumor. So, what his remark *really* meant was: ''What are you, Pallone—a *faggot?*''

Hallinan looked at me patiently, waiting for my response. I said, "I already know about that rumor. It's not true."

"Well, I've been checking it out, Dave, and I've got people that say it *is* true."

"That's very interesting, since it never happened. Who are these people?"

"I can't name anyone. But they were in the bar."

"Look," I said, trying to control my rage, "it's easy for you to sit here and tell me about nameless people who are spreading stories about me. And it's easy for me to say it's not true. But the fact is they're liars and it's *not* true, because it didn't happen. And that's all there is to it."

"Let me ask you this: have you ever been in that bar?"

"Yes, I've been in there. But I never tried to pick anyone up in that bar. I don't know why this rumor is being spread." I couldn't tell him my next thought: "Jesus, it isn't even a *gay* bar. I mean, come on—am I going to try to pick up a guy in a straight bar in Middle American Cincinnati? And why the hell would a gay person try to pick up a straight guy anyway?" So I just said, "This is really pissing me off. Who's telling you this? I think I have the right to know."

He said, "It's some people we interviewed in the bar. That's all I can tell you."

I said, "Well, it didn't happen, but I'll make it a point never to go in there again."

Hallinan stayed calm; he wasn't being a hardass. His attitude seemed to be: "I just want to hear your side of this." I wanted to believe he was trying to help me, trying to find the truth. But the league had investigated me before, and they always came up empty, because there was never anything to find. So something told me they were still trying.

"Lemme tell you something," I said angrily. "I don't know for sure what this rumor is all about or who started it, but I have reason to believe it was Bruce Froemming. You should check Froemming out."

Hallinan shrugged that off. He said he would report back to Feeney that I knew about the rumor. As he rose to leave, he advised, "Just be careful."

I said, "Make sure you tell Mr. Feeney I'm coming in to see him." And that ended our meeting. On my way home, I kept thinking, "Maybe they've been following my private life all year. Okay—but so what? I am gay and I have gone to gay bars. But I did nothing wrong. I mean, going to a gay bar isn't wrong."

It was like a sick, ironic joke. I was gay, yet this rumor was totally false. Here I'd hidden my secret from baseball for eight years, hoping no one would figure out the truth about Scott or my activities in gay bars—things I *had* done—and now my secret was leaking out for something I *hadn't* done. It made me crazy that a false story could have this effect. On top of that, I wanted so badly to work the playoffs, because I knew I was ready for them. I just hoped that this phony rumor wouldn't take that chance away.

That afternoon I met with Chub Feeney in his office—but not to talk about the rumor. I wanted to discuss the playoffs, because Runge, as president of the Umpires' Association, had heard I wasn't getting them. But the first thing Feeney said was, "I understand you talked to Hallinan today about the rumor."

I said, "Mr. Feeney, I don't care about that. It's just what it is—a rumor. It's not true." But I could tell by the expression on his face that he didn't believe me.

He said, "We've got people that say you did it." (I was continually amazed at baseball's willingness to assume the worst. I kept wondering what happened to fair play, due process, being faced by your accusers, "innocent until proven guilty.") I thought, "If they can crucify me over a false rumor, I hope I never get into anything *really* serious." But what I said was, "I don't give a damn what those people said—whoever they are. They're wrong. They don't know what they're talking about. Where are they? Let them tell me about it to my face."

Feeney leaned back in his chair. "There's only a few more weeks to go in the season," he said, relaxed. "Maybe it'll just blow over."

I was annoyed at how casually he was taking this. I said, "Mr. Feeney, I'm not here to talk about that anyway. I want to know what my chances are of working the playoffs this year.''

He had to think about it. Then he said, "I don't think I'm going to have you work them.''

"And I don't think that's fair. I had a great year. I deserve them." Suddenly his phone rang. He answered it, listened a minute, hung up, and got up to leave. He said he'd be right back.

I said, "Would you like me to leave?''

"No," he said, unconcerned. "You can sit there.'' When he left, I noticed the list of people assigned to work the playoffs lying on his desk. I couldn't resist sneaking a look—and I saw that neither Fred Brocklander nor myself was on it. I couldn't figure it out. Our 1984 contracts stated that every umpire must work at least one playoff series within four years after eligibility—which for both of us meant no later than 1987. Since Feeney was retiring at the end of the year, if he didn't work one of us in the '86 playoffs he'd be leaving the new league president with the prospect of having to use us both in '87. "Shit," I thought, "they wouldn't let two scabs work together during the regular season. They'd *never* use us together in the playoffs.''

When Feeney returned, I was burning. I said, "Mr. Feeney, I'd like to know what rationale you're using for the playoffs. I doubt anyone deserves it more than me this year.''

He said, "I just don't think you're ready. But I know I have to use either you or Brocklander—so let me think about it some more.''

I knew he'd already made up his mind to use Fred—and I'm convinced it was because of the rumor. He had no other criterion. It's funny; my career might have been threatened by the rumor, yet when I left there that day I was more disturbed about not getting the playoffs that I'd worked so hard to earn.

Around September 10 I found out that Feeney had given the playoffs to Brocklander. It was the biggest disappointment of my career, but there was nothing I could do about it. So I went to Boston, and, while Fred worked the Mets-Astros series, I went to a couple of the Red

Sox–Angels games at Fenway Park and brooded about my bad luck. But when the season ended, so did most of my bad feelings. I told myself, "I'm just glad I have Engel and Runge to go back to next year."

THE BAD LIFE

During the 1986 off-season, I fulfilled a promise I had made to myself years ago when a child I knew died of spina bifida (a congenital birth defect of the spine, lower body muscles, and nerves), and I arranged a celebrity roast in Washington, D.C., to benefit the Spina Bifida Association of America. I decided the person I wanted to roast was Tommy Lasorda. He and I had been on the outs through the years, but I got his number from a friend and I called him anyway. He said, "Absolutely. No problem."

We then set up a great affair with Barbara Bush as honorary chairperson, along with celebrity participants like Steve Garvey, Sparky Anderson, Frank Robinson, Angie Dickinson, Mr. T., and Larry King as host. Since the plane from California was late, I went to the airport in my tuxedo to bring everybody back to the hotel in my limousine. When Lasorda got off the plane, he looked at me and said, "I've been a lot of places, but this is the first time I've ever had anyone greet me at the airport in a tuxedo." It was great; he was in rare form.

When we got to the hotel, I showed Lasorda to his room—the Presidential Suite. He said, "Dave, this is tremendous. I didn't need anything like this." I said, "Tommy, we wanted to show you our appreciation for letting us roast you." We were running late, so I said, "I hate to be a pain, but if you could get dressed and come down as soon as possible . . ." He said no problem, he'd be right down.

About fifteen minutes later, I was downstairs greeting guests when Lasorda called me on the phone. He said, "Dave, you're not gonna believe this. I forgot my goddamn *shoes.*"

"Jesus!" I said. "You're kidding, right?"

"No, I ain't kiddin' you. I don't have any black shoes with me. I got *nothin'.*"

"Okay," I said, thinking fast, "what size do you wear?" He told me and I said, "Sit tight. I'll do everything I can in the next twenty minutes to get you a pair of black shoes." As soon as I hung up, I gave an assistant a hundred dollars of my own money and I said, "Give this to the bellman and tell him to buy a pair of black shoes. And tell him we need the shoes in fifteen minutes." I gave him the size, and off he went. Exactly fifteen minutes later we had the shoes, and I sent them up to Lasorda and we were all set.

Well, the roast was a big hit (Lasorda especially liked my one-liner calling him "a baseball that grew arms and legs"), and everybody was feeling great. We were all upstairs in my suite celebrating when a guy I didn't know came up to me and said, "Did Tommy get you for a pair of shoes?"

I said, "Excuse me?"

"Tommy have his own shoes?"

I thought the guy was drunk. "No," I said. "He forgot his shoes, so I bought him a pair. Why?"

He laughed. "Oh, Tommy pulls that all the time. He goes to events and says, 'I forgot my shoes,' and he gets a new pair to take home."

I said, *"What?* You gotta be shittin' me."

"No," he said, walking away. "It's a great shtick. Tommy's got more shoes than Florsheim."

I couldn't believe it. Even today, I don't know whether it really was a shtick, or if Lasorda just sent that guy over to me to bust my balls. Either way, *he* ended up roasting *me.*

To anyone else, this might seem like only what it was: a happy occasion for a worthy cause—with a little joke on me as a kicker. But as I remember it now, it also seems like the perfect analogy for a lot of what happened to me over the next two years. Because in so many instances during that time, the joke ended up being on me.

In February I started getting nervous about the crew assignments for '87. It was a new regime: Bart Giamatti—who, from what I'd heard, sounded like a great guy—replaced Chub Feeney as league president; and Eddie Vargo replaced Blake Cullen as supervisor of umpires. "Good riddance to Feeney," I thought. But I knew I would miss Cullen badly, because he had always been on my side. Blake had a hand in making up the crews, and he knew how important it was to me to work with Engel and Runge. So the first thing that went through my mind was: "Eddie Vargo's in charge now. He's gonna fuck me over bad. I have to arrange a meeting with Giamatti and talk to him about it."

I had never met A. Bartlett Giamatti before, and here in my first meeting with him I was going to bring him an attitude problem. I didn't want to start off on the wrong foot, but I felt I had to speak my mind. So I explained that I had come up through the '79 strike and that in the past few years I'd been happy working with Engel and Runge, and they were happy with me. I mentioned my problems with Vargo and that I felt he disliked me. "I know he's your new supervisor," I said, "but I think he's going to do everything he can to hurt my career. For one thing, he's a staunch union supporter. For another, we worked together in '80 and '82, and he never spoke to me. In 1983, I ran into him in a restaurant in St. Louis and he wouldn't even acknowledge me. And now he's my head supervisor—the guy who calls all the shots? I worry that he'll switch me to a crew that doesn't want me, and that'll make my life miserable."

Giamatti listened intently, eyes fixed on me the whole time. Compared to Feeney, who never looked at me when I spoke, this seemed like a giant step forward in itself. I said, "Mr. Giamatti, this is your first year. I'm not here to cause you problems, but I am here to let you know how I feel. I hope you understand." He gave me what I would later come to recognize as his fatherly look. "I'm glad you brought this to my attention,'' he said with interest. ''I do understand how you feel. And I will talk to Eddie about it.''

He struck me as sincere. But I thought, ''What's Vargo going to say—'Yeah, I hate that son of a bitch and I *am* gonna do everything I can to hurt him'? No, he'll say, 'I have nothing personal against Dave Pallone and I intend to treat him like everyone else.' '' What I really wanted Giamatti to tell Vargo was, ''I think it's important that we leave Pallone on Engel's crew.'' But I didn't suggest this to him—which I would later regret.

About a week later, Giamatti informed me that he had spoken to Vargo and that Vargo said not to worry, because there wouldn't be any problems. Even with that reassurance, I knew in my heart I was through working with Engel and Runge, and that Vargo would slot me on a crew that didn't want me. Not long after this, Vargo sent me my spring training schedule for 1987—which immediately triggered our first confrontation. He'd scheduled me to work about twenty consecutive days, despite the rule in our contract stating that umpires with five or more years of service did not have to work more than fourteen consecutive days in spring training. I had more than five years, and I didn't want to work more than two weeks because of the ostracism.

I told Vargo about this oversight and I explained that March 21 was the cutoff date. He got mad at me: ''You can't do it. I've got guys that don't want to work the twenty-second, and guys that don't want to work the twenty-third. I need someone to work—'' I cut him off: ''Wait a minute, Eddie. First of all, you got plenty of young umpires who don't have a choice that you can use after the twenty-first. There is no way around this; there's no choice with me. I don't *want* to work past the twenty-first, and according to the union contract I don't *have* to work, and I'm not *going* to work. So you might as well straighten it out right now.''

He said, ''Well, let me talk to Bart about it.'' That was fine with me; I knew I was right. Vargo called me later and left a message on my answering machine: ''I talked to Bart and you're through on the twenty-first. But don't forget, I still have you working that exhibition game in Washington, D.C., in April.'' Which was okay; I had agreed to that game, as long as I got the last two weeks of March off. I wanted to be able to spend those two weeks at my condo in Clearwater, enjoying the sun and relaxing before the season began.

On March 24, I got another phone message from an angry Vargo: ''Dave, this is Ed. You missed two god-damn games, and we were short an umpire. Where the hell were you? You were supposed to be there.'' Obviously, Vargo had miscalculated my schedule again. I was pissed that he blamed me for his own mistake. So I called Giamatti and left a message for him to call me back—which he did, but I missed it. Finally I reached Vargo and I said, ''Eddie, what is this about the twenty-second? You know I was through on the twenty-first.''

He said, ''No! You're through on the twenty-third.''

''Eddie, we agreed that fourteen consecutive days was the twenty-first. I was all done, remember? Except for the game I promised you in Washington. You were supposed to replace me on the twenty-second.''

''No! You were supposed to be done on the *twenty-third*. Fourteen consecutive *working* days—the twenty-third, not the twenty-first.''

I said, ''No, Eddie, not *working* days. It's right there in black and white in the contract. It says fourteen consecutive days, period. That doesn't mean working days. You can work me fourteen games, if you want, in those fourteen days. But it's *consecutive* days. How can you have fourteen consecutive working days? What do you do—work on the third, work on the sixth, work on the ninth? How's that consecutive? That's not consecutive, Eddie.''

It was hard to believe that I had to explain this to the supervisor of umpires. It started to sound like an Abbott and Costello routine: ''Who's on first?'' ''No, stupid—*What*'s on first. Who is on second.'' So I called Giamatti and he said he would look into it and get back to me. He did; the first week of April, I received a letter from him saying: ''You are hereby fined two hundred dollars for missing two games.''

The third week of spring training, I found out Vargo had switched me off Engel and Runge's crew for the season and assigned me to Lee Weyer's crew with Dutch Rennert and Eddie Montague. I called Engel and Runge to see if there was anything they could do, and they called Vargo to suggest alternative options. But Vargo wouldn't budge. This was a big emotional setback for me. I had been on Weyer's crew for a short time in my rookie season, and although he wasn't as unpleasant as the other crew chiefs back then, he definitely didn't want me around. God, it was depressing; I was losing two great friends who helped me grow as a person and to survive as an umpire, and now—for no apparent reason—I would have to prove myself all over again. I remember my first thought: "Jesus Christ. For three and a half years I lived the good life, and now I'm back in the bad life again."

Not a great year so far: a conflict with Vargo; a disappointing meeting with Giamatti; getting yanked off my crew, just like I had warned. The only thing I could do was throw myself into my umpiring and hope that things would smooth themselves out. But right away trouble found me on the field, too. My first week I had an exhibition game in St. Petersburg between the Mets and the Red Sox—their first meeting since the previous year's incredible World Series. Commissioner Ueberroth was there, along with Giamatti, and I worked home plate. The Red Sox still resented Mets outfielder Darryl Strawberry for his slow, "hotdog" trot around the bases after hitting a home run off Al Nipper in the seventh game of the Series. There was so much bad blood between them, it had been in the papers that Nipper would get Strawberry the next time he faced him.

And that's what happened. Strawberry came up and Nipper drilled him. I knew that Strawberry had the guts of a burglar; if he came after you, he was gonna blast you. So I grabbed him and walked him all the way down to first base. I said, "Darryl, you gotta let me handle this. I know how you feel. And you're absolutely right. I'd probably wanna do the same thing. But I can't let you go out there and start swinging. All that'll happen is you'll get fined and suspended. You don't want that." He said, "I don't give a shit anymore." I said, "I under-stand how you feel. But just let me handle this one." And somehow he calmed down.

After the game, I wanted to talk to Giamatti about the crew change; it had been on my mind since I spotted him in the stands. By chance, as I came out of the clubhouse to the parking lot, I ran into Giamatti on his way over to see me. So we talked out there. He said that both he and the commissioner were impressed with the way I'd han-dled Strawberry, which made me feel great, because now he knew what I could do. That's when I said, "You know, I'm really unhappy with the crew switch. I told you Vargo would do that to me."

He said, "Look, Dave, I know that you don't like the switch. But Eddie didn't do it to hurt you. He did it to try to help you. He thinks you'll be a better umpire if you work with Lee Weyer." This was probably what Vargo told Giamatti, and he bought it. That got me mad-der. But then he said, "I want you to give it a chance. If things don't work out, maybe around the All-Star break we'll review it and see if we need to make another change."

"Mr. Giamatti, I had almost four years of people lik-ing me, and talking to me, and not ostracizing me. And it was good. They really want me on their crew. And now you want me to take a step backward."

He said, "If you just give Weyer and his crew a chance, I don't think they'll be that way." Something in his man-ner made me believe he really did care about my welfare.

"Well, I feel bad because I'm getting off on the wrong foot with you. So far, I'm always complaining to you. I don't want you to think of me that way. I want to do what's best. And I know that's what you want for your umpires—so I'll give it a chance. I'll try it."

At the start of the regular season, I had a private con-versation in the dressing room with Lee Weyer. He said he'd heard I didn't want to be on his crew, and he was hurt: "It's the first time in my career that somebody didn't want to work with me." I said, "Lee, you have to un-derstand where I'm coming from. I know that you're a fair man and you're going to treat me like a professional, because that's your reputation. But we're not going to have the camaraderie as a crew that I had with Engel and Runge—and you know it. That'll just be a hardship for both of us. It's not that I don't want to work with you personally. I mean, you tell me we're going to have some kind of camaraderie, I'll be happy as hell. But you know it won't be there.'' He said, ''Yeah, I know it,'' and I said, ''That's why I don't want to be on your crew.''

But I think this talk helped. Because even though I constantly lobbied to get off the crew, Weyer, Rennert, and Montague were not vindictive people. They associated with me cordially both on the field and in the clubhouse (the union pact against associating with scabs had died years ago), so we worked together fine as a crew. Weyer wasn't a bad person at all; he treated me courteously and professionally and sometimes was even friendly. Dutch Rennert was a thrifty, cigar-smoking oldtimer who was pleasant enough when he had to be, but too meek and timid for my taste. We just had nothing in common. But Eddie Montague, particularly, made it bearable. Although he had disliked me in the early years, he was one of Paul Runge's best friends—and I knew that Runge kept telling him, ''Dave's a good guy. Give him a chance.'' So he did. He was a personable, intelligent, class guy. All in all, things were at worst comfortable (in July, I brought them all gifts when I returned from my vacation in Greece, and they really appreciated the gesture of friendship). On the other hand, throughout the season, they never ate with me, chummed around with me, or stayed at the same hotel. So there was nothing to replace the genuine friendship I'd developed with Engel and Runge—which made it very lonely for me again.

In early April, Giamatti came into our dressing room in Atlanta. ''By the way,'' I said, smiling, ''I got your letter about the fine. When do you want the money in your office?'' He said, ''I'd like to have it as soon as possible.'' I said, ''You know the contract says we only have to work fourteen consecutive days.'' He said, ''Yes. Fourteen consecutive working days.'' I knew that Giamatti was too intelligent to have misread the contract, so he must have gotten that interpretation from Vargo. I didn't want to press it here, so I said, "Well, I do want to have a meeting with you about this to explain my side of the story." He grinned. "I'll look forward to it. As I do to your two hundred dollars." His manner was so open and friendly, it reassured me that he would give me a fair shake.

I paid the fine that week but didn't get the meeting until later in the summer. I remember it vividly, because that's when another dimension of Giamatti's character emerged for the first time. I spoke first: "So you got my two hundred dollars?"

"Yes. Thank you. You took that very well."

"Not really. That's why I'm here. I don't know if you know the whole story, but I personally showed Eddie Vargo the basic agreement and it states verbatim: 'fourteen consecutive days.' "

Giamatti fished out a copy of the contract and skimmed through it. I showed him the passage in question and we debated interpretations, and he concluded that what had happened in spring training was just a "miscommunication." And he said, "I'm going to return half your fine at the end of the year." That seemed fair—although something else was bothering me.

"It isn't the money," I said. "I just don't want you to think I neglected my job and did something wrong when I did nothing wrong."

"I understand, Dave. And I appreciate your concern." We sat silent a moment, and then he shocked the shit out of me by asking, "Dave, do you really want to umpire?" He studied me, then added, "I don't mean you don't love your job. It's obvious that you do. But is it the life for you?"

"It's funny," I said, "but I've been thinking about that a lot lately. I'm not sure." I was surprised at how easily I revealed my real feelings to him. It was partly because it had been so long since anyone in baseball's hierarchy gave a damn about me, and partly because of Giamatti's warm, professorial aura. Talking to him was like talking to your father and your favorite teacher at the same time.

"You should go to school," he said flat-out. "You're too intelligent not to continue your education."

"But I never had college."

He nodded. "That's all right. There's still time. There are plenty of opportunities for you to go to school right here in New York. For example, you could take classes this winter at NYU. Or you could pursue it in New England, if you move back to that area. That's something you should think about. A good education is so important in this world."

On that note the meeting ended. I left more impressed than when I came in. Here was the president of the National League taking a personal interest in my life. I thought, "Boy, if he's any indication of where baseball's headed, maybe there's hope for the game after all."

I didn't feel that way in August, though, when Lee Weyer and Eddie Montague took overlapping vacations and the league gave us Bruce Froemming as a temporary crew chief. Everybody knew about our long-standing feud, so the feeling was that there would probably be a fistfight before his stint with us was over. I remember Montague getting ready to leave and telling me, "I wish I didn't have to take my vacation now. I really want to see this."

The antagonism between me and Froemming went back to 1979, but it originated in his own mind. The weird thing was that, for whatever reason, I seemed to preoccupy his life since then. I knew for a fact that he constantly bad-mouthed me to other umpires—especially to Runge, who pretty much told him he was wrong. So when he joined our crew in Cincinnati, I gave him a little speech: "You're gonna be the crew chief now, and I'll respect you for that. Whenever you want me to do something, all you have to do is tell me and I'll do it. Otherwise, if you leave me alone I'll leave you alone, and everything will be fine." He said, "That's the way I want it, too. That's the way it'll be."

There was no fistfight. Froemming treated me responsibly on the field, though he avoided me the rest of the time. Once—when Montague was back from vacation—Froemming threw Dave Parker out of a game for yelling at Montague behind his back. So I told him after the game, "I just want you to know that I've always admired your work, and you showed why today when you stepped in for Eddie and threw Parker out. You had the guts to jump in and not be blind to it.'' Reluctantly, he said ''Thanks'' and left it at that. I did this because Froemming really was one of the best—and toughest—umpires in the league, and I did admire the way he stood up to players who tried to give him shit. I also wanted him to see that although I didn't like him as a person, I could still appreciate his work. Maybe I thought it would help him realize he could appreciate me the same way.

But we did finally have an ''incident,'' in Montreal. We were in the dressing room, and I had known something would happen sooner or later because he still couldn't stand me, and I wanted just once to antagonize him before he antagonized me. It started innocently enough. Froemming mentioned an upcoming union meeting and said, ''Jesus Christ, we're not gonna have anything to talk about this year. Everything's going so smoothly.'' That was my opening. I said, ''Well, you could always tell them thanks for helping me spend my vacation in Greece this year. Since I'm not in the union and I don't have to pay dues, I used that money to go to Greece.''

All of a sudden, you could hear the proverbial pin drop. I could tell by everybody's face that they loved it—and they were just waiting for Froemming to erupt. But his face was expressionless and he didn't say a word. The next day I was thinking in the dressing room, ''I know he has to say something. This is not the Bruce Froemming I know. Why hasn't he said something?'' Finally he came over to me and said, ''You know, I didn't appreciate that fucking comment yesterday about the union.'' I stood up and said, ''Yeah, well, I don't appreciate what you have to say about me—which, by the way, is always behind my back. I agree that my comment was uncalled for, and I apologize, but I got tired of you bad-mouthing me all the time to other people. I know what you're saying about me, and I better not hear it to my face. You don't have to like me, Bruce. You don't have to do anything—just keep your mouth shut about me. That's all I'm asking you.''

On September 10, I got a call from Phyllis Collins, vice-president of the National League, to inform me that Bart Giamatti had awarded me the 1987 National League Championship Series between St. Louis and San Francisco. This should've been a big-deal call—my first playoffs, the second of my major goals in baseball—but it wasn't a surprise, because he *had* to select me this year or be in violation of my contract. Still, in light of my recent troubles, I thought if I could do a great job in the playoffs, it would go a long way toward showing Giamatti how valuable an umpire I was, and maybe shut up the hardline union guys who still resented me.

Then the hammer fell again. In late September, during a series in St. Louis, I went to a straight bar one night with Ned Stoner, owner of a well-known restaurant, and a couple of his friends. At the bar I was introduced as "Dave Pallone, a National League umpire," to two brothers I mistakenly took for other friends of Ned's. The older brother kept hitting on me all night with eye contact, and I wondered if I should respond. I thought about the Cincinnati bar rumor, and the fact that this bar was straight and so was Ned, and I thought, "Better not." But my personal life had regressed to what it was when I had first entered the league, and I could hardly stand it. In other words, I was desperate for the sympathetic company of another gay man, to say nothing of a lover. I wasn't going to be indiscreet, but I was feeling bolder than before.

Ned and his friends left early, but I stuck around drinking and talking with the two brothers. When it got late, they said they were stranded without a ride, so I offered to drop them off. They said they lived about thirty minutes away, in Illinois, but I didn't mind. I was feeling high and depressed at the same time, and I didn't want to go back to an empty hotel room. So I drove them home.

On the way, it did occur to me that something might come of this. Yet I kept wondering if I was doing the right thing. When we got to their home the younger brother said, "You look wasted. We have an extra bedroom; why don't you stay here tonight and drive back tomorrow?'' I was tired and it was very late, so I said okay and I went inside. Almost immediately, the younger brother went into the bedroom to make a call, while the other brother showed me the spare room. While we were in there he put his hand on my ass, and I responded. Abruptly, he left the room and got his brother, and they marched into the kitchen together. I was confused; I followed them in to find out what was going on. When I entered, the older brother said coldly, "We both want you to leave now." I thought, "Uh-oh, weirdness here"—and I left immediately.

Driving back to my hotel, I knew I'd committed a stupid indiscretion. First, the whole fiasco started in a straight bar. Second, it involved two people, not just one—and they were strangers. I should have declined to go into their house. Instead, I'd figured, "Here's a chance to meet someone new in St. Louis." But there was nothing I could do about it now. I just hoped it would disappear.

A few days later I got a call in Montreal from Paul Runge. He said, "I want to let you know what's happening. You'll be working the playoffs with Kibler and Quick, and they've heard a rumor going around that you picked up a guy in a St. Louis bar. So be prepared." I said, "Jesus, not again." I was so pissed, I just said, "Paul, it didn't happen," and I hung up. I couldn't understand how this rumor had started. The only answer was: the two brothers did it. But why? I didn't even *know* them. Was I paranoid—or did someone put them up to it?

October 6, 1987, I was excited to begin my first playoff series in St. Louis. It felt like the 1983 All-Star Game; excitement was in the air. Busch Stadium was one of the few places in any sport where the majority of hometown fans came dressed in the team colors. You always saw a lot of green in Boston Garden for the Celtics, but it was only a few thousand people. In St. Louis, especially for the World Series, maybe thirty thousand people dressed in Cardinal red—shirts, sweaters, jackets, hats. It added something special to the atmosphere. And it pumped me up the same way it did the players.

My mission was clear: they had withheld this assignment from me for three years, even though I was qualified, so I was going to try to make them look bad for that by having the best playoff series anyone ever had. I was determined to be in the middle of the action, no matter where they put me on the field. Our position assignments were based mostly on seniority, so Vargo assigned crew chief John Kibler to work home plate the first game. With a crew of six (four on the bases, two on the outfield lines), if the series went seven games they'd have Kibler at home plate in the first and seventh games—which didn't necessarily mean they had the best home-plate ump for those crucial games. It was just the way Vargo did things; he wanted Kibler to be his ace. And no wonder; they were two of a kind—old-school scab-haters still holding outdated grudges.

The first game, we had Eddie Montague at first base, me at second, Eric Gregg at third, Jim Quick on the left-field line, and Bob Engel on the right-field line. The game went innocently enough, with the Cardinals winning 5–3. But it was the start of what was to be an extraordinary series for me, because whenever there was a close or controversial call, I was destined to have it. Things started off in that first game with a tough call at second base. Cardinals shortstop Ozzie Smith took a throw on a steal and made a "phantom" tag on the runner's head, so I called him safe. Smith couldn't believe it, because the ball beat the runner to the bag. But Ozzie was in the air, and the guy clearly slid under his swipe. It was a gutsy call—yet nobody watching TV knew I was the one who made it. That was because the announcer, Vin Scully, called me Jim Quick—and that was because they had the wrong position list in the broadcast booth. It didn't bother me at the time, because I didn't know it. But when you get a close call right, you want to be known by your own name. When you blow one, then they can use somebody else's name.

After the game, I had dinner at the Marriott with Pat and Bob Engel. During the meal, Bob said, "What happened in St. Louis? What about that rumor?" I don't know what came over me, but I couldn't lie to him anymore. He and Runge had been defending me against rumors for too long, and I was feeling guilty about it and frustrated that there was no one I could confide in. I guess, at that moment, I felt it was time to tell *somebody* I could trust.

So I said, "Bob, you know I consider you and Pat two of my best friends in the world. I have to tell you that I'm gay." They didn't even blink. I said, "I hope this stays between us, because it would create a lot of problems for me. I believe in my heart that it doesn't make a difference to you and Pat."

Pat said, "I knew."

"You knew? How?"

"Let's just say woman's intuition. But I love you just the same. You're still Dave Pallone to me."

Bob wasn't surprised, either. He said, "Well, I sort of suspected it. I never saw you with women."

"Yes, you did." And I named a couple of my female friends.

"I just thought that was for cover. But look, it doesn't make any difference to me."

I said, "I've wanted to tell Paul, too. But I don't get a chance to see him, and I don't want to do it over the phone. I want to tell him in person—straight out."

"I think you'll have a little problem with Paul. It'll take him time to get used to it. But I think he'll come around."

I said, "Well, that's why it's taken me so long to tell anyone. I didn't want to risk losing anybody's friendship. I just couldn't take the chance."

We continued the conversation up in their room, and I explained how difficult it was to be gay in baseball. They were very sympathetic. Bob said, "Yeah, and these fuckin' umpires hate you because you're a scab. Jesus Christ, if they ever find out you're gay, they'll bury you." He was right, but it was a great relief to know that *he* was on my side.

In the second game, Giants starter Dave Dravecky pitched a brilliant, two-hit shutout and won 5–0. I worked first base, but every call was routine. Although nothing unusual happened in the game itself, at the start of the seventh inning something memorable happened between me and Bart Giamatti. He called me over to the president's box by the Cardinals' dugout and he pointed to a speck on the infield. "Dave," he said, concerned, "you see that piece of wood out there? It's been bothering me. Would you please pick it up for me?" I went over and picked it up and gave it to him. It seemed a little odd, because it was a minuscule chip. But Giamatti was a perfectionist; to him, a wood chip on the artificial turf during the playoffs was an imperfection.

As usual, after the game the Cardinals had a get-together at the Marriott, where everyone involved in the series went to eat. I went with the other umpires—except Kibler. I stayed away from him the same as if he were Bruce Froemming. He might as well have been Froemming; when it came to maturity and professionalism in dealing with the scabs, they were clones. Plus, I knew from other umpires that he constantly ridiculed me behind my back. I wanted nothing to do with him. In the meantime, while I was getting a drink at the bar, Chub Feeney wandered by and said—with a dig in his tone—"Well, Dave, you had a great game today. You didn't miss any close calls." That was a typically sarcastic Feeney remark. He knew I didn't *have* any close calls, so that's why I didn't miss any.

The next day was a travel day. I ran into Jim Quick at the airline office in St. Louis, and it was obvious he had something on his mind. He took me aside and said, "Look, you know there's another rumor about you floating around, right?"

I said, "Right. And that's what it is—a rumor."

He said, "Okay, but it's the second one, Dave. I don't know what to think. I want to know if you *are* gay, because I don't really appreciate that kind of a life-style."

I hadn't seen this side of Jim Quick before. I said, "Lookit, you don't have to believe me if you don't want to, but the rumors aren't true. That's all I can tell you." I didn't tell him the truth, because I wasn't ready, and because—with his attitude—I knew if I told him, he'd say something to somebody else and there'd be trouble for me during the playoffs. There was no way I would let that happen if I could help it.

Game three was in San Francisco, and here came the pressure, because I finally had home plate. The epitome of a major league umpire's career, of course, is working a World Series. Well, the playoff series is only one step away. So, the first great thrill would be working home plate in the playoffs. Then: working home plate in a World Series game. Finally, the ultimate: working home plate in the seventh game of the World Series.

At the time, I knew this would be my one and only chance in the playoffs to have that special feeling, so I wanted it to be the best job I'd ever done. It would be tough, though; I had butterflies before the game the size of hamburgers. And I knew that Candlestick was a terrible ballpark because of the cold and wind, and also that Giants fans were the loudest, most abusive fans in baseball, not only to visiting players and umpires but also to their own players. Yet they were knowledgeable; they knew the game.

It took me two full innings to relax. I remember telling Giants catcher Bob Brenly, "Bear with me, Bob. I'm a little tight." He said, "Yeah. I am, too." It wasn't that I was doing badly; I just wanted to let him know that I wasn't myself yet. Early on, I had my first tough call. The Giants had a man on third with Robby Thompson up. A breaking ball got away from Cardinals pitcher Joe Magrane and landed by Thompson's foot. I didn't see where it actually hit, so I didn't react immediately. The ball bounced and Thompson took two steps toward first, like he'd been hit in the foot. But when he saw the ball roll to the screen, he came back, because he wanted the run to score (he knew that if he was hit, the ball would be "dead" and nobody could advance).

Since I didn't see the ball make contact with Thompson's foot, I had to rule wild pitch—and the run scored. That brought Cardinals manager Whitey Herzog out to argue with me. I said, "Whitey, I didn't see the ball hit him. And if anybody else had seen it, they'd have helped me out." I thought that was so ironic because of all the years nobody helped me out. Now, second baseman

Tommy Herr came in to tell me he saw the ball hit Thompson's foot. But how the hell could he have seen from second base what I couldn't see from three feet away? Obviously, he was trying to get the call reversed so the run wouldn't score. Well, the call stood. And despite watching the replay over and over later on, I never did find out whether the ball hit Thompson. In fact, I asked him the next day and he said he didn't think so. That's how close that call was.

In the fifth inning, I had another tough call. The Cards had a runner on first and Terry Pendleton on third. When the batter chopped one toward third, Kevin Mitchell fielded it and got Pendleton in a rundown. From third base, Bob Engel had pointed "fair" on the chop but put his hand down quickly, so I didn't think anyone saw it. It was my call anyway, and I knew the ball was foul when it was fielded. There were fifty-five thousand people making noise, and the players had a rundown going, so nobody heard me yelling, "Foul! Foul! Foul!" I yelled it about six times to really sell the call, because if anybody had seen Engel's signal we were in for one big argument. If that happened, I had to be prepared to say, "Hey, it's my call. I saw the ball go foul, I called it six times, and that's it." But I'd sounded so convincing yelling "Foul!" that nobody questioned it. I was very proud of how I sold that call.

I had another key call to end that inning. With two out and the Cards down 4–0, they had the bases loaded with their big stick Jack Clark up. Possible turning-point situation. Clark went to a 3–2 count, and you could cut the tension with a knife—and then I called him out on a perfect strike. That was a very big pressure call. If I had buckled under the pressure, or if I had been having a bad game, I might have missed that strike and called it a ball. Occasionally, in regular season games, you found yourself missing perfect pitches like that, and you didn't know why. In a playoff game, though, that wasn't acceptable. You had to psych yourself up so you *couldn't* miss a crucial pitch.

Just before the start of the eighth inning, I was standing at the plate when I noticed a piece of wood in the dirt—probably a bat splinter. I picked it up, called the batboy over, pointed in the direction of Bart Giamatti's box, and said, "You see the man in the beard over there? I want you to bring him this and tell him I said that now he has a piece of wood from each ballpark." The kid ran over to Giamatti, gave him the wood, and told him what I had said. Giamatti smiled and nodded at me; now we had our own private joke.

Things were going along great; it was 6–4 Cardinals now, the game was almost over, I'd done a good job, and I was feeling confident and relaxed enough to kid around with the new National League president about a piece of wood. I had never felt so totally in command of my skills. I was like the guy who'd just hit for the cycle, or scored his fifth goal, or thrown his sixth TD pass. It was like, "What's next? Give me something *really* tough now." I didn't want the hard calls to end. And they didn't.

In the top of the eighth, Vince Coleman was at first with Ozzie Smith batting. Smith laid down a nice bunt, but Will Clark couldn't handle the throw at first because Smith got in his way running up the line. When the throw got away, Smith took second and Coleman took third, and they were excited to be in scoring position. But wait a minute. There was Dave Pallone calling Ozzie Smith out for running out of the baseline, and bringing Coleman back to first base.

Herzog came out like a shot to argue, and then coach Nick Leyva came all the way over from his third-base coach's box. I turned to Leyva and said, "You get the hell back to the coach's box. You have no business being over here." Then I told the first-base coach to get his ass back to *his* box. Finally, I turned to Whitey and said, "I'll talk only to you." Whitey said, "How can you call him out?" I said, "Whitey, you know damn well he's gotta run inside that forty-five-foot lane. He wasn't in the forty-five-foot lane, so there's nothing to discuss. Interference—he's *out.*" I started to walk away, but I sensed Herzog following me, so I turned around. "Hold it right there, Whitey," I said. "I am not gonna stand out here and argue this all night. It's over with." He knew I meant business, so he returned to the dugout without a word. That's where reputation helps you when you need it.

I didn't know it at the time, but the TV announcers praised me on that call. It's easy for me to say this because it's about me, but most umpires wouldn't have made that call. It was too gutsy, too controversial. Even though it should have been called, no one would have argued if it hadn't been. I know that someone will say, "That fuckin' Pallone. *All* umpires make that call." But that's just not true. I saw umpires deliberately avoid it many times. Like Dutch Rennert—and yet he kept getting rated number one.

Some guys don't make those calls because they're timid. The less trouble they get into, the better they feel about themselves, and, unfortunately, the better the league feels about them, too. That encourages them to stay timid—because that's how they get rated number one. When you don't make a controversial call, everybody loves you and no one argues with you. When you make a controversial call, everybody hates you and everyone argues with you. Controversy is the ratings meter. It's the old adage: "You did a great job if nobody remembered that you umpired the game." Well, that might be right. But if you're out there doing the job and you see this play, are you supposed to ignore it? I didn't ignore that stuff. I didn't ignore balks, either. Dutch Rennert never called a balk. John Kibler never called a balk. They didn't want the controversy. On the other hand, it was such a pleasure to work with men like Bob Engel and Paul Runge. You knew when you walked out on that field that if something controversial happened, they would *see* it.

After the third game, we went to our dressing room and I was feeling great. I got accolades from Engel, Montague, and Quick. Then Giamatti stopped by to congratulate me. Ed Vargo came in, looked down, said his basic "Nice job, Dave," and gave me his usual wishy-washy handshake. Of course, Kibler didn't come near me. I got more attention in the Giants' postgame reception tent. Of all people, Ralph Nelson—the Giants executive who had helped spark my fight with Nick Colosi—made it a point to say, "Dave, you did a hell of a job.'' His team lost, yet he said this sincerely. I guess he'd changed his mind about me over the years. That impressed me. Bart Giamatti came by again with Vargo and said, ''Nice work, Dave.'' When I talked later to Whitey Herzog at the bar, he explained that he didn't object to my out-of-the-baseline call; he just objected to the rule. He added, ''You had a great game anyway.'' Boy, I was flying high. What a switch after nine years without appreciation!

I arrived at Candlestick early for game four. Kevin Hallinan came up to me and said, ''The commissioner said he's never seen an umpire control a game like that. I thought you'd like to know.'' It was interesting; here was the head of league security, the guy who'd investigated me on the Cincinnati rumor, bothering to let me know what the commissioner had said about my work. I thought, ''It might be hard not to trust this guy now.''

I worked the right-field line in game four, and it was relaxing—nothing controversial, no tough calls. The Giants won 4–2 to tie the series at two games apiece. I received one memorable compliment afterward. As I walked past Giants general manager Al Rosen, who was talking with some people in the reception tent, he excused himself from his friends and came over to me and said, ''I wanted to tell you that you had a hell of a plate job last night.'' Here was the general manager of the losing team telling me I did a great job. I started to feel like people were finally seeing me for the umpire I was, and not just as ''Dave Pallone, the scab.'' It made me feel that maybe the bad life might end sooner than I thought.

In the fifth game I worked the left-field line, and, again, nothing unusual happened. The Giants won 6–3 and were now just one victory away from going to the World Series. In game six, I worked third base and made a couple more close calls. In the sixth inning, with St. Louis leading 1–0, the Giants had runners at first and second with nobody out. Kevin Mitchell attempted to bunt them over, but Terry Pendleton's throw beat the runner to third for a force out. The Giants' third-base coach, Don Zimmer, went nuts, and so did their manager, Roger Craig. I told

Zimmer to get the hell back to his coach's box, and I told Craig, "No way he was safe. The throw beat him by a foot."

In the bottom of that inning, a line drive down the third-base line went foul by a hair, and I called it immediately. I found out later that after my call, Vin Scully remarked on TV, "The eyes of a diamond cutter." But down on the field I was thinking, "God, my wish before the series to be involved in all the action is coming true in spades. I'm getting *all* the close calls."

After the inning ended, as Giants pitcher Don Robinson headed for the bullpen, he said to me, "Great fuckin' call, Dave." Then Don Zimmer, who was on his way out to his coach's box, stopped to tell me, "I saw the replay on that force at third. You were right, I was wrong. I'm sorry." I felt great, of course. I hadn't been wrong in six games of controversial calls—and everybody was recognizing that.

The night before the seventh game we were in the clubhouse eating, and I was trading gibes with Bart Giamatti about my clothes. (I wore seven different suits to these games. Before game two, when Giamatti saw me coming in my newest Hugo Boss suit, he'd teased me, "They can definitely hear you coming, Pallone—and not by your footsteps." He was a Yale conservative, but he appreciated style.) Then Giamatti said warmly, "Pallone, shut up, sit down, eat your pasta, and listen to my wife praise you for the great series you're having. I'm even hearing that at home."

Game seven was uneventful for me. I worked second base and I watched John Kibler destroy the strike zone, as usual, and I thought, "So much for Vargo's theory of saving the senior umpire for the last game. Obviously, 'senior' doesn't mean 'best.' " St. Louis won easily, 6–0, and I survived all my controversial calls. I thought I proved to my peers that, without a doubt, I belonged.

After we dressed, I said my goodbyes to everyone on the crew. As I headed toward Kibler, he shook my hand and said, "We'll never be friends, but you did a great job." I said, "Well, that's all I've ever asked—to be respected for my work." But once I got outside I thought,

"Here's a guy I worked seven crucial games with, and he doesn't have the class to compliment me without sticking it to me first." I shook my head, thinking, "I'm lucky he feels that way. I wouldn't want to be his friend anyway."

Once I got home, I reflected on how important it was for me to hear all that praise. I realize that no matter how I talk about this now, it will sound like I'm making myself out to be the best umpire in the history of baseball. I don't want it to sound that way. I mention it to point out that in order to survive the first nine years of my career, I had to praise myself. If I hadn't been labeled a scab back in 1979, people would have long ago discovered my real ability, and I wouldn't have had to keep proving myself year after year. All the praise from people who knew the game reinforced what I believed about myself all along.

But my biggest motivation during the playoff series was proving that I was worthy of a World Series. I thought, "God damn it, I showed all those guys who ostracized me and hated my guts and rooted for me to screw up—like the Froemmings, the Tatas, and the Kiblers—that I can umpire with anyone." It's one thing for people to hear that you're a good umpire from someone else, like Engel and Runge, but it's another thing when they can see it for themselves. And you better believe that every major league umpire watched those playoffs.

Another thought occurred to me for the first time. Next year would be my tenth; maybe that would be a good time to end my baseball career and walk away from all the bullshit. I would never have considered that until I'd proved to everyone that I was a good umpire. But now I *had* proved it, and maybe that was enough. Maybe it was time to get my private life in order permanently, and start a new career. I wanted the World Series first, but how long could I fend off all the rumors and the talk behind my back: "Did you hear the latest about Dave Pallone?"

I made up my mind that Bart Giamatti would be the person to talk to about this. Unlike Chub Feeney, he had told me his door was always open to me. And he not only knew my quality as an umpire now; he'd also shown me that he had sympathy for me as a human being. I just sensed that he was the right person to give me the inspiration and advice I needed to go forth from baseball in another direction. So I called Giamatti's office to arrange a meeting for January, and then I went to London for New Year's.

I stayed two extra days in London and came back with a renewed sense of purpose. But something was strange when I got home—I had thirty-eight calls on my answering machine. I thought, "God, that's weird. How could I have thirty-eight calls in five days? What the hell's going on?" But I wanted to wind down from the long flight home, so I relaxed for a couple of hours and sorted through my mail. Then, finally, I sat down to play my messages back.

Before I could start, the phone rang. It was a friend from Florida. He said, "Dave, this is Joe. Where have you been?"

I said, "I just walked in the door. I was in London for New Year's."

"Well, I've been trying to call you."

"I was just about to turn on my answering machine to see who called me. I have thirty-eight calls."

"You haven't checked it yet?"

"No. I was just going to do that."

"Have you listened to your outgoing message lately?"

"No. But it's the same as it's always been."

"No, it's not. It's a very weird message. It doesn't sound like you at all."

"What do you mean? What's it say?"

"I don't even want to repeat it. Listen to it."

So I turned it on—and I heard a portion of the filthiest, most obscene message you can imagine. So I said, "Jesus, let me call you back." I hung up and listened to the whole message, and it made me sick. It was another man's voice saying, "Francis, I want to fuck you, and I want your big cock up my ass"—and it went on like that. It was unbelievably vile. I didn't recognize the voice on the message, but it had to be someone who knew I was gay because that message was obviously about being gay.

Plus, I had only one close friend named Francis, so it had to be someone who knew both of us.

I started replaying my messages in dread. Close friends had called, including Francis. He was beside himself; he didn't know what to do. When I hadn't returned home as planned, he called up and heard the message. He said, "What the fuck is going on?" and hung up. Then he called back to double-check.

The secretary in the National League office called, too. She was unbelievably nonchalant; she actually left a normal message: "David, this is Cathy. Please call me when you get in." Jesus Christ, could anyone be stupid enough to think that the message they heard was really *mine?* (I asked her later, "Cathy, how could you possibly leave me a normal message like that? Did you really think that was *me* talking?" She said, "No. But I didn't know what else to do. It's a good thing Mr. Giamatti didn't call." Understatement of the year.) There were also a few calls from a guy doing a survey. Finally, he got the operator involved and she said, "Sounds like *she's* in trouble. Maybe we should call the police."

I phoned Francis immediately to let him know I was home. He said, "Jesus Christ, Dave, if you weren't home by today, I was going to get the police to open up your apartment. I was really worried that someone had broken in and killed you, and did this to your machine." Francis and I discussed the phone message and tried to puzzle out the mystery.

That was all I knew until a week later, when I got my phone bill and noticed that someone had charged long-distance calls from Atlantic City to my AT&T credit card, and the dates of those calls were identical to the time I'd spent in London over New Year's. How anyone had gotten my credit card number was a mystery. But I called AT&T, and they traced the number that had been most frequently called from Atlantic City; it was the home number of a gay acquaintance of mine named Lane. He'd obviously called his home to get his own messages. I knew Lane only casually from the gay bar scene, and he had never been to my apartment. But a friend of his named Mac—whom I dated a few times but recently had a falling out with—*had* been to my place before. Mac must have told Lane the kind of answering machine I had; and since Lane had a devious mind, he must have figured, ''Dave's code is probably something simple, like his umpire number.'' Which it was: number 26. Then they tried it until they accessed my outgoing message.

Francis knew Lane, too. He said, ''My advice is to ignore it. Pay the $240 phone bill. It's $240 out the window, but it would cause you more problems than you need if you pressed the issue. This kid is evil. He's got a very sick mind. So it's money well spent. Let the kid get away with it.'' I thought it over and took his advice—which I usually did. I couldn't afford this kind of aggravation now.

When I finally did run into Lane again about a month later, he greeted me with a strange smirk—like he was expecting a reaction from me. He was probably hoping I'd come right out and say, ''You'll never believe what somebody did to me,'' so he could get satisfaction. But I just said, ''I went to London for New Year's and I had a great time. I'm really happy with the way it went.'' I had a nice smile on my face, which I think annoyed him even more.

But there was a negative aftermath to all this. A host of people who called me didn't leave messages because they were so shocked. I mean, who knows the subconscious effect the message had on people who knew me? A couple of people I knew pretty well stopped calling me altogether and never talked to me again. And I didn't find out about some of the others who'd called until the baseball season four months later, and then I had to explain it all over again. I had to lie to everybody: ''I don't know what the hell happened. And I don't know anyone named Francis.''

This really drove home how incredibly vulnerable you are if you're gay in this society. The only reason for leaving a message like that was to humiliate and expose me. Lane capitalized on my secret life by knowing how scared I was of exposure. Our mutual friend Mac—who knew me so much better—probably told him, ''Dave's scared shitless of being found out.'' So Lane was cocky enough to charge all those easily traceable calls to my credit card to flaunt how much power he had over me. He was right; I was totally trapped behind my mask. My vulnerability left me paralyzed.

The real problem wasn't *being* gay; it was the fear of people *finding out* I was gay. Aside from the loneliness, that fear was the main reason my life was so miserable. The thought of being at someone else's mercy like that gave me the most sickening feeling I ever had, next to losing someone I loved. And it was double jeopardy for me—who would ever have bothered to leave that kind of message on the phone of a shoe salesman? What if Bart Giamatti *had* called? Or Eddie Vargo? Or Paul Runge? Or just a newspaper reporter?

This horrifying fear of exposure is the Achilles' heel of every hidden life. No matter how thick the mask, someone can always yank it off. With one stroke, even a stranger could strip away every defense, every piece of armor I spent a lifetime hiding behind. That's why it's so important for gay people to take off their masks themselves and at least try to live the truth.

One other thought on this event: it made me understand that the time *had* come to change my life. It strengthened my feeling that I should leave baseball after I got my World Series. But I didn't see the wisdom in coming out of the closet in baseball yet. If I did, I knew I'd face tougher recriminations than when I had crossed the picket line. (Jim Quick's insensitive response—even after he'd spent so much time with me—told me that.) Besides, I'd dodged so many bullets before, I felt I could just dodge another one for now. Also, if I came out, they'd never give me a World Series, so my career would be incomplete.

Meantime, as far as I was concerned, I was going to tell Paul Runge and that would be it—because then I would have revealed the truth to the only people in baseball who really mattered to me anyway. Also, there was no safety net in baseball. No gay had ever come out, so there was no pattern of acceptance. If the Froemmings,

Kiblers, Vargos, Tatas, and even Quicks were the measure of baseball's mentality, then it wouldn't be worth it. They would absolutely crucify me—and I wasn't about to go through that now. Christ, I'd been there before.

(17)

THE ROSE THING

My new year started with a jolt. During the second week of January, I got a strange call from my friend Sam Gennaro in upstate New York. We had become casual friends five years ago when we both lived in Boston. He wanted to tell me that Bill Desadora and Larry Blodgett—two Saratoga Springs men he introduced me to the previous October, and whom we visited briefly in December—were in serious trouble. He said, "Dave, you're not gonna believe what happened. Larry and Bill got arrested. It's a big thing up here. It's in all the newspapers."

I said, "Why? What do the papers say?"

"That they're part of a sex ring with teenage boys. They're accused of running it out of their homes. The media's calling it the 'Saratoga sex scandal.'"

"You gotta be shittin' me. Thank God nothing went on while *we* were there. That could've cost my career. Jesus Christ, how the hell could you introduce me to these guys and bring me to their house?"

"I didn't know anything about it. I feel terrible; I never would've taken you there if I knew what they were into."

When I hung up, I thought about it briefly. Although I was shocked, I just counted my blessings that I'd only been at Larry's house one time for about twenty-five minutes, and I wasn't one of his or Bill's close friends. And I dismissed it without a second thought. I refocused on my upcoming meeting with Bart Giamatti to discuss my future.

The next week, when I walked into Giamatti's office dressed in a suit, he gave me a broad smile, a friendly tease about the suit, and a hearty handshake. I loved feeling so at ease with him; he made me feel like I could talk about anything. The first thing out of his mouth was what an amazing playoff series I had. He was impressed also with something Whitey Herzog had told him the day after game three: "Talk about umpires having a great game. Dave Pallone had a *career* yesterday." Giamatti grinned at me: "It isn't every day that Whitey Herzog bothers to compliment an umpire like that." It made me feel great; I could see in his smile that he was proud.

That's when I said, "You know, this is my tenth year, and I've been thinking about my future in the game."

He lit a cigarette. In his paternal tone he said, "David, you strike me a person who wants to do more than just umpire for the rest of your life. I've mentioned school to you, but you didn't go this winter like I suggested, did you?" I said no, and his brow pinched in. "God damn it, Pallone, you're too intelligent not to be in school. I just don't think baseball is for you anymore."

I said, "Well, that's really one of the reasons I'm here. I *am* thinking about leaving the game. But I always promised myself I would never leave until I got my World Series ring. I've worked the All-Star Game, and I proved in the playoffs that I'm capable of working important games under pressure. Wouldn't it be great to round off my career with a World Series?"

He thought it over. "I can't promise you anything, but if you come to me during the season and you tell me you're really ready to retire, and if the opportunity presents itself, I will do everything in my power to help you round off your career with a World Series."

I thanked him and changed the subject. I said, "You know, I felt some remorse last year over bringing you my crew problems. I really believe you were thinking of my best interests. And as far as the 'fourteen consecutive days' thing with Vargo, I guess it *was* just a lack of communication."

"I'm glad to hear you say that. It makes me feel that you're thinking things out more clearly. That's why I decided to return half your fine."

I laughed. "By the way, I'm still waiting for my money."

"You didn't get your check?"

I said no, and he got up and marched me right out to Phyllis Collins's office and had her write me a check for one hundred dollars. Then the three of us chatted about my plans to vacation in Spain. Giamatti said, "He's always traveling to somewhere exotic." As I shook his hand goodbye, I said, "Well, I think traveling is very *educational.*" He grinned and shook his head as I left.

In the elevator, I felt confident that I now had a real chance to get the World Series in '88. I was feeling so good, I promised myself that, no matter what, I would not give Giamatti a hard time about the crew I was working with, and I would do everything possible to get along with Eddie Vargo.

Those promises were tougher to keep than I expected. Hard to believe, but even after getting the fiftieth-anniversary All-Star Game and doing a great job in the league championship series, spring training was the same old crap. Once again I got the cold-shoulder-and-sarcasm routine from the union umps. It was tough to accept that baseball hadn't taken any steps to banish the ostracism. The game just kept shitting where it ate.

One thing I started doing a few springs before to escape the ostracism was treating some of the minor league umpires to an evening out. I remembered all the years I struggled to live on forty dollars a week, so I took these guys to a nightclub that features a comedian I knew, and I put their food on my tab. Whether or not they looked up to me, I don't know. I just felt good giving something back—and making new friends at the same time. And to be honest, it was a little ego trip. I was a major league ump, and they were trying to get there, too, and they knew me, so it gave me a sense of worth I never got from most of my peers.

For some reason, Eddie Vargo gave me a great spring-training schedule. Most of my games were close to Clearwater, and I wasn't slated for more than fourteen consecutive days. He was so cooperative, it gave me hope that maybe he would return me to Engel and Runge. But then I got my crew assignment for the '88 regular season: Vargo had put me on John Kibler's crew with Eric Gregg and Jim Quick. So much for Vargo's goodwill. I was upset—and I'm sure Kibler wasn't thrilled, either. But I remembered my vow at Giamatti's office, so I told myself, "I'll make the best of it."

When Kibler learned I was on his crew, he left a message for me in Florida to be at our opening game at Dodger Stadium for a meeting two hours before the game. I thought it was a step in the right direction; if he was bothering to call me, maybe he was trying to make things easier for me. On the other hand, I still had a foul taste in my mouth from his "We'll never be friends" remark after the playoffs. Little did I know how true that remark would prove to be—because in a few weeks John Kibler would play a central role in the strangest, most controversial game of my career.

Just before that, though, I had other business. In late April I had a day off in L.A., waiting to work the next series after Bob Engel's crew left. I stayed at the same hotel as Engel and Runge, and we caught up on things. The night of one of their games I had dinner with Bob's wife, Pat, and Paul's wife, Stasia, in Hollywood. After dinner we went back to the hotel for cocktails. Pat had excused herself, leaving Stasia and me alone to talk, when out of nowhere, Stasia said, "Dave, I have to ask you a question. You don't have to answer if you don't want to."

I said, "What is it?"

She said, "Are you gay?"

I was shocked that she would ask me in that manner—but I wasn't angry, because she was my close friend. In fact, it made it easier for me to say "Yes." She touched my arm. I said: "I always told myself that if anybody of significance in my life ever asked, I would tell the truth. I put you in that category."

She said, "I'm so glad you told me the truth. It doesn't make a difference to me—or to Paul. I don't even think it will bother the kids. You know they love you."

"Will you tell them?"

"I could never lie to them."

"I wouldn't want you to. You should always tell your children the truth." (Stasia eventually did tell her son, Brian, who was eighteen at the time. He's a big, strong, athletic kid; Paul would tell me later, "Brian was such a macho redneck, he didn't even like to go to San Francisco." Brian's response to Stasia was, "No way." She said, "He is." Brian said, "You're believing all those stories, but he is not." She said, "Yes, he is." Brian said, "How do you know this?" She said, "He told me." Brian said, "He did not." It took a while before he believed it, but he eventually accepted it beautifully.)

Revealing your true self to a friend is a wrenching experience that most people never go through. It toughens you, but it also reminds you of your vulnerability. Because a truth like this can devastate people you love and ripple down to people *they* love, and that can end up costing you a lot of people's love and trust. And you have no defense against it.

Stasia gave me a big hug and thanked me for trusting her enough to share my secret. I told her I planned to tell Paul the next time we were both in New York—but I knew in my heart that she would tell him first. I thought that might open the door a little, but I was still worried how he would react. His respect and support were still very important to me.

That was the main thing on my mind the last two weeks in April. Then came Saturday night, April 30, 1988: the most unforgettable game of my career. It was the Mets against the Reds at Cincinnati's Riverfront Stadium before a crowd of forty-one thousand. Gregg had home plate, Quick had third, Kibler had second, I had first. Early on, Gregg called a Reds runner out on a close play at the plate, and manager Pete Rose bolted out of the dugout to argue. I noticed how mad Rose was; his face was puffed with rage before he reached Gregg. He argued vehemently, got nowhere, and returned to the dugout. It's one of baseball's ritual dances; the ending is always the same.

Rose liked to check the replays a lot. He did this time,

too, then came back to the rail and gestured to Gregg that his call had been correct. When Rose yelled, "Hey, Eric, if the next call goes *for* me, I'll send you some champagne at dinner," I remembered that Gregg had told me before the game that Rose promised to set him up for dinner at his restaurant, the Riverfront. So everything was pretty loose at this point.

Then the fire ignited. In the sixth inning, the Reds' starting pitcher, Tom Browning, threw a gopher ball to Darryl Strawberry, giving the Mets a 4–2 lead. Two batters later, Browning sailed one into Gary Carter, even though he hadn't hit a batter all year. After that, I had a tinderbox sensation. And sure enough, the next inning was the spark. Mookie Wilson connected off Browning for a two-out triple, bringing Tim Teufel to the plate. Just as Browning went into his windup, Teufel stepped out of the batter's box—without calling time out—and Browning stopped his motion. Gregg immediately called a balk, and the run scored.

But Gregg blew the play. Normally, stopping your pitching motion constituted a balk, but the rule book also stated that if the batter stepped out of the box intentionally to cause a pitcher to balk, then the balk would be nullified. Maybe Gregg forgot the rule. Out came Rose, really pissed—and he had a right to be pissed. He reminded Eric about the rule, but I heard Eric say, "No, that's not what happened." That *was* what happened— and Rose knew it. So he was mad at Eric, but even madder at Tim Teufel. Pete Rose didn't believe in "pussy" baseball; his philosophy as a player was more like: "Hit, hustle, make it happen." Yet here was Teufel *backing out* of the box to try to get a run home. Rose's disdain was written across his face like a newspaper headline: YOU PUSSY, TEUFEL.

But he didn't say a word to Teufel. Instead, he marched from home plate directly to the mound. You didn't have to be a brain surgeon to figure out what he was saying to Tom Browning. Sure, he might have been telling him to calm down, or reminding him of the situation. But do you suppose he might also have said something like, "I want you to drill that little fucker''? That would have been characteristic of Rose's fiery, competitive nature.

Well, guess what? On the next pitch, Browning uncorked a fastball that drilled Teufel in the back. Browning was a control pitcher throwing a control game until then; I think everyone who knew baseball realized that Rose ordered him to hit Teufel. Instantly Darryl Strawberry exploded out of the dugout in a beeline for Browning. I thought, ''Uh-oh, here we go,'' and the benches emptied and players started swinging away in a full-fledged donnybrook. The fans got hot, the players got hot, the managers got hot, the umpires got hot.

Eventually we cooled everybody down. Then we had to decide: ''Who gets tossed and who stays?'' It was obvious that Strawberry had to go for instigating the fight. And Browning had to go for drilling Teufel intentionally. I noticed that Browning—who'd been thrown to the ground during the melee—was sitting in the dugout. So I went over and informed him he was gone. He said, ''Why are you throwing *me* out?'' I said, ''You intentionally threw at the batter. You have to go. And Strawberry's gone, too.'' Browning didn't say a word. He just looked at me sheepishly, got up, and left the dugout. That confirmed for me that Rose *did* order him to throw at Teufel. Otherwise, Browning would have raised holy hell.

I went back to Kibler and I said, ''John, I think we should run Rose. He told Browning to hit Teufel.'' Kibler looked surprised. ''No!'' he protested. ''You're crazy. I'm not gonna do that.'' I said, ''He told him to hit the guy, John. How can you ignore that?'' Kibler looked at me like I was a rookie arguing a called third strike. ''We're not doing that,'' he barked—and he walked away.

That offended me. I had ten years' experience; where did he get off dismissing me like that? Granted, he had twenty-three years; but I knew what I was talking about. I knew it was because Kibler didn't want to take advice from a scab—and least of all from me. So now I was pissed that he wouldn't listen to me, and he was pissed that I was trying to tell him what to do. Meantime, we got everyone back to their positions and we finished the inning without further damage.

The score was tied 5–5 when the Mets batted in the ninth. They had two outs, Howard Johnson on second base, and Mookie Wilson facing Reds ace reliever John Franco. Wilson grounded into the hole at shortstop, but Barry Larkin scooped it up and made the long throw. It was slightly wide, so first baseman Nick Esasky had to stretch for it, lifting his foot off the bag. I didn't make the call right away, because Mookie Wilson hadn't reached first base yet. Once Wilson reached the bag, I pointed at Esasky's foot and yelled, "No. You're off the bag. *Safe.*" As I pointed, Mets first-base coach Bill Robinson stepped into fair territory, yelling, "He came off! He came off!"

Meantime, as Esasky turned to me and protested, "Why's he safe?" Howard Johnson kept running for home. If Esasky hadn't lost his composure, he would have seen Johnson racing home and nailed him easily. He probably assumed time was out, but he was wrong. No one called time, and it wasn't automatic just because he decided to argue. Rose stormed onto the field, incensed. His first words to me were, "Why'd you wait so goddamn long to make the call?"

I tried to explain. "Pete," I said calmly, "I had to wait until the play was over."

He said, "You waited too long to make the call." He paced back and forth, his anger building. "Jesus Christ, it's *your* fault the run scored."

I said, "It's not my fault your first baseman fell asleep. Instead of arguing the call, he should've thrown home."

Rose snapped. He screamed, "You blew it!" and pointed his finger at my face. Until then I was calm. But when I saw that finger in my face, I flashed back to my "Pallone, stick that thumb up your ass!" days from umpire school, and I said to myself, "Stick that finger up your ass, Rose"—and I started pointing my finger back at him. I knew that if I didn't do something, it would look like I had let a manager get the best of me.

So now we were both pointing fingers at each other. I

said, "Pete, his foot was off the bag, the runner was safe, and that's all there is to it."

He brought his finger closer to my face and he screamed, "It's *your* fault! You stole the goddamn game from us! You waited too goddamn long!"

I was boiling now; I pointed back and said, "Get your fuckin' finger out of my face. Put that fuckin' hand down."

He totally lost it; he leaned in and gave me a shove. I said, "You're fuckin' gone," and I threw his ass out. But as I turned around to walk away, he shoved me from behind with his forearm. I turned around to face him, astonished he'd done that. I said, "You're in a lot of fuckin' trouble, Rose."

He pointed to his own face and screamed, "You touched me! You touched me!" He was so out of control, I knew I shouldn't do anything in response, that my crew had to step in and take control and get him settled down—which they did by helping to restrain him and get him off the field. It was then that I first noticed the mood of the crowd. All hell had broken loose; people were booing, screaming, throwing things onto the field. (I didn't know it then, but the Cincinnati radio broadcasters were fueling the fire by badmouthing me.) I thought, "My God, we're gonna have a riot on our hands."

When we tried to get the game started again, John Franco stuck it to us by walking off the mound and refusing to pitch. That agitated the crowd into a frenzy of cursing and booing. For about fifteen minutes, it felt like a fuse had been lit for a bomb. Debris rained down on the field from everywhere: golf balls, baseballs, food, seat cushions, toilet paper, hats, even coins. (Coins are dangerous. One time in San Francisco, the umpires were standing at home plate before the game when a fan tossed a coin that hit Eddie Montague in the face, causing a deep cut. I picked up the coin—a quarter—and showed it to Montague, and then I saw the blood. I said, "Hey, you're *bleeding*." He was a little shocked, but he took it lightly. "Well, a quarter's good," he said. "I can use it to call an ambulance.")

When a ghetto blaster flew from the stands and landed

in the on-deck circle, the crew decided to leave the field and call the public-address announcer. As we ran off, people dumped beer on us; it was like a feeding frenzy all around us. Safely under the stands, Kibler called the PA guy and told him to warn the crowd to stop throwing things. I told Jim Quick, "We should really forfeit this game right now. We're gonna have a problem when we go back out there." Quick looked at me helplessly. "Hey, I'm not in charge," he said. "Kibler's the man you have to talk to."

Well, you never want to forfeit a major league game if you can help it. So I decided to hold off with Kibler and wait and see. When we returned to the field and got ready to resume play, John Franco refused to pitch again. This reignited the crowd into throwing things again—especially at me. I would have loved to deck Franco; if he had started pitching right away, the fans would have calmed down—and he knew it. Meantime, up in the Reds' radio booth, the Reds' announcers, Marty Brennaman and Joe Nuxhall, were taking shots at me. Nuxhall called me a "scab" and a "liar" on the air. (This was later documented, because their broadcasts were fed into the clubhouse TV, so it got taped along with the game. In fact, they were so unprofessional they got a reprimand from the commissioner's office for "inciting the unacceptable behavior of some of the fans.")

Well, shit, I wasn't going to stand out there much longer dodging everything but bullets. Finally, I took a few steps toward Kibler at second and yelled, "John, they're still throwing things. I have to come off the field." He gestured at me and yelled something I couldn't hear through the boos. I looked at the first-base stands, where people were gesturing and cursing and recklessly tossing things, and I said, "Fuck this," and I trotted toward the Mets' dugout. I felt my safety was endangered—and I assumed the whole crew would be trotting off behind me. But when I got to the dugout and looked back, nobody else was coming. I could hear fans yelling things like, "You asshole, Pallone!" and "You're gonna die!" And there was Kibler, still at second base, staring at me in disgust.

By leaving the field alone, I had shown Kibler up. At the time I didn't care. I cared about my safety—and he hadn't done a thing about that. As crew chief and a twenty-three-year veteran, it was Kibler's responsibility to oversee the safety of not just me—whom he detested as a scab—but also every person on that field. Had it been my call, I'd have forfeited the game on the spot. They had their warning; the fans kept littering the field; the Reds' own pitcher deliberately stalled the game and incited the crowd. Forget it. You couldn't invent a more classic forfeit situation if you tried. But, in my opinion, Kibler didn't want that black mark, that scar, on his record. And he definitely didn't want *me* to be the cause of it.

That was what went through my mind as I left the dugout and hurried up the runway. When I entered the Mets' clubhouse, I saw Strawberry, pitcher Bob Ojeda, and the clubhouse man watching the game on the TV monitor and listening to Brennaman and Nuxhall's account. Ojeda said, "Dave, you wouldn't believe what these guys are doing to you. They're calling you everything in the book. It's unbelievable." Strawberry said, "They're rippin' you, man."

I went into the umpires' dressing room and turned on the TV. There was no picture, just the radio broadcast, so I listened and seethed. The crew was finishing the game without me—ironically with Kibler taking my place at first base. When the top of the ninth ended, I heard Brennaman say, "The score is 6–5 on a call by an incompetent umpire named Dave Pallone." I was so goddamn mad, I turned off the TV, yanked my shirt off, and sat there in the cubicle directly across from Kibler's, pumping adrenaline and waiting for the game to end. Everything went through my mind: "How can those assholes talk like that on the air? . . . Why the fuck didn't the crew follow me off the field? . . . This is the worst ordeal of my career. . . . Is somebody gonna try to kill me when I leave the stadium? . . . Maybe I waited too long to make the call. . . . Was I right to leave the field? . . ."

The game ended about twenty minutes later, and in came Quick, Gregg, and Kibler—all visibly shaken.

(Kibler later admitted in *Sports Illustrated*, "It was as unruly a crowd as I have ever seen. I was afraid when I went to first base.") Kibler locked the door and asked me heatedly, "You think I handled that wrong out there?"

I said, "Yes. I think you should have forfeited the game."

"Why did you leave the field?"

He was ready to detonate, and I didn't want to start a big fight, so I said, "When you motioned to me, I couldn't hear you. I thought you were *telling* me to leave the field."

Jim Quick chimed in, "I told you it was a miscommunication. He never would've left the field."

That helped calm Kibler down. He thought it over and said, "Okay. We'll let the reporters talk to me. I'm going to say that I told you to leave the field." For a split second I thought he was trying to protect me. Then I realized he didn't give a shit about me; he was just trying to cover himself.

Meantime, while we were having this conversation, Pete Rose was over in the Reds' clubhouse, holding court for the press. He told them, "I don't understand why an umpire needs four seconds to make a call. Molly Putz could have scored from second base. Howard Johnson runs good, but he's not the wind. Plus, if Nick goes to make the throw to the plate, he hits the coach. What's he doing on the field?" He was wrong about all of this. It didn't take four seconds for me to make the call; it took more like two. And Bill Robinson was nowhere near Esasky, so he couldn't have interfered. Esasky interfered with himself by losing his cool.

Rose did say he was sorry he bumped me, but also that I had started it by poking him first with my finger. With TV cameras trained on him sitting behind his desk, he pointed to a big red mark under his left eye and said, "Get that on camera. Get a picture of that. Zoom in on that." Many fans don't know about this dramatic performance—or about my reaction to it, because I never told my side of the story publicly. Well, here it is.

First of all: *I never touched Pete Rose.*

Second: Does anybody have a tape that shows any kind

of mark under Pete Rose's eye immediately after he says I touched him there? I have yet to see one. The tapes I *have* seen shows nothing.

Third: I happened to have clipped my fingernails in the dressing room before that game. With my nails that short, there was absolutely no way my finger could have made as big a scratch as Rose showed off to the cameras—a little too eagerly and *after the fact.*

Fourth: If you study the game tape, you can see that at the moment when Rose claimed I touched him, his head never moved backward. That's an important issue. I realize we're not discussing the Zapruder film here; but if my finger had nicked Rose as close to his eye as where that cut later appeared, and with as much force as it would have taken to mark him like that, how could his head *not* have jolted back? Nobody's that strong. But, for argument's sake, let's say I *did* nick him with my finger, and that we forgive Rose for the first push on the grounds that I provoked him. What provoked the *second* shove—when I had my back turned and I was walking away?

For me, the $64,000 question is: How did that big scratch end up under Rose's eye? In my personal opinion, after Rose left the field and had time to consider the consequences of shoving an umpire *twice,* either he or someone in the clubhouse who was advising him inflicted that big scratch to make it look like I provoked the incident, and to get him off the hook.

Meantime, back at the umpires' dressing room, immediately after the game the Reds' security people placed a guard outside our door and told us not to leave until they could ensure our safety. Police offered me a ride back to my hotel, but Kibler said he would take me. So for the first time I would actually ride in the same car with my own crew—even if it was to a different hotel. Then the stadium's security chief came in and told us he'd driven our car under the stands near the players' parking lot and cleared the area for our exit. He said it was safe to leave, because there was no one out there except security people, and that the police would follow us until we reached our hotels. We said no to that; a police escort might draw too much attention to our car. That's how paranoid we were.

We left the dressing room cautiously, hurried through double door 7 into the parking area, and started toward the car. All of a sudden, somebody yelled, *"You really blew it, Dave!"*—and I literally jumped. I spotted the guy standing next to a cop, and the first thing that flashed through my mind was Jack Ruby shooting Lee Harvey Oswald. It sent a chill up my spine. I couldn't believe that this guy was standing ten feet away—next to a goddamn cop yet, who only then grabbed him and arrested him.

I blasted the security chief: "I thought you said there was no one out here! What if this guy had a *bottle* to throw, or a *gun?* Jesus Christ, you told us it was safe!" I lost control; I was nervous and afraid for my life. I said, "You people are telling us security is tight, and there's a guy that has no goddamn business being here. He could've been a *Jack Ruby!*" He said, "We're sorry. You're right. We don't know how that happened." Then they ushered us to the car, and we got the hell out of there.

Up in my room, I phoned around until I located Bart Giamatti in Boston. I said, "Bart"—I was so juiced, I didn't remember to call him "Mr. Giamatti"—"this is Dave Pallone. I'm calling you because we had an incident in Cincinnati tonight. Did anyone get in contact with you about it?" He said, "No. I just walked in the door." I said, "Well, I hate to tell you this, but you better sit down. And you might want to turn on your TV." Then I told him what had happened. His response was, "Jesus, David. I'm really sorry this happened to you. Let me start making some phone calls. Stick around and I'll be back in touch."

So I turned on the TV and waited. After about fifteen minutes the phone rang, and I thought it was Giamatti. "Pallone," a stranger's voice said, "you screwed up, you asshole. If you go on the field tomorrow, you're dead. I'll kill you." I hung right up. A few minutes later the phone rang again. A different voice said, "Pallone—" and as soon as I knew it wasn't Giamatti, I hung up. I thought, "I have to get out of this room." So I went downstairs to the hotel bar. I had stopped drinking scotch after ballgames because I'd gained weight, but I needed a drink now to calm myself down.

That year I had no close friends in Cincinnati, so I was alone with my anxiety. If I had been any other union umpire, the rest of my crew would have rallied to my support and said, "Dave, you're coming out with us tonight." But not one of them so much as called or left me a message at the desk. I can't say I expected their support; I guess I just hoped they might offer it for once. Maybe riding in the same car with them caused me to drop my guard.

While I sat at the bar, I spotted Arthur Richman, the Mets' traveling secretary and a great guy. He invited me to join him and his friends. When I did, they wanted to talk about the game. Arthur told me, "You made the right call at first base. I feel bad about the way things turned out." But then everybody realized it was best to drop the subject. I proceeded to have four double scotches while I talked with one of Arthur's friends, a woman who was working as Dustin Hoffman's secretary while he shot *Rain Man* in Cincinnati. We talked about Hoffman, acting, and the movies, and it was a great release.

Finally, I went back to my room and turned on the TV to catch the late sports news. Sure enough, there I was arguing with Pete Rose and tossing him out of the game. The phone rang and I thought it was definitely Giamatti. But it was another crank with a death threat. I hung up and unplugged the phone and tried—unsuccessfully—to sleep.

At seven A.M., I dragged myself out of bed and plugged the phone back in. A few minutes later it rang, and it was Giamatti. He told me he had called back last night but couldn't get through. I explained what happened and he said, "I kind of thought that might be it. I really feel bad about it. But I talked to Kibler last night, and Phyllis Collins, and also Kevin Hallinan. He's on his way to Cincinnati now with Eddie Vargo. They'll be there before the game starts. We've all agreed that you should not work home plate today, as scheduled. We'd like you to work second base.'' I didn't like the idea, but I was nervous about the death threats and what the fans might do, so I said, ''Whatever you think is right.''

I went down to breakfast, where some of the Mets greeted me and asked if I was going to show up for the game. I said, ''Of course, I'll be there.'' They asked if I was working the plate, and I said, ''They told me not to. They want me to work second base.'' I felt terrible saying that; it sounded like I'd been intimidated and had caved in to the pressure. That could cost me the players' respect on the field, too, so I began to change my mind even before I finished my eggs.

At the ballpark that afternoon, I met with Vargo and Hallinan in the dressing room. I told Vargo I thought I should work the plate but that he could decide what was best. Hallinan reassured me that security had been tightened and that police would be in both dugouts, in the stands, and outside the dressing room at all times. Then the phone rang; it was Paul Runge for me. He asked me what was going on, and I explained. Then he said, ''You're still working the plate, right?''

''No. Everybody wants me at second base.''

''Who's everybody?'' He was disturbed.

''Giamatti, Vargo, Kibler.''

''Dave,'' he insisted, ''you cannot do that.''

I said, ''Paul, I don't *want* to do it. I think I belong behind the plate, because if I work second it'll look like everyone intimidated me.'' He asked me to put Kibler on the phone, which I did, and I knew exactly what Paul was telling him: ''John, if this was you, where would you work? You know damned well you'd work the plate. Forget the fact that Pallone's nonunion. This is important for the union, and it's important for *us*. He *must* work home plate.''

Well, Kibler and Vargo ended up agreeing, so I called Giamatti and told him. He said, ''I don't want you to do that.'' But I insisted that we all agreed and that I felt very strongly about it. He said, ''All right. If you feel that strongly, go ahead. But I want it absolutely clear— and you tell Runge this, and Vargo, and everyone else—

that it was the *union* that made you work home plate, and that I was firmly against it.''

Game time approached. Security was visible everywhere, and tension was thick. As soon as I stepped onto the field, the boos thundered through the stadium. Although nobody threw anything, some of the threats people screamed at me I wouldn't have expected to hear in a prison yard. The fans were wound up, like they were looking for something to happen. I remember thinking, ''God, it feels like everyone is here for *blood* today.'' So I was very wary. For example, I immediately noticed some fans sneaking down through the box seats and draping a white sheet over the rail that had a message scrawled on it in big red letters: FIRE PALLONE. Security nabbed the culprits and removed the sheet, but I was really upset that they had allowed anyone to get down there so easily.

I scanned the crowd anxiously, thinking about the ''Jack Ruby'' guy who had slipped through security last night. And I remembered a game years ago in New York when I threw out Mets manager Joe Torre. After the game, riding the subway to my hotel, I overheard two guys sitting across from me. One said, ''What do you think about that guy Pallone throwin' Torre out?'' His buddy said, ''Shit. I'm gonna go to the game tomorrow and *shoot* the fucker.'' The next day I got a call in the dressing room: ''If you go out on the field tonight, I'll shoot you.'' That reminded me now of the calls I got in the hotel the night before.

I had told the police about those threats before the game, but I knew it wouldn't make much difference. If someone was out there with a gun, how could you stop him from taking a shot? My theory was: if someone really wants to shoot you, they certainly won't call to warn you in advance. So I didn't believe it would happen here today. Even if I did think so, I couldn't let a threat keep me off the field. On the other hand, any umpire who says it doesn't affect him is a liar. Subconsciously, it *has* to bother you. I mean, you'd hear a balloon pop and, okay, you wouldn't be dead, and you'd realize it was just a balloon—but you'd get a hell of a jolt.

Just before game time, I noticed the Reds' owner,

Marge Schott, in her box with Dustin Hoffman. He nodded at me with that famous grin, as if to say, "I know you had a tough game last night. Good luck today." And it occurred to me that because he was such a celebrity, he was in the same boat as me when it came to crackpot death threats. Anyone in the public eye was a target.

This game was a rout; the Mets were leading 9–0 in the seventh. I was having a great game—there were no arguments, and I was calling solid balls and strikes. I was feeling very confident about my calls when, in the Mets' half of the inning, with a man on second, I called Reds pitcher Pat Perry for an unusual balk. In 1988 we had the "discernible stop" balk rule, which required a pitcher using a stretch to bring his hands to a discernible stop before delivering the pitch. Perry was in the process of intentionally walking the batter when, on one of his pitches, he failed to come to a discernible stop. Out-and-out balk, so I awarded the runner third base.

The Reds had been trying to set up a force play at third with the intentional walk, so the call took that away from them. The fans booed like crazy, and Rose got hot. From the dugout steps he yelled to Kibler, "What the fuck is goin' on? How come he's calling a balk on that?" Kibler didn't respond. Then I heard a Reds bench jockey yell, "That's a bullshit call! Pallone's sticking it to us!" In a sense he was right. Perry did balk (the replay confirmed that clearly), and I happened to be the one who called it, and I felt good that it happened, because it screwed the Reds. But I didn't invent it, and it didn't affect the outcome, because the Reds lost 11–0.

When we got back to our dressing room, Gregg and Quick congratulated me on a good game. I started to remove my shirt when in came John Kibler, loaded for bear. He told the clubhouse guy to leave, lock the door, and turned to me. "Who the fuck do you think you are?" he said.

I said, "What're you talking about?"

"Were you trying to get us killed out there? What the fuck are you doing calling that balk?"

That did it. I stood up and fired back with both barrels. "That *was* a balk," I yelled. "You haven't called a fuckin' balk the whole fuckin' year, and all of a sudden you're gonna tell *me* how to call a balk? *Fuck you.*''

Kibler's face turned red. ''You cocksucker!'' he said—and he lunged for me and grabbed my shirt. Jim Quick got between us and pulled him away. I said to Kibler, ''Don't you *ever* fuckin' touch me again. You fuckin' asshole, you're such a horseshit umpire you couldn't carry my jockstrap.''

Then he said something I didn't expect: ''Who would want to *touch* your jockstrap!''

That registered. Maybe he believed I was gay, and he was spreading some of the false rumors about me. So I said, ''Fuck you, you ignorant asshole!''

He lunged for me again. Just as Quick and Gregg stepped in, I swung at Kibler, but it got deflected, catching him on the shoulder and knocking him sideways. He stumbled near the table, regained his balance—and all of a sudden calmed down. But I didn't; I was ready to tear him apart.

At this point Vargo knocked, someone let him in—and I unloaded on him. ''I ain't workin' with this fuckin' crew again. Today's my last day of workin' with this crew. And I don't give a shit *what* you do about it.''

Kibler said, ''I don't *want* you on this crew anymore.''

Quick and Gregg kept us from getting at each other. Then Vargo said, ''Dave, do what you want. But you better be in Philadelphia tomorrow.'' He didn't suggest, ''Let's talk about this outside''; it was just, ''You better be in Philadelphia.'' As far as I was concerned, Vargo could kiss my ass along with Kibler, for all the good he did me.

Coincidentally, at that moment Bart Giamatti phoned the dressing room. He wanted to find out how things went in the game. Vargo talked a minute, and then I got on. Giamatti said, ''Eddie says things went well. I'm very pleased.''

I said, ''Well, we got a problem here. Are you going to be in your office tomorrow?'' He said yes, and my temper got the best of me again. I said, ''I'm comin' to see you. I am not workin' with this fuckin' crew after today.''

"Dave," he said calmly, "you can come here if you like, but I'm not going to switch you, and you must be in Philadelphia for tomorrow's game. What is it?"

I said, "We're having problems over the balk I called."

"As a matter of fact, I'm a little confused about the balk you called as well." That made me feel even blacker, so I signed off and told him I'd talk to him about it tomorrow.

But the next day I didn't go see him, and I didn't call. Instead, I went to Philadelphia, where Quick, Gregg, Kibler, and I had a closed-door meeting before the game. I spoke first to Kibler: "Lookit, we were all under tremendous pressure the last two days. I apologize for my actions." He didn't respond, so I continued. "You know, I can take criticism. I have respect for a crew chief. If you felt I did something wrong, if you felt it was not a balk, why couldn't you have come in and said, 'Dave, I don't think that was a balk. I think you should've used better judgment on the call'? I would've listened to you; I would've respected your opinion. But you came charging in accusing me of deliberately trying to cause you trouble. I don't take that from *anybody*."

He said, "Well, I shouldn't have yelled at you. If you want to stay on the crew, it's fine with me."

"I'm here," I said, "and I'll just stay." And that was how we left it. There was a chance that Kibler was being sincere, but there were other factors. For instance, if I had left his crew, that would have caused him some problems. It might have indicated to the league that he couldn't handle me. And he would not have wanted that mark on his record, because it was no secret now that he wanted to become a supervisor.

One final note about that meeting. As we were leaving, Vargo told me, "I saw the tape of the Rose thing. You never touched him." I said, "Thanks. I didn't think so."

Rose had a different view. That same day he'd told reporters, "I pushed him and I was wrong. But if he doesn't touch me, I don't touch him. I'd say it would be fair to suspend both of us." But my view was confirmed the next day when Bart Giamatti announced that he was suspending Rose for thirty days (the longest suspension since Leo Durocher had to sit out the entire 1947 season for activities "detrimental to baseball") and fining him ten thousand dollars. Giamatti said, "The National League will not tolerate the degeneration of baseball games into dangerous displays of public disorder. Nor will it countenance any potentially injurious harassment of any kind of the umpires."

I got this news when I was in Philadelphia. I was shocked. I figured he might get a week or, at the most, ten days. But thirty days and ten thousand dollars seemed incredible. I felt vindicated; I thought, "Giamatti really backed me to the hilt on this." But I also knew the press would be all over me at the ballpark that night. So I prepared a statement and went to the stadium. When I came around the corner leading to our dressing room, there were about fifteen reporters and camera crews waiting for me. I took a deep breath and waded into the crowd. As I shouldered through, I remarked, "I wonder what you people are here for"—and I expected to be mobbed. But incredibly, no one knew me. So I walked right past them into the dressing room.

Fifteen minutes later, I emerged with a security man and I addressed everyone: "Gentlemen, my comment on the thirty-day suspension of Pete Rose is 'No comment.' I have nothing to say about how the league handles its business. My responsibility is on the field, not off it. I just turn in a report. It's Mr. Giamatti's responsibility to decide the fate of that report." Faces sagged; they were hoping I'd say something rash to bury myself or, better yet, to bury Rose.

That same night Rose and the Reds announced he was appealing the suspension. He said, "No player or manager has greater respect for umpires than I do, and while I expected to be suspended, I am shocked by the length of the suspension. I also feel I should have been given the right to tell the league president my side of the story." I think Pete Rose *did* respect umpires. He and I had had many disagreements, but I had always found him reasonable and fair-minded. I remember when he was playing with the Phillies, and I called him out on a foul tip, and we had a big argument. Yet in the papers the next day he said, "Hey, Dave's a very good umpire. He just made a mistake." He didn't lash out at me personally, or even at my work. He only criticized one call, and he did it graciously.

I respected him for that—and even after the shoving incident I still respected him. In his heart, I bet, he still respected me.

ANOTHER PALLONE
INCIDENT

Beginning the day after Giamatti's announcement, the
media ran with the incident like it was big news. The replay
appeared on probably every sports show in the country.
And for a short time, wherever I went, I took abuse.
Since Rose had played in Philadelphia, they booed
the crap out of me there. Next we went to Montreal, and
the same thing happened, because Rose had played there,
too. It was like his ghost was haunting me for a while.
From Montreal we went to Chicago, where I went to eat
at Morton's—one of my favorite steak joints. People recognized me from TV, and the bartender kept introducing
me as "the Pete Rose guy." Afterward I escaped to a
favorite jazz bar, figuring that there at least I could hide
in obscurity. But when I entered, a singer I knew named
Brownie spotted me. She stopped the band, pointed me
out, and started singing her rendition of "The Rose." I
had to laugh; it looked like I was going to be stuck with
"the Pete Rose guy" tag for now.

For three solid months my face and name were in every
major newspaper in the country, and TV kept replaying
the tape of the incident. Friends called to ask if I had
seen my picture in *People* and *Newsweek* and *Sports Illustrated*. Reporters kept trying to line me up for interviews, and I did a couple, but then Eddie Vargo and I
agreed that I shouldn't do any more. Even so, I started
getting hate mail, including some from kids. One

scrawled in crayon, "Since you did a terrible job for Pete Rose I think you should learn to use crayons instead of being an umpire." Another letter said, "Your incompetence as an umpire was proved even more during the April 30th game in Cincinnati against Pete Rose. You really should consider a new line of work. Do yourself and the National Pastime a favor and leave." Throughout the winter, I received letters every day at my home with my baseball card enclosed and requests for autographs. I thought, "I'm finally a household name with kids—but for the wrong reason." It got me strangely depressed.

One other related, weird event: On Friday, April 29— the day before the Rose incident—I had gone to a clothing store in Cincinnati, where I purchased a navy-blue sport coat and a pair of white linen slacks, and arranged to have them sent by UPS to my home in New York. The package never arrived. The clothing store had it traced, and it turned out that the package never left Cincinnati. It was found in the UPS office, ripped open, the sport coat stolen, and the pants shredded and decorated with the words PETE ROSE in red ink. My best guess, at the time, was that someone at UPS who recognized my name did the damage. So for the rest of that year, whenever I had anything mailed to me, I had it addressed to a friend's apartment in my building.

I had a lot of time during that season to review the Pete Rose thing, and I did have some regrets. For one thing, I shouldn't have left the field alone, because the only one who looked bad was me. I should have gone up to Kibler and said, "Let's leave. We're gonna get killed." And if he didn't do it, then I should have said, "I'm holding you personally responsible for our safety" and let John Franco keep sticking it to us until Kibler *had* to forfeit the game, or the other umpires told Kibler they agreed with me that we should leave. The other thing I regret was my reaction to Kibler in the dressing room. I was too emotional and out of control—like Rose was with me.

I was an explosive personality; everybody I worked for had said that about me—Pat McKernan, Chub Feeney, Blake Cullen, Eddie Vargo, Bob Engel, Paul Runge, and eventually Bart Giamatti. None of them was wrong. I could never excuse my temper; it was terrible. I had one of the shortest fuses a human being could possibly have. But no one can know how badly I wanted to go out there every night and have a perfectly calm game—no controversy, no arguments, no temper tantrums. I honest to God wanted people to like me as well as respect me. I always had a wide range of friends outside of baseball, and I rarely turned any of them off because of my temper. That was because I didn't *have* that explosiveness off the field, or that pressure of constantly being tested to prove myself.

Yet I blamed my temper on the emotional turmoil in my personal life. I had gone almost five years without a lasting relationship. I'd had the short affair with Rick, brief encounters with a few ballplayers, and some one-nighters with men in the gay bar scene. But no one had quite filled the void left by Scott. And that got to me over time. I was so distressed, day to day, it created a kind of undertow in my baseball life that started dragging me down. That was a big reason why I sometimes didn't think straight on the field.

Right after the Pete Rose incident, I got a call from Bart Giamatti's secretary informing me that Mr. Giamatti wanted to have me come in for a review of the incident the next time my crew was in New York. So on May 30 I went in to see him. Eddie Vargo was also there, so before we entered the conference room, I told Giamatti I wanted to speak to him privately afterward, and he said fine.

Then we went in and sat at a long conference table and watched the replay of the events of April 30 in Riverfront Stadium. Giamatti had an amused but concerned expression on his face—as if to say, "Well, another Pallone incident." He said, "You don't need to see any more of this, do you?" I said no, because I'd seen it a million times. Giamatti shut it off and said, "David, what do you think? Do you think you threw a little wood on the fire? Do you think you could have walked away? I've tried to tell umpires to walk away from an argument, but I can't seem to get that into your heads."

I said, "I know I've been told time and time again about my temper. But if you study the tape, you can see that I don't really get hot until he starts pointing at me. That's when I lost my temper and started pointing back at him. If you're going to say I should've walked away and prevented this from happening, how can I say that you're wrong? You're right; it never would've happened."

Giamatti nodded. "Do you feel that since you were a factor in this thing, you should be reprimanded?"

"I won't say that I should be reprimanded, because I really don't think I was at fault here. But I can see where I might've put wood on the fire."

Giamatti got up and paced away from the table. "So, you would not be upset if I fined you, say, a hundred dollars?"

I pulled out my checkbook. "I thought you might do that, so I came prepared."

He laughed. "I've always liked your style, Pallone. I knew you were an astute person. Now, we will follow the league policy of not divulging that you were fined or reprimanded. But I do have one other slight problem. I have an owners' meeting coming up, and I do work for them, and if they ask me if I reprimanded you, I must tell them."

I don't know what came over me, but then I said, "Well, you have *another* problem."

Both Giamatti and Vargo looked puzzled that I would say this. "What problem is that?" Giamatti said.

"Your door has always been open to me whenever I needed to talk to you. You've always treated me fairly, so now I think it's time to be fair to you. I think if you were to fine me a hundred dollars and you told that to the owners, they'd say, 'Are you nuts? How could you fine this guy just one hundred dollars?' I mean, guilty or not guilty, there's no in-between on this." Giamatti looked at me, surprised. I said, "Far be it from me to tell you what to fine me. But if you gave Pete Rose thirty days and a ten-thousand-dollar fine against what he makes a year, how does a one-hundred-dollar fine look against what I make a year? They're certainly not equivalent."

He said, "Do you think something like a thousand dollars might be more appropriate?"

I said, "I won't tell you what to fine me. But yes, that might be more equivalent." So, in essence, I ended up fining myself. I felt like I was repaying Giamatti for backing me up with the thirty-day suspension and for always being on my side. And although it cost me a thousand dollars, I thought it might end up being the best thousand I ever spent, especially if it made Giamatti think that much more of me.

After the meeting, Giamatti and I went into his office for a private talk. We started by kidding about all the flak I'd been getting over the Rose incident—which reminded him of the balk I'd called in the game the day after that. He said he and his wife were watching that game, and he got upset when I made that call. She had said, "Why are you so upset? Dave is having a good game." He said he told her, "I don't understand why he called that balk. That's the Italian in him. He's got to show them, 'See, I called a balk.' But he didn't have to call it."

I told him it wasn't just the Italian in me but also the *umpire*—and we shared a laugh. Then I changed the subject to my future. He asked if I was still planning to go to school, and I said yes, and I asked him if, as a past president of Yale, he had any influence to get me in there, or if he thought I should go to a junior college first. We threw ideas around awhile, and then I mentioned that I might like to be a lawyer someday.

He said, "I can see you as a lawyer. I could see something of the lawyer in you at work when you suggested the thousand-dollar fine." He complimented me on how I handled that situation, so it seemed the perfect time to say, "You know, I still want to retire at the end of the season. But I really want a World Series before I go."

"Pallone," he said, "get that out of your head. You're not working the World Series this year."

I didn't need a Ph.D. to know why: the Pete Rose thing threw it right out the window. There was no way he could reward me with the World Series and not catch hell from the supervisors, other umpires, almost certainly the press. But that was a letdown, because now I had to change my plans. A little depressed, I said, "That means I'll have to stay another year. And I honestly don't know if I can take it."

He said, "Tell me why you feel that way."

I had that father-and-son feeling again, so I said, "I have so much pressure with the ostracism and some of the things going on in my personal life. My personal life is a shambles."

"What *about* your personal life?"

I looked at his unjudging eyes and the words just rolled out: "I'm gay." He didn't flinch; he wasn't shocked. I said, "You know, Bart, one reason I told you is I think you can understand. In your career at Yale, you had a very vocal gay element in the student body."

He said, "Yes, that's true. In any case, your personal life is your own, Dave. I am not concerned about it—as long as it doesn't interfere with the game itself."

I said, "It doesn't. I would never do anything to hurt baseball. I love it too much. I have tried, all these years, to live my private life privately. All I ever wanted was for people to let me do that. But, unfortunately, you can't do that in a public life."

"Yes," he agreed, "you have to be discreet." He studied me a moment, then leaned toward me. "What the hell happened in St. Louis? How could you be so naive? That was a setup, Pallone. Don't you know that?"

He caught me off guard. I said, "Maybe. I don't know." Then I changed the subject: "I know I need to get on with my future."

"I wish I could help you with that."

"I believe you. But I just want you to feel that you've got a good umpire here, and a good person. I don't want to cause you any problems, yet that's all I feel I've done since you've been in office—problem after problem."

"I understand that you feel you need someone to listen to problems that others might consider petty. I know you don't have fellow umpires to go for that, and you don't have the union, so you have to come to the horse's mouth—which is me. I understand that, and I don't have a problem with it."

His compassion came through strong. I said, "Thank

you. I really appreciate hearing that. In the meantime, you just cost me a thousand bucks, so I think you owe me a lunch.''

He laughed and promised to buy me lunch whenever I wanted. So I picked a date in July after the All-Star Game, and we concluded the meeting. When I left, I was relieved that I had finally told him my secret and that he was still on my side. I felt very good about it; now that he knew the truth about me, maybe he would even be a stronger ally than before.

I remember the next four months more for meetings and revelations than for baseball games. After I unmasked myself to Giamatti, I felt it was time to do the same with my close friend Paul Runge. Stasia had informed me that she had already told him, and that he had taken it well. But I needed to hear it from Paul. So I arranged to meet him for lunch at the Loew's Summit Hotel in New York. Paul was very much a man's man; he had a hard, tough exterior and traditional macho ideas about men to go with it. But inside, he was a very sensitive and caring person.

I knew he wasn't comfortable with the idea of homosexuality, and that he didn't know much about it, so I was prepared for a cool reception. But he wasn't cool; like Bob Engel, he was warm and understanding. Essentially, I said that I'd wanted to tell him for a long time, but the right opportunity never presented itself. He said Stasia helped him understand that I was still the Dave Pallone he'd always treated like a brother, and he had no problem with that. I said I felt bad that he and Bob had always defended me against the rumors that I was gay, but that I couldn't take the chance of losing their support at the time. He just said, ''Don't worry about it. Your personal life is your business, and it won't make a difference to our friendship.'' And, as I continually found out through that year, it didn't. For the moment my world was still intact.

Then, the third week in July, the roof over that world began to fall. I went to the National League offices to meet Giamatti for the lunch we'd arranged back in our May 30 meeting. I was eagerly looking forward to talking about what I'd have to do to get a World Series in 1989 and to talk about possibly beginning school in the off-season. I was waiting for him to come out of his office so we could leave when he emerged and summoned me in. I just thought he was running late and he wanted me to wait in his office with him. But when I entered, he caught me by surprise by asking, "Did you see Kevin Hallinan out there?" I said, "No. Was I supposed to?" Then he explained that Hallinan had called him that morning and wanted to talk to us about something important, so Giamatti invited him over when I would be there.

"What's going on?" I asked, mildly curious.

"I don't know. Let's wait for Kevin." And within five minutes Hallinan was there. So I repeated my question to him.

Hallinan said, "Well, Dave, there's an investigation going on in upstate New York, and your name is involved. Do you know anything about it?"

I said, "Jesus Christ, no. I have no idea. What is it—drugs? Or did I rob a bank, or what did I do?" I was kidding, but he wasn't.

"I don't know. We don't have the details yet."

Now I was worried. "You gotta be shittin' me. I've done nothing wrong. I mean, why would my name even be up for investigation?"

"I'm in touch with a police officer who knows what's going on, and he's going to let me know where things stand."

"I don't understand this," I protested. "I'm totally in the dark." Neither he nor Giamatti reprimanded me or warned me to watch my ass, so I couldn't figure it out. I was also upset because I came there that day for a different kind of meeting; I was there to go out to lunch with just Giamatti and myself. That was when Giamatti said, "I'm sorry about this, David. Do you want to go to lunch now?" I said sure, and he said, "Why don't we go to that Italian place you like?" Then he invited Hallinan to come along.

So the three of us lunched at Anche Vivolo and talked of everything except baseball and the investigation. I remember that Giamatti liked the food so much, he had two orders of pasta. So I said, "I know another great Italian restaurant, called Oggi. It means 'today.'" Giamatti stopped eating. "Pallone," he said, staring arrows through me, "I know what that word means." It was revealing; his intellect was offended.

As we left, I kidded Giamatti about picking up the tab, which he did. Outside, before Hallinan went his separate way, I asked him when he thought he would know something more about the investigation, and he said to call his office in a couple of days.

My next series was in Philadelphia, so while I was at the airport the next day waiting to leave, I called my lawyer, Joe Fiore, in Boston. I told him what was going on and he said, "Has anyone contacted you about it?" I said, "Not one person." He said, "Then let's not worry about it until they do." Afterward, I couldn't get it out of my mind. I remembered Sam Gennaro's phone call back in January about the sex scandal in Saratoga Springs, and I wondered if these two things were somehow connected. So I called Sam.

I said, "What's going on with Blodgett and Desadora?"

Sam said, "I haven't heard anything. But it's still big."

"Has my name been mentioned in any way, shape, or form?"

"No. Why should it be?"

I didn't explain. I said, "I just want to make sure my name hasn't been dragged around in the mud for no reason. Nobody's been talking to you, right?"

"No. Everything's been quiet lately. I would call you right away if something like that happened."

I hung up, thinking, "What a relief; there's nothing going on. These two events can't be related. If for some weird reason they were, why wouldn't they come and talk to me personally? I'm not the hardest person to find." But just to be sure, I called some friends of mine in the FBI, explained the situation, and asked if they could find out if anyone was investigating me. They said they'd try. And then I put it out of my mind.

For the next couple of weeks, I kept calling Hallinan's

office and he kept telling me he didn't know anything
more. On August 8, I was working the first night game
ever at Wrigley Field, and Hallinan was there, along with
Commissioner Ueberroth and Giamatti. So I asked Hallinan again, "Have you heard anything?" Again he said,
"Nothing." Once more I reassured myself that I hadn't
done anything wrong anyway, and if the police *were*
looking for me, they certainly would have contacted me
by now. "Fuck it," I thought, and I tried to focus again
on baseball games.

But real life wouldn't leave me alone. Weird things
kept disrupting me off the field and making me paranoid.
I couldn't put my finger on it, but I carried a sensation
of disaster with me throughout the summer. It just seemed
like I was stepping blindly over huge cracks in the ice in
the middle of a lake. One of those cracks widened in
early September when a strange woman left me a strange
message on my answering machine. She said, "Dave Pallone? My son bought a dining-room set from you, and
he's having problems with it and I wish you would please
call me"—and she left a number.

At first I dismissed it as a crank or a wrong-number
call. But the next day I got the same message. I thought,
"Well, I never sold anybody a dining-room set." And
then, all of a sudden, it clicked that I *did* sell a dining-
room set, years ago, to Sam Gennaro, but I knew it
couldn't be Sam's mother, because why wouldn't he call
me himself? I called this woman back, and I said, "I
don't understand what you're talking about. I never sold
a dining-room set to your son. Who's your son?" She
said, "That's just what Sam Gennaro told me to tell you,
because he thought you'd remember the dining-room set.
I'm not his mother; I'm his friend. . . . Are you talking
from your home phone?" I said yes, and she said,
"Maybe you shouldn't. Your phone might be tapped. Can
you call me back from a phone booth? It's very important."

I decided to do it. I brought my friend Francis with
me to La Stanza restaurant, because I'd been confiding
in him all summer and I wanted someone I could trust
there when I made the call. I dialed the woman from the

restaurant phone booth, and I said, "What are you talking about? What do you mean my phone is tapped? What's going on?" (I let Francis listen to all this, and he said, "Don't say anything.")

She said, "Sam needs to talk to you, but he thinks the phones might be tapped, so he can't call you from his office or at your home. He needs you to give him another number where he can call you."

I said, "Just tell Sam to call me at home," and I hung up. Later, Sam did call—in a panic. A newspaper guy had been tailing him at work and at home, trying to get him to talk about Larry Blodgett and Bill Desadora and their arrest in the sex-ring case. Sam thought this guy had tapped his phone, and maybe mine, too. I asked why. "Because," he said, "the DA's office sent someone to talk to me—and he asked about *you.*"

"What?" I said, scared now.

"I didn't know what to say. I didn't want anybody going after you for no reason, so I said I didn't know you."

"Why would you say something like that? That's stupid. If they come and talk to you again, tell them the truth. Tell them you know me."

Sam was concerned that my name might be linked with the sex scandal. I was, too. I realized now that this was what baseball was investigating. I knew I hadn't done anything wrong, but if the papers ever linked my name with a sex scandal—guilty or innocent—I could kiss my career and my reputation as a person goodbye. It hit me that while I hadn't taken this investigation stuff seriously when Hallinan first mentioned it to me, it was suddenly as serious as poison.

(19)

SARATOGA
SPRINGS

For most of the first two weeks of September, I juggled the pressures of a pennant race with the stress of worrying about why baseball was investigating me and how I could clear my name of something I hadn't been accused of before something terrible happened. Nearly every day my routine was the same: working baseball games and making phone calls to Sam Gennaro ("Any more contacts from the DA's office? Has my name come up again?"); my FBI friends ("Did you find out what's going on?"); and Kevin Hallinan ("Any more news on the investigation?"). And every day I ran into the same brick wall: "No." "No." "No."

A few weeks earlier, my main concerns were surviving the rest of the season and possibly going to school in the off-season at NYU. Now I was obsessed with one thing: overcoming this new invisible obstacle. But I was in a holding action; I just kept rationalizing that as long as no one contacted me directly, I must be okay. Then, on Wednesday, September 14, things changed. I had just arrived in Philadelphia for the second game of a three-game series when Eddie Vargo came into the dressing room to tell me that Giamatti wanted to see me in his office the next day at ten A.M.

The idea of an emergency meeting worried me, but I assumed it was baseball-related. Since I had a "businessman's special" afternoon game on Thursday, I called

Giamatti's office to find out what was going on. He wasn't in, so I left a message for him to call me at my hotel. He did call—around midnight. I told him my situation and asked if we could reschedule. He said, "No, David. This can't wait. I need to speak to you tomorrow." That got me anxious: "Well, what is it about? Is it what we talked about in July—the investigation?" He said, "Yes, I'm afraid it is." I said I'd take the first train to New York in the morning.

I was upset, apprehensive—I felt like I was heading into a war zone. So I called my lawyer. He suggested going with me, but I said I'd rather go alone and let him know what happened. He advised me to be careful about what I said. "Don't worry," I told him. "I have nothing to hide." When I hung up, I felt like I needed to talk to someone else. I phoned Paul Runge and told him what the meeting was about and that I thought something bad was going to happen. "I'm really scared about this thing," I admitted. "It's too secretive. What can I do about it?"

Paul said, "Did you do anything wrong?"

"Absolutely not. Jesus Christ, I barely know those people!"

"Then don't worry. If you didn't do anything wrong, there's nothing to worry about." That was his general attitude in life: there's nothing to fear but fear itself.

It calmed me down a little—but I couldn't sit still in the hotel. So I went out to a gay bar called Key West to have a few drinks and collect my thoughts. I drank beer at the upstairs bar, feeling depressed and alone. The only other times I ever felt this despondent were when my parents died and when Scott was killed. More than anything else, I needed to talk to someone who loved me. But there was no one in my life, so I sat there dwelling on the things I feared. I envisioned being forced out of the closet in a way I'd never dreamed of, and losing my career and my reputation as a decent human being. Then I thought about my mother: the day she drove me to the baseball camp; how proud she looked when I completed umpire school; how sure she was that I had chosen the right profession. And I thought of Scott: the first time we made love; the times he came on the road with me; the great mood he was in the night he died, when he put on my brand-new jersey and flashed me that smile that always said, "Hey, don't worry. Everything's going great."

I dragged myself into my hotel room around two A.M., but, needless to say, I couldn't sleep. When morning broke, I was worn out. In the train I was so nervous, and it was so humid outside, I sweated profusely all the way to New York. I arrived at the league office, soaked and drained, at exactly ten A.M. When I entered Giamatti's office, I was surprised to find Lou Hoynes there. He was the league counsel—an instant danger sign. Giamatti's face was creased with concern. He said, "David, we have a problem in Saratoga Springs, New York. They're conducting an investigation into a homosexual sex scandal involving teenage boys, and the assistant district attorney wants to talk to you about it. His name is Thomas McNamara. Do you know him?"

I said, "No. And I don't understand. If there's a problem, how come they haven't come to me?"

"I don't know. But they came to us, and you must contact this man."

"I don't even know what this is all about. I've heard rumblings about it, but I am not involved in any way whatsoever."

"Nevertheless, you need to attend to this. The season's almost over, so we feel you should take a leave of absence, with pay, and take whatever time you need to get it straightened out."

"Jesus, I don't want a leave of absence."

"I'm sorry, Dave. Either you take it or I have to give it to you—and I don't want to do it that way." He showed me two letters dated September 15: one granting my request for a leave, and the other directing me to take a leave. "I had both letters written up for you," he said. "But I think it will be better for you if you take the leave voluntarily, rather than if I give it to you."

I was confused. I said, "Well, Jesus Christ, I can't make this decision now. I have to talk to my lawyer."

He then escorted me into the conference room and showed me the phone. "Use it for as long as you like."

I called Joe Fiore and explained the options I was offered. Joe said, "Take the voluntary leave." I said, "You think it's the right thing to do?" He said, "Yeah, take it. I don't see any problems with that." I wasn't sure, but I figured I wasn't paying a lawyer not to take his advice. So I went back into Giamatti's office and told him I would take the leave.

"Good," he said. "I'm glad you made that decision." He gave me the appropriate letter, and we agreed that if anyone inquired about me, the league office would say only that I took a leave of absence for "personal reasons." Then I blurted out, "I can't believe this is happening. What about next year?"

Giamatti said, "Let's not worry about next year. Let's just get over this first."

On that note I left. I had second thoughts immediately. When I told Runge what had happened I felt even worse, because he was against the leave. He said it would look like I was guilty of something. I said, "Well, all I know is I'm not. And I hope this doesn't affect our friendship." Dead serious, he answered, "You don't make it easy. Every time you take a step, the whole world falls in behind you."

Little did I know that in just a few days, I would feel like the whole world had fallen *on* me. On Friday, knowing I would need an attorney licensed in New York, I asked Joe Fiore to refer me to the best one he knew. He lined me up with E. Stewart Jones, Jr., a renowned defense attorney from Troy, near Albany. A meeting was arranged for the following Wednesday in Troy, and another one was scheduled for Thursday between Jones, Fiore, myself, and Assistant DA McNamara at McNamara's office in Saratoga Springs.

My main concern was to give McNamara my side of the story before my name got leaked to the press. I knew that if the papers found out I was being investigated in a homosexual sex scandal, I was dead. They would absolutely crucify me. Most people believe what they read. Innocent or guilty—it doesn't matter: "Well, the paper

said so. It must be true.'' Even if you didn't do it, once
the papers say you did it—or even that you're suspected
of doing it—you're through. It raises too much doubt in
people's minds. But if you're cleared and they print that,
does anybody see it or remember it? No. They only remember that you were linked to the problem, one way or
another. I understood the mechanism, because for ten
years I was "Dave Pallone, the scab umpire," and now
I was "the Pete Rose guy." Those labels stick. That's
why my thinking was, "Christ almighty. Imagine what
I'll be labeled if *this* gets out."

In the meantime all I could do was lie low and wait
until Wednesday. But the big news that weekend was that
Dave Pallone didn't work his scheduled games in Cincinnati. Because of the Rose thing, that was a very big deal
there. The press interviewed Kibler; they called the National League office; and they tried to find out where I
lived. One AP jockey, Ben Walker, found my apartment,
left me messages, even sent me a telegram. But my lawyer told me, "No interviews," and I agreed, because I
didn't have any details yet, and I knew that no matter
what I said, the media would end up distorting it. So I
instructed my doorman to tell people I wasn't in the
building, and I kept sneaking out the back door to my
friend Francis's for some privacy.

I was distraught—and also petrified that the fact I was
gay would almost certainly come out. It was hard enough
for me to think about telling relatives and lifelong friends
face to face, so what would it be like if they read it in
the papers—and in this kind of story? But after a weekend of nonstop worry, I was relieved when the major
article on Monday, the nineteenth, mentioned only my
baseball problem. I was pissed, though, because the same
article—by Ben Walker, the AP guy—was pure bullshit,
including the completely false headline: CONTROVERSIAL
UMPIRE PALLONE RESIGNS. In part, it said:

New York, Sept. 19—Umpire Dave Pallone, who
feuded with players and fought with Pete Rose, has
resigned from the National League staff under pressure, the Associated Press has learned.

Pallone, who reached the majors in 1979 during a strike by big league umpires, was told by league officials he could either leave now or would be fired at the end of the season, sources close to the situation said.

Pallone umpired his last game Thursday night in Philadelphia. . . .

"He has asked for a leave of absence for personal reasons," National League spokeswoman Katy Feeney said. . . .

Pallone was subject for review by the league at the end of the season and either had to be rehired and given tenure or released. . . .

This fifth-grade crap was the product of a major wire service; AP stories are picked up by every major daily in the country. Yet almost all of it was slanted and wrong—and the information he got wrong was easily attainable without talking to me. First: Why did Walker identify me as "Umpire Dave Pallone, *who feuded with players and fought with Pete Rose*"? Why not just "Umpire Dave Pallone"? Why were these unrelated things even mentioned, except to imply, "He did this and this, so he must also be guilty of *that?*" It was deliberately slanted to suggest that I deserved to be out of baseball. Second: Although Walker quoted Katy Feeney saying that I only took a leave of absence, *he* said I had resigned. That was a ridiculous contradiction; obviously, he didn't know what he was writing. Third: I was never told I had to leave now or be fired at the end of the season. If Walker had bothered to check the facts with the league, he would have known I was on leave only for the remainder of the season. Fourth: Thursday's game was in the afternoon, not at night—and I didn't work *any* game on Thursday. Last: At the end of the season, I did not have to be "rehired and given tenure or released." That was more Walker nonsense; the league gave me no such ultimatum, and there was no such thing as "tenure" for umpires.

Walker's story was 99 percent false—yet it provided the whole country with the first information on my situation. Unfortunately, it also set the standard for the outrageous garbage that followed.

On Tuesday, September 20, I was again relieved to see only stories and blurbs about my "resignation" from baseball. But the press screwed up again. Every paper I saw rehashed the false information from Ben Walker's phony AP story. Even *The New York Times* compressed that piece in their "Sports People" column and headlined it UMPIRE RESIGNS. Obviously *they* never checked the facts, either—which is significant, because it tells us all: "Don't believe what you read in the press. A lot of it is lies."

That night, while Francis and I had dinner at La Stanza and discussed my upcoming meeting in Saratoga Springs, I said, "Francis, why do I have this gut feeling that I'm gonna wake up tomorrow morning and see my name spread all over the papers? I feel a tidal wave coming my way." He said it was probably because that was the one thing I didn't want to happen; and he tried his best, as a friend should, to convince me that it probably wouldn't.

But it did—full force. Wednesday morning, September 21, I was at La Guardia Airport on my way to catch my plane to Albany when I decided to check the papers. I picked up a *New York Post,* and there, in bold print across the whole back page, was this sickening headline: RE-PORT LINKS UMP PALLONE TO SEX SCANDAL—PAGE 52.

For a few seconds I couldn't breathe. I turned to page 52 with dread—and this is what I saw:

REPORT LINKS UMP PALLONE
TO SEX SCANDAL
BY LEO STANDORA

Umpire Dave Pallone is under investigation in a sex scandal involving teenage boys, a Schenectady TV station reported yesterday.

The bombshell revelation came on the heels of Pallone's resignation from the National League staff under pressure.

He gave no reason for his exit.

League officials, who announced the resignation late Monday, also declined comment.

But WRGB-TV said last night Pallone's resignation may be connected to an investigation into the so-called "Saratoga sex scandal."

A number of men accused of having sex with teenage boys already have pleaded guilty or been convicted in the case.

WRGB-TV capital bureau chief Judy Sanders—quoting unnamed sources—said Pallone recently was "in the company" of a number of the boys and men involved in the case.

Sanders then did an onscreen interview with a man who said he was an eyewitness.

During the interview, the man's face and voice were disguised and his name was not revealed.

He told Sanders that Pallone came to Saratoga Springs last December "at the request of homosexual friends who promised him a good time."

He said teenage boys also were there.

The TV witness said he told his story to Saratoga Springs cops and the District Attorney Friday.

When asked, he said, he was able to identify Pallone from baseball cards.

The witness said he came forward now because of who Pallone is—"an umpire and a role model for kids."

Neither the DA nor the Saratoga Springs cops would comment.

During his career, Pallone has feuded and fought with players and umpires alike.

Pallone joined the NL staff in April 1979, one of eight minor-league umps to make it to the majors during the seven-week strike by big-league umpires.

Some umps still won't talk to him because he crossed their picket line.

"Oh, my God," I thought. "My life is destroyed." And my heart hit the floor. Even though I'd sensed it coming, I still wasn't prepared for this kind of jolt. I had put my whole adult life into baseball, and in the time it took to read a single newspaper story, my career—and my reputation—were wiped out. A million things went through my mind: "Who do I call first? What do I say? How do I explain this newspaper story? Will they believe it's true? Even though it's false, as this story unfolds, people close to me will realize I'm gay. How do I explain why I never told them?"

But then, as I paid for the paper and started walking to my gate, I suddenly had the most incredible reverse reaction. I thought, "Well, at least now my secret is out." How can I explain what that was like? One minute I had felt totally ruined. The next minute I felt almost relieved—like two thousand pounds had been lifted off my shoulders. That feeling caught me by surprise. Was that my subconscious need to be my real self? Was it my guilt over living a hidden life? I didn't know; I just knew that, for a brief moment, I felt profoundly relieved. It was like, "Now I don't have to hide anymore. Now I'm free."

But almost immediately, I knew that reaction was a mirage. My secret wasn't really out. The article only implied I was gay—and attached that to the worst possible connotations. It suggested I was gay: (a) because I was being investigated in a sex scandal involving teenage boys; (b) because I was supposedly seen "in the company of" a number of the young boys and men involved in a teenage sex-ring case; and (c) because I supposedly went to Saratoga Springs last year "at the request of homosexual friends who promised [me] a good time." (This was the kind of slanted, biased reporting I'd hoped to stay clear of by not giving interviews. The logic here is that adult male homosexuals are degenerates who corrupt innocent young boys—exactly the sort of ignorant stereotyping that has forced many gays to stay in the closet. This kind of thinking is a major reason why gays in high-visibility careers—like politics, entertainment, and professional sports—know they can't come out. If they do, it will very likely cost them their livelihoods. I believe that this is why you don't see anyone in major league baseball coming out, even today.)

Before I boarded the plane to Albany, I realized I was

flying into a nightmare. I knew this scandal would force my hidden life into the spotlight—in the wrong way, at the wrong time—and that once people accepted I really was gay, most would also assume I was involved in this sex ring. I thought, "Christ, I *gotta* clear my name. Nothing else matters."

A couple of hours later, I met my new lawyer, E. Stewart Jones, Jr., in his office. He was a tall, dark, self-assured man who wore glasses and a no-nonsense expression. I was impressed; he was just what I'd been told—understanding, probing, tough. Plus, he was also representing Bill Desadora, one of the Saratoga Springs men Sam Gennaro had introduced me to the previous Halloween. Desadora was scheduled to go on trial in mid-October on charges of sodomy. So, obviously, Jones was the right lawyer for me; no other defense attorney knew more about this case.

I was distressed about the *Post* article, so I showed it to him. After he read it, I said, "This is terrible. I did nothing wrong; why are they going after me? And how could it ever get in the newspapers? Why do the newspapers know when *I* didn't even know?" I asked him who had been questioned so far in the investigation, and he named the people I was with the one time at Blodgett's house, as well as a bunch of other men who weren't there and who I didn't know. I said, "In any kind of an investigation, even if something gets leaked, *somebody* comes at you. They went after all these other people, and they asked *them* questions. Yet they haven't come after me. Why? This investigation has been going on since January, yet not once did anybody from the assistant DA's office approach me; not once did anybody question me; not once did they come to my home; not once did they call me; not once did they send me a letter. I mean, *nothing*. They did it all behind my back. And I didn't hear anything about it until September fifteenth. I don't understand that. How can they let something like this get in the newspapers without even talking to me, never mind charging me? Doesn't that seem very unusual?"

Jones agreed that these methods were reckless and irresponsible, and he intended to present that point of view at our meeting with McNamara. Then I told him my version of the events of the weekend of December 5–7, 1987. Afterward, Jones and I discussed our strategy for the meeting with McNamara. Suddenly he was buzzed by his secretary and he left the room. When he returned, he looked surprised. ''We're being besieged by the press,'' he said. ''We have to move you.'' Apparently the press had found out he was representing me and they wanted a statement. So Jones escorted me to his upstairs office and asked me to wait while he made his statement. Twenty minutes later, he returned and told me he thought it was a good idea if I stayed somewhere out of town that night. I knew by looking at him that he didn't realize until just then the pressure I'd been under the last few days.

An hour later I was driving my rental car behind Jones's secretary, who led me to a small colonial lodge on the outskirts of Albany. I felt like a criminal, a fugitive hiding from the law. She left me there alone, but after about an hour I was climbing the walls with anxiety. I decided I had to get out of there for the night. So I threw my things in the car and drove to Pittsfield, where I knew I could stay with my old friend Connie Bianchi, whose late husband, Al, had been a friend of mine in my minor league days. I told her about my predicament. She suggested that I calm down and tell her the whole story in detail. So, in effect, this is what I told her:

''My friend Sam Gennaro and his lover, Paul—whom I knew from Boston—had been after me for years to come visit them in upstate New York, where they now lived. In late October of '87, they came to my place for a visit over Halloween. During that visit, they invited me to a party on the Upper East Side, and that's where I met two of their acquaintances from Saratoga Springs, Larry Blodgett and Bill Desadora. Larry had a successful insurance business and Bill was a real estate broker. Sam told me they were highly respected in the community, and that's how they behaved around me.

''The next day, Sam, Paul, Desadora, and I met downtown for brunch. They said, 'You have to come visit us soon.' They wouldn't let up. Finally, I said I would come, but I had to pick the right time. We talked it over and agreed the weekend of December fifth was best. So that Friday, I flew up and stayed at Sam and Paul's house in Clifton Park. The first night, we met with Bill and Larry and went to a gay bar—which are few and far between in that area. We also hit a few straight bars. At the end of the night, we agreed to meet up the next day for lunch. Next day, we woke up to a beautiful Saturday morning. Since Paul had to work, Sam said, 'Why don't we take a drive to Saratoga Springs? You've never really seen it in the daytime. It's beautiful; they have the famous race-track and some incredible estates. Then we'll call Bill and Larry and go out to lunch.' And that's exactly what we did.

"After seeing the sights, we swung over to Larry's house, but he wasn't home. We drove around and saw more of the area. Then we came back to Larry's—still nobody home. It struck us as odd, because his car was there yet no one answered the door. So we decided to go to Bill's house. When we knocked there, a man with a foreign accent answered the door and said he was a friend of Bill's and that he was staying a few days. We asked where Bill was, and the guy said he was on his way over to Larry's house. He said, 'I was going over there myself. Can I catch a ride with you?' We said yes, and we all drove over.

"When we knocked at Larry's door, this time he answered it and let us in. We went straight into the large living room, where a football game was playing on TV. They offered me a beer and showed me around the downstairs—it was a big Victorian house with huge rooms. Then we came back to watch TV and talk. At that point there were just five adults in the room—Larry, Bill, Sam, me, and this foreign guy. About ten minutes later, a teenage boy came down the stairs. He was wearing a jacket with a backpack, and he looked maybe fourteen or fifteen. Larry introduced me as 'Dave, the ump.' I didn't like that, but I didn't mention it. The kid shook my hand and said, 'Hi, how are you?' and sat down on the couch with us. I didn't know who this kid was or what he was doing there, or even if he knew we were gay. I was concerned about that, and I remember commenting to Bill, 'He's so young'—meaning that maybe he shouldn't be around us.

"About ten minutes later we got up and left to go to lunch. Larry and Bill went to their car; Sam and I went to our car; the kid and the foreign guy went their own way on foot. That was the only time I ever saw either of them. I never saw the upstairs of the house, and I was only in the house for a total of about twenty-five minutes."

When I was through, Connie said, "I can't believe these people lied about you. How will you fight this?" I was too exhausted to answer, so we said goodnight and I spent a sleepless night on the couch.

Thursday morning I picked up Joe Fiore at the airport, drove to Jones's office, and introduced them. They talked alone awhile, and then I joined them and we drove over to McNamara's office. Jones explained to me that this meeting was being conducted to establish everyone's position. He said it would also give McNamara a chance to evaluate me as a potential witness in terms of my demeanor, credibility, and character. Jones's hope was that McNamara would see I was telling the truth and be discouraged from filing charges. He reminded me firmly that all they had at present were flimsy allegations, not charges. In other words, there was no case against me.

After everyone was introduced, McNamara apologized about my name being leaked to the newspapers. I controlled myself, but I did say, "Well, it just ruined my life." Then McNamara explained that he was investigating me for having sex with a minor. He told me that a teenage boy claimed he performed sexual acts with me at Larry Blodgett's house. I said, "That story is a lie. I did not do it. I don't know what your information is at this point, but I have only been to Saratoga Springs once in my life, and I saw these people one day and I was there twenty-five minutes, and I did not have sex with a minor."

Fiore got emotional, too. He made a statement like, "I've known David since he was a kid. I have had dealings with him and his family throughout his whole life, and there is no question in my mind that this man is a moral person, and that he would never be involved with such a thing as this.'' McNamara seemed more inclined to deal with Jones, whom he knew better. But I know *I* appreciated Joe's support. One of the investigators was in the room, and he said he had conducted the interviews with the teenage boy, and that everything the kid said about the other people investigated so far had checked out. I said, ''Well, he's not telling the truth this time. We have other people who were in the house who contradict his testimony.'' At this point Jones and McNamara left together to talk it over. When Jones came out again, he, Fiore, and I went back to his office, where Jones explained to me what McNamara's investigation turned up on me:

- I was named as part of the sex ring by a fourteen-year-old boy—referred to as ''J''—and an anonymous adult male who claimed to be an eyewitness to the events of Saturday, December 5.
- ''J'' said he was introduced to me by prearrangement at Larry Blodgett's house, where he performed oral sex on me in an upstairs room, followed by ''mutual masturbation.''
- The previous Monday night, an adult male witness appeared on local TV with his face and voice disguised, and said he saw me in the company of boys and men in the sex ring, and that when I met ''J'' at Blodgett's house, I said, ''This kid's too young.'' But I was told, ''He knows what he's doing.'' Then I went upstairs with the boy, where I was alone with him for some time.

Jones said that none of these allegations was corroborated by anyone else in the case, and that if this was all McNamara had, it wouldn't stand up. He seemed confident that I would not be charged and that the investigation would be dropped. I said, ''I wish I felt as confident as you.''

I flew back to New York that afternoon, totally exhausted. I remember thinking about how hard it would be to face the people I cared about who would be reading all this crap about me. When I got back to my apartment, I had literally dozens of phone messages from family and friends from all around the country. What a great revelation those messages were; the overwhelming sentiment was, "We know it's lies. We're here for you if you need us." They were basically calling to give me their support. I was so touched, I listened to some of the messages twice. I knew it would still be an uphill fight, but at least now I also knew the right people were in my corner. I collapsed on the couch and, within minutes, fell into my first deep sleep in a week.

Over the next week to ten days, I explained the situation to people close to me. The first thing everybody asked was, "Did you resign?" I said: "I did not resign. I took a temporary leave of absence." Then I explained about the sex scandal: "I am not involved in any teenage sex ring. I don't know where they got their information, but I have to clear my name from that." It was interesting that several people asked, "Do you think Pete Rose had anything to do with it because of your run-in with him?" I said, "Absolutely not. No way."

It was amazing; not one person came right out and asked me if I was gay. Either they were too afraid to ask, or they surmised I was gay, or they didn't read between the lines. The subject only came up once, and it wasn't spelled out. I was talking to my godmother, who, from reading the newspaper articles, now assumed I was gay. She said, "Now I understand why you've had all these inner problems all these years." And I said, "Well, I've been wanting to tell you for the last three or four years, but every time I tried, I got cold feet. I could not come out and tell you, because I always felt I was going to lose your love. I just could not take that chance."

Through September and October Jones kept insisting publicly, "There is no truth to these allegations. He did not do anything wrong. He committed no crime. He was not involved with a sex ring. I predict we will convince the district attorney's office that there is no truth to the allegations, and no case, and that the investigation of my client should be dropped." At the same time I learned from the newspapers that since January '88 eight men in the case had been accused: one had been tried in the summer and found guilty; four had pleaded guilty to sodomy; one had pleaded guilty to endangering the welfare of a child; two others had been indicted. Meantime, no charges had been filed against me.

I found out something else, too: Saratoga Springs police confirmed that Kevin Hallinan had been in Saratoga Springs on July 29, and that he had brought "official identification" (baseball cards) of me with him. That identification was given to Assistant DA McNamara. Now it was clear to me that Hallinan had known all along. Why, then, did he tell me as late as August 8—at Wrigley Field—that he still knew nothing more about the investigation?

By mid-October there were still no charges against me. In the meantime, Larry Blodgett had been sentenced to up to eight years in state prison on sodomy charges (but was free on bond pending the outcome of his appeal), and Bill Desadora had admitted to third-degree sodomy and was awaiting sentencing of up to three years. Both of them corroborated my version of what happened that Saturday at Larry's house. They confirmed that I was never part of the sex ring; I had never met "J" before he was introduced to me that day, and the meeting was not prearranged; I never displayed any sexual interest in "J"; I was never out of their sight the whole time "J" was there. Sam Gennaro also confirmed my version of the story.

At the end of October, my attorney informed me that the anonymous TV witness—the foreign guy staying at Desadora's that weekend—had just been arrested for breaking and entering, and was also facing a drunken-driving charge, and that he had a previous criminal record. Jones also went directly to District Attorney David Wait and told him that they had already ruined my life, had absolutely nothing on me, and were banking on an unreliable witness. In effect, Jones said they had no case.

I was convinced that the district attorney's office came after me for one reason: I was a public figure in the wrong place at the wrong time. My guess was that the foreign guy probably offered up my name to get himself out of other charges, and the DA's office wanted to believe him—maybe because of the notoriety they thought they'd get if they nailed a celebrity. If I wasn't a public figure, even if they had proven beyond a shadow of a doubt that I was in the sex ring, since I was only there that one day they probably would have said,

"Let's forget it. We're not going after him. He's nobody." But because I was Dave Pallone, National League umpire, they went after me big time. And no one can tell me that my name didn't draw *more* national attention because of the Pete Rose thing.

As for the teenage boy, I cannot explain why he would say what he did about me. Maybe the foreign guy threatened him; maybe the kid was so active in the sex ring that he really thought he did those things with me; maybe he just wanted to brag about having been with a celebrity. I have no idea; I'm not a psychiatrist. But I do know he used me as a scapegoat.

Well, it didn't work. On Tuesday, November 1, the DA's office quietly dropped their investigation of me without every having filed a single charge. Even today, the majority of baseball fans who knew about this case in the first place still don't know that I was never charged in the case and that I was cleared—and they still believe that I resigned from baseball.

In retrospect, maybe it was bad judgment for me to have gone to that house, especially given the rumors that were already floating around about me. But I would never have gone there if I had known what they were involved in. I remember Leona telling me afterward, "You never should've gone there to visit your gay friends." I said, "I don't understand. Does that mean if you have lunch with a thief, then you're a thief, too? Suppose you go next door to visit neighbors and you walk in, and all of a sudden the door slams back and there's the FBI arresting everyone for possession of cocaine. You might get arrested, too—even though you're an innocent bystander. But forever after that, you won't be remembered as the innocent bystander. You'd be remembered as the guy who got busted for cocaine."

In other words, it really didn't matter that I was a gay man visiting other gays. What happened to me could have happened to anybody—gay *or* straight. And it frequently does.

20

LIFE AFTER BASEBALL

It took a while for the thought "It's really over" to sink in. At first, I felt numb: "How could this have happened?" Then vindicated: "Now they know I was telling the truth." But there was also the bitterness for suffering through forty-five days of hell for no reason at all. The first thing I considered was telling everyone close to me—everyone who didn't already know—that I was gay. But I changed my mind. I had just been through a trauma, and I wasn't ready for another one.

I started worrying about baseball: "Will I get my job back? If I do, I know how the umpires will react, but will the players and fans shun me now, too?" Yes, I had wanted to retire—and if I had gotten the World Series in '88, I would have retired. But when I didn't get it, I started looking forward to working for it again in '89. And I definitely couldn't retire under *this* kind of cloud. It was important now to be back on the field in April, because that would be an acknowledgment from baseball that I had done nothing wrong.

So I concentrated on one thing: clearing my name with baseball. That was why, right after my lawyer phoned on November 1 to tell me they'd dropped the investigation, I called Bart Giamatti's office and set up the meeting for 11:30 on November 30. Over the next twenty-nine days, other than going to the gym, I sweated it out at home. Too many people knew me, and I didn't want to answer questions. Mostly I worried about what Giamatti would say and whether he would still be on my side.

November 30 finally arrived, and here was Giamatti starting me off with "I know you're not going to like what I have to say." He was right; that meeting was the biggest disappointment of my life. How could they banish me for something I didn't do? Why wasn't exoneration from the DA's office good enough for them? Where was their loyalty after I'd devoted ten years of my life to the game?

It hurt me that Bart Giamatti was the one holding the gun to my head and saying, "We don't want to fire you. We'd like to see you retire voluntarily." After all the support he'd given me in the past, it felt like a betrayal. Yet because he'd touched my life in so many ways— especially by being a father figure when I needed that— I wondered if he believed this was for my own good. He'd always taken the long view with me and treated me with compassion. Maybe he figured I was better off out of baseball now, and that this whole mess might be a blessing in disguise.

I became convinced that Giamatti sympathized with me and wanted to help, but the league tied his hands. The owners were concerned about the game's image, not Dave Pallone's personal problems. They must have told him, "Look at all these things that happened to Pallone the last three years. Look at the notoriety he got from the Pete Rose thing. And now this sex scandal. It's in baseball's best interests not to rehire him." I could understand that. Bart once told me, "No individual is bigger than baseball"—and that probably guided him here. Add the pressure of being commissioner-elect and the fact that the owners knew I was the type of person who might take them to court, and Giamatti had no choice. I realized that although he held the gun to my head, it was the owners who pulled the trigger.

The first week of December, when my lawyer received the letter from Lou Hoynes spelling out the reasons baseball was terminating me, I was distraught. None of the reasons was valid:

1. *Concern about my involvement in the Saratoga Springs scandal:* I was cleared. What more did they want?

2. *The Cincinnati bar rumor:* They had investigated this rumor and found absolutely nothing.

3. *Low 1988 ratings:* The joke of jokes, even to Giamatti. Plus, how could I get high ratings after the Pete Rose incident? And if I was so bad, how did I do such a great job in the Championship Series? How did I go from that good in October of '87 to bad enough to fire in November of '88?

4. *Concern about my ability to function under pressure of publicity from the Saratoga Springs case:* Pure speculation, especially given my past performance under all kinds of pressure for ten years.

These reasons were camouflage for the real reason: I was gay, and they didn't want the publicity surrounding that to tarnish baseball's macho image. In other words, they were prepared to sacrifice a proven, veteran umpire so they wouldn't *look bad*.

That ate away at me. Baseball always talked about how open, fair, and inclusive it was—the All-American Game that gave us Jackie Robinson. But the lesson I learned on November 30 was the biggest irony of all: baseball was living a hidden life, too. Publicly, it pretended to be inclusive and fair, but it was close-minded and biased behind its mask. They believed I was gay and therefore guilty of everything—and that's why they wouldn't hire me back. Yet they allowed Cesar Cedeno to continue playing for thirteen years after being charged with manslaughter in the shooting death of a nineteen-year-old woman in the Dominican Republic, for which he paid only a hundred-dollar fine plus court costs. They let Lenny Randle play six more years after he shattered his manager's cheekbone with a punch, plea-bargained a felony down to battery, and paid a thousand-dollar fine and medical costs. They allowed George Steinbrenner to operate a franchise after being convicted of making illegal campaign contributions. They didn't care when pitcher Bryn Smith was arrested for solicitation or, in 1989, when outfielder Luis Polonia was convicted of having sexual relations with a fifteen-year-old female minor. And how come baseball did virtually nothing more than slap the wrists of all those players who recently admitted publicly to buying, using, or selling illegal drugs?

I don't understand how they could possibly let all those other transgressions go by the board. How could they allow people who were guilty of breaking laws to continue their careers, but then turn around and force me out for being *innocent*? What was the message there—that baseball considered manslaughter, political corruption, solicitation, and sex with a female minor more acceptable than being gay?

Let's be clear: I want players who have a drug problem or an emotional problem to have a second chance. But the policy should be fair and consistent for *everyone*. How was it fair to single me out as different from all those others? And what was baseball afraid of, anyway? What threat did a Dave Pallone pose to the game? What threat did Jackie Robinson pose? If anything, his presence finally started baseball on the road to becoming a truly "American" pastime. But until the game accepts gays openly, it can never really be "American."

Some gays have come out of the closet in professional sports. It's interesting to me that all but two that I know of are women. Yet it's obvious that gay men participate in professional sports as well. But where's the problem? Owners who fear male homosexual athletes are like those ignorant people who feared "witches" in seventeenth-century Salem, or the fifteenth-century sailors who believed that if they sailed to the horizon they'd fall off the earth. In today's world, most people are not concerned about what athletes or sports officials do with their lives off the field. In 1989, fifty-five million people paid their way into major league baseball games. Can you imagine any of then returning season tickets because they found out that one of the umpires or players on the field was gay?

It's time someone pulled the mask off baseball and shined the light on its real face. Baseball doesn't accept gays; and if what the game did to me is any measure of where it's headed, then it's going backward. I personally know of about a half-dozen gay major league baseball players—including some of the best-known and most accomplished players in the game—and the only problem they have is that they must lead double lives because baseball refuses to address the issue openly. And until there are drastic changes, they will stay in the closet. That's why it's important to know that what happened to me wasn't about performance on the field, or ratings, or ability to handle pressure. It was about *discrimination*.

And that was the subject of discussion with my lawyers all through December as we planned our strategy. They kept asking me, ''Do you want to sue to get your job back, or do you want to swing a monetary settlement?'' I wasn't sure. I wanted to retire, yet I still wanted my World Series. I had regrets about taking the leave of absence, too. It made it look like I was guilty and then resigned, and I wanted to counter that false impression. I also figured that if I went to court and won my job back, I'd have a lot of back pay and I could work one more year and then leave on my own terms. Some of my gay friends said it would be easier for me in baseball now that everyone knew I was gay. But I wasn't convinced everyone *did* know, because I hadn't admitted it publicly. Other friends asked if I'd be able to handle the double dose of ostracism if I went back. It was a very difficult decision.

My first inclination was to fight for my job. But I'd already drained my savings to pay my lawyers, and I didn't have a war chest or a job to replenish my funds. How was I going to pay for a long-drawn-out court case? Then my attorneys explained that even if I won, I would only be entitled to my job with back pay and benefits— no damage award. That was a big factor, because I was almost broke and I had no idea where my next dollar was coming from. Finally, I said, ''Start negotiations. See what they offer.''

My lawyers computed how many years of future service I would have had up to the age of fifty-five, and the appropriate salary, benefits, and pension numbers I would lose—and they came up with a beginning negotiation figure that was substantially more than Giamatti's original offer. That's why negotiations dragged on through January and February. Meantime, I fell into a depression: "I can't believe how bizarre my life is. What's gonna happen next?" If a light bulb blew, or the mail came late, or the subway stalled, I had fits of rage. I took long walks along the East River or through Central Park, not stopping, not hearing, not really seeing, just feeling numb again. I thought, "How am I going to get through the year without baseball?"

On February 15, 1989, I made what I hoped was the first step toward a new future. I took a friend's job offer and moved to Washington, D.C., to work for Events Management, Inc., a company that arranged charity functions and social events. My job was to bring in new business and coordinate logistics: hire caterers and entertainment, arrange security, even help with decorations. It was my only full-time job other than umpiring since high school. The first morning, I wore a sport coat and tie and I felt like someone else. The last time I dressed for work that way, I was working the '87 Championship Series. But every day for two weeks, I got up early, put on my new "uniform," and reported to work like millions of other people. It was awkward; I was the classic fish out of water. Yet for a while I felt good, because it looked like there really might be life after baseball.

In late February I started dreading the idea of spring: warm air, chirping birds, kids playing ball in the parks. My attorneys were still going back and forth with the league, and I needed a vacation from the turmoil, so I flew to St. Maarten to swim and relax on the beach. It was working miracles—until my lawyer called and said, "They're ready to close. This is their final offer and we think you should take it." So I searched my heart and sifted all the input from family and friends, and I decided to accept the settlement and move on with my life. They were offering a tempting amount—much less than our starting figure but enough for me to start a new life. It also meant no more legal bills, no more tension and worry about what baseball would say or do and how I would fight it, no more ostracism and having to stand alone at home plate again, acting out a farce. I'd had it with all the conflict. It was time for a change.

It wasn't an easy call. Once I took the money, I'd be facing the unknown. And I would have to reconcile myself to the fact that I was going to be without baseball for the first time in nineteen years, and that people would think either that I was guilty or that I sold out for the money. I *did* sell out for the money—because I didn't have a bottomless pit of funds to fight baseball in court, and I desperately wanted a life again. It wasn't the noble road, and it let baseball off the hook for screwing me out of my career. But it was the only choice I had.

Before people judge me, they should know two things: First, the legal agreement I signed with the league doesn't permit me to divulge the specific figures of the settlement. Second, in a letter to me in early January '89, Bart Giamatti wrote that "among the reasons for the League's decision to terminate your employment were substantial allegations that you engaged in certain conduct which could be characterized as serious misconduct or acts of moral turpitude. Under our Collective Bargaining Agreement, the League would be entitled to terminate you without any severance pay under those circumstances." Yet they *did* give me my severance pay. Why? Out of the goodness of their hearts? Hardly. In fact, in my mind they gave me not only the severance pay they said I wasn't entitled to but also my entire next year's salary plus a substantial amount on top of it. What was that—a *bonus* for "moral turpitude"?

If I really had done something illegal or violated the morals clause of my contract, and if baseball could have nailed me to the wall for it, would they have ever offered me a dime? Why would they pay me *any* money—never mind the hefty sum they did pay—if they were right? What their payment said was: "We know we're wrong, and we know it would hurt us in court. But we don't want you in baseball, so we'll give you this not to sue us."

From the moment I signed the papers, I second-guessed myself: "Maybe it was a mistake to take the money. Maybe I should've said, 'See you in court.' " I still wonder about that today. But I didn't take them to court—and the result was that baseball was lost to me forever. That's why, when March came, it was very painful to me. I knew that spring training was going on without me. I tried to ignore it, but a little voice kept saying, "What are you doing here? You belong in Florida." So one day I forced myself to watch the spring-training reports on TV. It hurt like hell. Every day TV took me to another familiar field. I thought, "I should be *there*." Then I'd read about the games in the papers and go, "I should be *there*."

That first week of spring training I had a meeting in downtown Washington with a businessman who was planning a party to celebrate the opening of his new bank. I pitched Events Management, but he'd already arranged everything himself. He said he used to be President Reagan's "advance man," and that he arranged all the details before the President traveled anywhere, so he didn't need our help. He kept talking, but I never heard a word. I remember looking right through him, out a window, and saying to myself, "What a beautiful day. Jesus, why am I cooped up in a building listening to someone I don't know tell me he doesn't need my services for something I don't *care* about?"

I got up, left his office, took a taxi to my apartment, yanked out the Yellow Pages, and looked up a moving company. By March 21 I was back in Boston—my third residence in three months. It was the right decision, even though I disappointed my good friend who had hired me at Events Management. But I still had to face the truth: something crucial had been taken from me and I couldn't adjust. Depression set in again; I missed baseball like I would an arm or a leg. When April arrived, I wasn't working. To vent my frustration, I pumped weights, rode my mountain bike practically around Massachusetts, and worked into the best physical shape of my life. But I still had nervous energy—especially at night, when something inside me kept yelling, *"Play ball!"*

I tried to ignore it. But in April in Boston, baseball was as impossible to ignore as the sky; it was everywhere. I'd be standing in the grocery checkout line and there were people ahead of me in Red Sox hats. I'd meet a friend in a café for lunch and I'd hear people discussing tickets for games. I'd switch on the car radio and get the one o'clock baseball notes, the two o'clock exhibition notes, the three o'clock Red Sox roundup, the four o'clock major league review. . . . It was like a fastball to the ribs; I couldn't get out of its way.

Finally, I made a big emotional decision. I figured my baseball avoidance was like the fear of elevators or fear of heights. You conquered those fears by facing them, right? So I said, ''The best way to eventually *avoid* baseball is to *go* to baseball.'' And what better game to go to than opening day at Fenway Park? I called a friend who worked in the ticket office and lined up a seat, and since I lived so close, I decided to walk to the field.

It was a typical Boston spring day, clear and cool. As I came to Landsdowne Street, fans converged on the hot-dog and peanut vendors, and I could smell the sausages grilling, which reminded me of the times I came here as a kid with my dad. At first I felt invigorated, because it hadn't sunk in yet that I wasn't going to be umpiring that day. In fact, the strangeness didn't hit me until I had to show a ticket to get in, as opposed to walking right through and hearing the security people say, ''Hi, Dave. Good to see you again. Have a good game.'' I mean, the baseball field used to be my home, my refuge from reality, the one place in the world where I had some control over events. Now it was just a place to watch a baseball game.

All of a sudden there I was, three rows off the field behind the plate. Immediately, another stinging irony: I looked at home plate and automatically thought, ''Shit, these seats are so close, I can almost call balls and strikes.'' When I first saw the umpires step onto the field, a nauseating feeling came over me: ''What the hell am I doing here? I'm only thirty-seven; how can I be retired? I belong on the field.'' During the national anthem, I thought, ''Well, at least we don't have to go through *two* anthems.'' Reflex response: whenever we had games involving Montreal, we had to wait through the American *and* Canadian anthems, which prolonged our pregame nerves. I just couldn't stop thinking like an umpire.

In the first inning I watched only the umpires, knowing what they were thinking and feeling. Opening day is a fresh start for every umpire. After spring training, you can hardly wait to get the season going. It's like a player who's anxious to come up and get his first hit. Well, we umpires can't wait to see our first pitch and make our first call. Then the anticipation and anxiety disappear, and we're back in the swing of it again. And we're not tired yet; we're not weary of getting on an airplane every three days and getting off in a different city. Everything feels new at this point; everything is possible.

I remember thinking about the people I would probably never see again because I wouldn't be working in their cities anymore. I would miss the Sunday barbecues with Chuck, Mary Lou, and their kids in Pittsburgh; dinner and conversation with Roger and Sue in San Diego; talking about the Hollywood scene with Maura and finding her "Welcome Back to L.A." gifts waiting for me in my hotel room; chatting between innings with Don and Pat in their Wrigley Field box seats so close to the dugout that they could shake Don Zimmer's hand; kidding around with the airline personnel who always did me little favors; and getting into the finest restaurants because I was Dave Pallone, National League umpire.

I thought about how much I would miss the nonsense of the Philly Phanatic, the only mascot I ever let joke with me on the field, because he never made me look foolish; and the fat lady behind the San Diego dugout who always screamed the same thing at me—"Pallone, you oughta get a lunch bucket and go to work"; and Jimmy, the clubhouse man in Chicago, who always went out of his way to wash our clothes and shine our shoes and run incidental errands for us; and the satisfaction of giving autographed baseballs to kids waiting around after the games. (When I was a kid, I always waited to catch that foul ball in the stands, but I never got one. Then I became an umpire and I had as many baseballs as I wanted.) It was interesting; until this game—probably because of the trauma in my double life—I never fully appreciated how rich my baseball life was.

I couldn't take it; I lasted only two innings. As I crossed Boylston Street on my way home, I could hear the crowd cheering in the stands and I thought of Bart Giamatti. Our relationship had ended on a sour note, and I was sorry about that. Part of my settlement, though, called for us to have a private meeting sometime during that season. At that meeting, I planned to ask Bart if he believed me about the Saratoga Springs scandal, and if he really thought that things had worked out for the best. I wanted to reestablish our rapport, because I still valued his friendship and advice. And I felt I had something more to prove to him.

Bart Giamatti died on September 1, 1989. We never had our meeting. When I called to give my condolences to his wife, she said, "Dave, I just want you to know that Bart was very upset for months about your situation." I said, "Thank you for telling me that. You will never know how much your husband meant to me. He was a great human being. I needed to tell you that."

That phone call was an ending for me. In a way, it might also have been Bart's final gift of advice—because when he died, so did my anguish and regret over the loss of my career. I realized that I had the rest of my life to live, and that I owed it to myself and all the people who ever cared about me to make something good out of it.

And that's what I'm trying to do.

AFTERWORD

In June 1988, during my mid-season vacation, I was lying on a Spanish island beach thinking, ''The old-time umpires could never have imagined vacationing here during the middle of the baseball season.'' Then it occurred to me that, like my other trips away from baseball, this wasn't so much a vacation as another escape. I was still hiding the real me from the world and from myself. That's when I first considered writing a book and calling it *Behind the Mask*. But I didn't have the time to sit down and do it. Then a nightmare called Saratoga sex scandal wrecked my career and almost my life, and I had time to tell the story you've just read.

I had several reasons for doing it:

1. My side of the controversies plaguing my baseball career has never been told. Whenever I tried to explain myself publicly, my words and thoughts were taken out of context. After the Saratoga sex scandal, reporters were more interested in distorting the truth than uncovering it. So this book sets the record straight and allows people to judge me fairly now.

2. I believe it's time for gay people in the public eye to come forward and say, ''This is who and what I am.'' I want this book to say, ''If you're gay, think about removing your mask. Because

unless more of us do that, the back-room politics of prejudice will continue to destroy productive careers and lives.'' I realize that some people will think, ''That's easy for you to say. You have nothing to lose.'' But that's not true; I have a *lot* to lose. For one thing, I have never come out publicly and admitted I was gay, so I am risking many important friendships by revealing myself so completely here. Second: I am still searching for my new career. While I hope this book helps both gay and straight people to rethink their values, I also know that it will shock some potential employers and cost me opportunities.

3. Our society expects its male sports figures to be ''macho,'' and many heterosexuals still cling to the myth that all gay men are effeminate ''nellies'' working as hairdressers, fashion designers, dancers, or artists. In this book I wanted to dispel those myths and make it clear that gays are just as ''macho'' as straights, no matter what career they're in.

4. As of this date, not one gay major league ballplayer has come out of the closet—and it's obvious why not. I hope this book conveys to heterosexuals the terrible scrutiny gays in public life are under, and how vulnerable we are to prejudice in society.

5. I hope that gays who read this book will be encouraged to be themselves, tell their secret to the people they love, and be proud of their humanity. The book should say to them, ''Have courage and pride and be true to yourself. Let people close to you help you. Let the world see you for who you really are.''

One final note: There has been a lot of tragedy in my life, which I talked about openly in this book. But I want to be clear that I am not asking for sympathy. I am not asking anyone to shed a tear for me. What I am asking of people who read this book is what I've asked of everyone I've ever known: accept me for who I am—a decent human being, just like you.

There's an epidemic with 27 million victims. And no visible symptoms.

It's an epidemic of people who can't read.

Believe it or not, 27 million Americans are functionally illiterate, about one adult in five.

The solution to this problem is you... when you join the fight against illiteracy. So call the Coalition for Literacy at toll-free **1-800-228-8813** and volunteer.

Volunteer Against Illiteracy. The only degree you need is a degree of caring.